"Most of the problems
in Scuba diving
come from ourselves"
Jim Crockett

"Never assume
an unexploded goat
is evidence of a good
decompression profile"
M. Edmonston

First published in 2012
Quetzal Publishing
42 Devereux Road
London SW11 6JS

© Julian Eden, 2012

ISBN 978-0-9553467-2-9

Distributed by
London Diving Chamber
Hospital of St John and St Elizabeth
60 Grove End Road
London NW8 9NH
+44 (0)20 7806 4028

—

Designed by Fivefootsix
Set in Futura
Printed and bound by Empress Litho

—

DISCLAIMER

We would like to point out (because our lawyers made us) that this book is intended to outline some of the medical issues concerned with diving and fitness to dive, and is not a substitute for actually being seen by a doctor, in much the same way that reading a dive guide to the Thistlegorm is no substitute for actually diving it. And watching a documentary on Guantanamo Bay is no substitute for being water-boarded for six years. If you're going to sign yourself or anyone else off for diving solely on the basis of what you read in this book, then you're mental. And mental people aren't allowed to dive.

FOREWORD

As someone who dives professionally, I would nevertheless prefer my birth certificate to be less ancient. I fall into that bracket where male medical procedures are more likely to provide material for Jack Dee's droll stand-up routine than the intellectual scribes of the Lancet.

So when it comes to diving medicine, it is rather comforting and even welcoming that the team at the London Diving Chamber appear to possess the rudimentary skills of the former but fortunately a great deal more of the latter.

They probably won't print the fact that they may feel justifiably proud one day of saving someone's life, while the next recovering from the tired and emotional consequences of a dive show with the aid of a saline drip. I have no direct evidence for this but it makes for good, salacious copy.

As well as requiring my own annual HSE endorsement of fitness to dive, when making a documentary for the BBC which required a suitably telegenic diving doctor, Jules Eden was my first choice without hesitation. Nothing to do with the fact that I knew he would leap at the chance of appearing on camera without a fee; and he only required a limited amount of make-up.

In all seriousness, the film was about the BBC's Security Correspondent Frank Gardner and the challenges of returning to diving after being paralysed in a terrorist shooting. Jules understood the medical issues fully and made an important contribution to the programme, not least by addressing Frank's genuine concerns, giving him the confidence and the all-important certificate to allow him to return to a restricted level of diving.

John McIntyre is a former BBC Correspondent who reported on the big stories around the globe for the Six O'clock News; now a successful underwater camera operator journalist. He was the principal underwater camera for the award winning cinema film 'The End of the Line'. Other credits include Blue Peter, Massive Nature, Wild Caribbean, Sports Personality of the Year, Ancient Britain, Nature's Top 40 and BBC World's Fast Track programme.

As for Oliver Firth, clinically proven to have two brains, he wields his reflex hammer with great finesse when testing a diver's medical competence. Not to mention the distracting charm tactics he employs when politely requesting the said diver 'cough' while rummaging delicately in his nether regions.

What the LDC have cleverly managed to achieve over the years is a level of integration with the diving community that not only provides an invaluable service but has also helped demystify many of the important medical issues.

Even if you don't need a recompression chamber because you've overcooked it on a deep dive, this particular LDC double-act are in a class of their own when it comes to medical FAQs.

John McIntyre

INTRODUCTION

Many of the Q&As in this volume appeared in Sport Diver magazine or the internationally acclaimed Tanked Up: the magazine formerly known as London Diver. Many others are siphoned from the enormous number of email queries an institution like the London Diving Chamber can't help but accumulate over a decade or so.

In answering these queries, Jules Eden and Dr Oliver 'The Diving Shaman' Firth have brought their unique expertise in diving medicine to bear on subjects ranging from "How do I equalise properly?" through to "Can I dive with a gunshot wound?" and covering perennial favourites such as asthma, diarrhoea and fire coral in between. What we've tried to create is something you can read at home or take on a liveaboard and which will be both practical and entertaining. That way, you can refer to it if you think you're developing a nasty ear infection and amuse yourself reading it if it turns out you won't be diving as a result.

We all love diving, and whilst we may not claim to be experts at the activity ourselves (I do: I'm brilliant at it. Except when I forget to put my weight belt on), we each probably know at least a hundred different people who do. This is why it may come as a surprise to discover that there aren't that many experts on diving medicine around. GPs rarely know anything about it: there's no reason why they should as they have to spend the majority of their days sitting in an office examining people's itchy bits; most divers aren't doctors: being able to drag someone out of the water and perform CPR, whilst undeniably useful, isn't the same as being able to assess somebody's fitness to dive after a heart bypass; and as for divers that are doctors: well, they won't necessarily be able to tell you whether it's OK to dive on warfarin or whether the tingling in your hand is due to nitrogen bubbles or a herniated disc, unless they're hyperbaric specialists.

That's what you get with Jules and The Shaman: specialist diving knowledge backed up with years of experience. That's why we made a book about it. It's what they do.

"What we've tried to create is something you can read at home or take on a liveaboard and which will be both practical and entertaining."

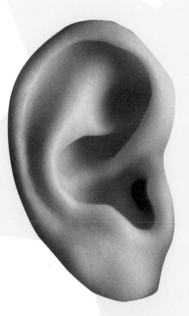

All I did, on the other hand, was hack my way through hundreds of these Q&As and pick out the Qs that were either most FAsked or which I thought were most interesting, and then try to make them coherent. You'll see the As strike a nice balance between explaining clearly (and medically) what the issue is and what the answer is, whilst often being amusing at the same time.

So, you'll find out what a PFO is, why it's a problem for divers and how to fix it alongside practical advice for avoiding things like insect bites and treating various stings. There are guidelines for what will and won't keep you out of the water and how to improve your chances of getting wet, backed with interesting true tales of curiosities like decompression sickness, what such things are and how to go about not getting them. There are a couple of longer pieces on pertinent subjects as well.

I should warn you that the introductions to each section contain no useful information whatsoever, because I wrote them and I know less about medicine than Cristiano Ronaldo knows about humility. A while ago, I advised a DM friend to put olive oil in his ear, for what the pair of us had diagnosed as 'some sort of ear infection', on account of I half-remembered reading something somewhere about it being useful. He perforated his eardrum on the next dive.

This is just one example I can think of where a book of Diving Medicine Q&As would have come in useful in my immediate past. Another is that it would have taken my mind off the monotony of the subsequent house-reef night dive I had to do to cover the now half-deaf DM. Except it was dark and the book isn't waterproof.

Apart from that, though, I think you'll enjoy it.

THE BENDS

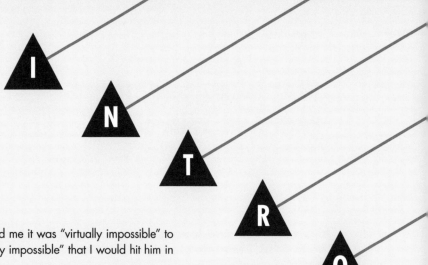

An instructor in Thailand once told me it was "virtually impossible" to get DCI. I told him it was "virtually impossible" that I would hit him in the face, and then did it anyway.

Oh, OK, I didn't really, but I think it's that attitude which stops a lot of people from calling the chamber. Or calling just to let the doc know they have a case of 'diver's elbow'. Sometimes it comes with 'diver's excessive fatigue'. I don't know, perhaps when shot during battle, members of the armed forces pop in to the medic's tent to see if they have anything for 'soldier's hole in the leg'. I've yet to speak to anyone that thinks they have 'diver's tingling, numbness and paralysis' but, as you will see in the following chapter, they have emailed.

I don't know why we're so often reluctant to admit we might have a hit and The Shaman has performed entire lectures on the subject, so it's unlikely you'll discover the definitive answer in this intro. Just kidding, of course: DCI denial afflicts those born on a Tuesday.

I suppose people worry they'll never be able to dive again or will be told off for having done something wrong, or they'll be stuck with a huge bill, none of which are true. Also, it's possible to come up with an alternative cause for almost any symptom; like putting your arm out of joint whilst punching an instructor in Thailand. And no one thinks it will happen to them, particularly when they've dived within their limits; but then I never thought I'd get off with a supermodel. Mind you, I haven't. Which is totally unfair. Maybe it's because I'm always lifting tanks.

So, I tried to separate this chapter into Type I and Type II bends which, as you will see, turns out to be a bit arbitrary, since the cause is the same. That's the problem with the body: all the bits insist on being interlinked rather than existing in separate, distinct categories, which makes diagnosis difficult.

It's far from a unique problem though. On iTunes, they have The Smiths listed under Britpop.

Tip: If a representative of the company you've been diving with assures you that, despite your symptoms, you can't have DCS because your dives haven't been "deep enough for long enough", call your local chamber anyway.

TYPE I – MUSCLE, JOINT PAIN AND SKIN BENDS

Three days ago, I returned from a holiday in Tenerife where I did a dive to 30m. Afterwards, I found that my computer had a diver attention symbol showing and that I had gone over the no-decompression limit by approximately one minute. My computer is set to a conservative setting and I had only done a safety stop of five minutes before surfacing.

Since then I have developed pain in my left shoulder joint that comes and goes especially after lying on it. I may have done something to cause this whilst passing my equipment back to the boat crew but wasn't aware of any injury at the time. I have no other symptoms at all. Could you advise of any prognosis?

"It's like hitting your thumb with a hammer. For your thumb to still hurt X days later, you have to hit it Y hard. And you would notice that at the time."

Pay attention everyone, this is interesting. It encompasses so many aspects of bends issues, as well as conflicting stuff that can throw doctors.

The bottom line is you have shoulder pain after a dive. It's still there and so must be suspected as a bend. On the other hand, you could have hurt it on the kit hand over, shoulders do hurt when you lie on them, and finally when you set a comp to a lesser physiological state than you really are, it can put you into deco when you are probably OK. I did this once, deciding after a big brekky in Grenada to see what P3 on the Suunto Stinger would do on my next dive. Well, I reckon it was more conservative than a bunch of spotty faced Eton boys at a BNP rally. Within five minutes of a 23m dive it was a-pinging and a-beeping on my slow ascent. I kinda knew I was well within limits, experience being the greater truth, but it did make me realise that you really have to be over 16 stone and unfit to use that setting.

So that could count on your non-DCS side, but the one curve ball you have is this: if it still hurts this long after the dive, and it was related to kit passing, then you sure would have felt a pang when you were handing over. It's like hitting your thumb with a hammer.

For your thumb to still hurt X days later, you have to hit it Y hard. And you would notice that at the time. My gut says it's a 50/50 DCS call here, but you do need to see a doc with experience.

Having never played a round of golf in my life, I have been diagnosed with 'Golfer's Elbow', or a case of tendonitis. I work in a dive centre and so the cause is easy to guess: lifting cylinders, kit and anchors. I have been given anti-inflammatories, and have an appointment with a traumatologist this week.

Relaxing the lifting is easy as I can just get the customers to do it, but I'm concerned with the uptake of nitrogen in the 'traumatised' tissues. I generally dive twice per day, six days per week. The morning dive is the deepest with a 30m max depth, multilevel profile, and an average 50 minute dive time. After a three hour break, the afternoon is usually taken up with another 50 minute multilevel dive to a maximum of 20m.

Should the diving stop for a while?

You're right: we should re-name this 'medial epicondylitis' as 'Tank Lifter's Elbow'. This is one of those perennial diving concerns, which seems to stem from many anecdotes of recurrent symptoms in previously injured areas of the body. I have to say that I've yet to see any convincing evidence that DCI is more likely at the sites of old trauma or scarring. That said, I do not dismiss the fact that many divers seem to get aches, pains and odd sensations in areas of prior damage. Quite why this happens is a bit of a mystery.

It is likened in a way to the old granddad whose arthritic knees begin to play up just before rain. In the 60s, a rheumatologist called Joseph Hollander built a special climate chamber to investigate this phenomenon and found that what was previously thought to be an old wives' tale was a demonstrable clinical reality. The currently favoured explanation goes like this: uninjured tissue is relatively elastic, compared to scar tissue, which is stiff, fibrous and dense. Hence pressure changes will cause expansion and contraction in healthy tissue, allowing gas to diffuse as normal. The scar tissue in old injuries distorts and is pulled about, often causing pain and inhibiting the easy movement of gas. As a consequence, one could postulate that once nitrogen is taken up by scarred areas, it lingers and increases DCI risk. A nice theory, but one not supported by experiments so far.

"...divers seem to get aches, pains and odd sensations in areas of prior damage. Quite why this happens is a bit of a mystery."

The bottom line then, is that we don't really know whether this connection between scar tissue and DCI exists. It's probably safe to say that in small areas, for example broken digits, healed cuts etc., there's little to worry about. When we're talking major surgery though, especially that around regions prone to DCI anyway (eg spinal operations), it might be prudent to take a few extra precautions with regards to conservative diving: minimising bottom depths and times, using Nitrox, keeping profiles square and avoiding deco where possible.

I recently went to Dahab for a dive trip where we did three dives in one day but with just five dives overall.

Due to poor buoyancy control, on dive four I was ascending and descending fast from 10m up to almost one metre and then down to seven and so on. My bottom time was about 40 minutes when we started to ascend. While ascending there was a sudden cramp as though my knee had locked itself up, with acute pain on the upper left knee joint.

Back on land I was limping. Thinking I had perhaps hit my knee against the dive boat, I went in for dive five. Again, I was bouncing up and down in the deep. Afterwards, I limped to my room and applied deep heat over the joint. The next morning, I could not walk straight. The pain was unbearable and continued for a week before it subsided. I did not suspect DCI as the depth was not more than 12m and I had no other significant symptoms.

Is it possible I was wrong?

I think you did have a bend. What you were doing has different names such as bounce diving or yo-yo diving but I prefer the term 'sawtooth profile'. You can see where the name comes from when you see the printout of this sort of dive from the computer, but whatever you call it, the end result can be the same: a hit.

When you breathe nitrogen as a composite of the air, the deeper you go the more is absorbed into your tissues. The reason why we have to have slow ascents and safety stops is to let the nitrogen slowly move from the tissues back to the blood and then be exhaled. Anything that speeds up ascent will mean that the nitrogen can come out too quickly and form bubbles instead of being evenly absorbed back into the blood for removal. Imagine a diver doing

"Again, I was bouncing up and down in the deep. Afterwards, I limped to my room and applied deep heat over the joint. The next morning, I could not walk straight."

multiple dives in a day. Now imagine that the surface interval time between dives is not hours but seconds. Where does that put you on your PADI tables? That's what sawtooth profiling does for you, so a bend it most likely was, and you should have had a recompression or surface oxygen at the very least.

The best way of avoiding this in the future is to buy your own BCD and wetsuit so you always carry the same weight. The more you dive the better your buoyancy control will be too; it was the same for all of us when we started. But promise me one thing. If your buoyancy has an error factor of 7m at the moment, please don't go anywhere near coral until you have it truly sorted, as it's likely you will plough through it as you crash back down again.

I returned from a diving trip in Sharm last week. During my last day, I did two dives: the first to 29.5m and the second to 23.4m with a one hour 11 minute surface interval between them. During the second dive I started to experience a stiff neck, but put this down to diving posture. Since I've been back, I have experienced minor discomfort in my left elbow and my neck is still stiff and heavy. What could this be?

It's time for you to see a dive doctor to have a check as to whether you have the bends. Back to the old mantra: any abnormal symptom that wasn't there before a dive but is there afterwards, has to be assumed to be caused by the dive.

Yes, of course it might be that you were constantly looking over your shoulder, looking for a missing buddy and that's why the pain developed in water. But for it to still be there, and to then get an elbow pain as well, makes me raise my suspicious eyebrow.

A point worth noting is that a lot of dive docs may not be that familiar with DCS. They just sign off medical forms, so the best one to see is someone who works at or alongside a recompression chamber, so contact your local pot and get seen there.

I had a Type I bend in Scapa Flow and was treated with a Table 6 recompression. I have since seen my diving doctor, who gave me a check up and a HSE Certificate without any restrictions on my diving.

I plan to go to Scapa again next April, and would like to know what the chances are that I will get bent again. (I will be doing

similar repetitive dives... two dives a day for six days). Should I do more deco or reduce my bottom time? I plan much slower ascents now (no more than 6-8m per minute).

I think a Type I that needed only one treatment in the chamber is fairly minor on the bends ladder. Is there a chance you could get bent again? Well there is a chance of a hit every time you dive. However I would say that Scapa with its depths, bottom times needed and coldness can be more of a risk than say the good old Dredger in Portland with its 10m maximum depth and tropical warmth.

So, to be really safe just use Nitrox and set your computer for air. Keep well hydrated, and if your deco stops are a bit chilly then increase the time by a few minutes to compensate for cold veins constricting and not letting the blood flow so easily, which can decrease off gassing.

Or, what about waiting for Hollywood to make the movie of Scapa? They'll say the US military single-handedly scuttled the entire German fleet, shoot it with full size re-creation in Palau, and stick it in 10ft of water. Historically inaccurate, but a much safer dive.

Three days after completing my Divemaster Course, I started having a dull ache in my right knee which comes and goes. Today my right elbow is aching. I only had three dives last weekend. On Friday I went to 7.2m for 11 minutes and on Sunday I went to 14.4m for 43 minutes, followed by a one hour 24 minute surface interval and then down to 4.5m for 23 minutes. On the first dive on Sunday I felt cold and a bit ill (red wine and beer the night before), so 25 minutes into the dive I surfaced for three minutes, after which I felt completely fine and went back down.

Apart from the aches I feel completely fine. Should I worry or is this just the pesky English weather?

It would be the pesky English weather if you had arthritis, or one of those conditions that always seems to worsen with the weather, but I assume you are a fit young bloke embarking on getting some pro-dive qualifications, and not my granny, so we have to assume the worst I'm afraid. The three dives would have surely been fine, except for that bounce dive on the second. I know it was only a shallow dive but reading between the lines, you may have been dehydrated from your alcohol combination the night before and on top of that,

"Keep well hydrated, and if your deco stops are a bit chilly then increase the time by a few minutes to compensate for cold veins..."

being cold on a dive can affect your off-gassing of nitrogen. Your peripheral vessels will constrict to retain heat, and don't perfuse the tissues like they are supposed to. Add all this up and it could well be DCS. Good news though, if it's just in the joints and you have no neurological symptoms, eg tingling or numbness, then it should get better in no time in the chamber.

I took up Scuba diving about six months ago and very shortly afterwards developed pains in my muscles, which was diagnosed as being a virus called Polymyalgia Rheumatica. I have been taking steroids for this ever since.

I hadn't dived in the intervening period and the pills have given me a pain free existence, but I went diving again about three weeks ago and the next day felt the muscle pains again, even though I was still taking the same dosage of steroids. Could it be that I got the virus as a result of Scuba diving or that by diving I am reducing my chances of getting rid of it?

Hmmm, a big long scratch of the head here. Here's what goes through my mind:

You develop muscle pains "shortly" after diving. It is vaguely diagnosed as PMR, for which the true causes have not really been elicited. When you're not diving and on steroids, you feel OK, but as soon as you dive the pains come back. This sounds like a bend, misdiagnosed, and then another hit next time you got in the water. Yes, it could be PMR, but let's consider the alternatives. I think you need to see a diving rheumatologist, if they exist. Failing that, a complete blood work up and even a trial of recompression if it occurs again after a dive.

My wife and I went to Stoney Cove last weekend to do a dry suit course. My wife had a membrane suit, hood and 2mm gloves, skiing underwear and thinsulate undersuit. The first dive was to a maximum of 20m for 31 minutes in 13°C water. She was cold on surfacing and realised afterwards that her drysuit leaked at both the neck and wrist seals. During the surface interval she was shivering, complained of being wet and had lost dexterity in her hands, but didn't warm herself up or change her undergarments. The second dive, after a 49 minute surface interval, was for 20 minutes with a maximum depth of 7m.

After showering, drying off and getting into warm clothes, she

complained that her hands had some numbness but also hurt. She also said that she felt a little 'spaced out'. The pain in her hands began to wear off after about four hours but she noticed that she had a red blotchy rash coming up on her cheeks and chin. These disappeared by the next morning. She's adamant these symptoms are due the cold and the hood rubbing but I'm concerned they might be due to DCS.

Well this is something we say a lot to divers: you must always seek advice about any feeling of being unwell after a dive, and the best people to seek this advice from are the hyperbaric experts. The problem with going to your local casualty department is that there probably won't be a doctor with a good understanding of DCS and in my experience most people walk out with a diagnosis of middle ear infection and a handful of penicillin.

Your wife could easily have Type I DCS as this is associated with a rash and fatigue over and above what is expected from a weekend at Stoney. The biggest problem with DCS is denial, which is unnecessary in the UK as the treatment is free, and there are plenty of well run chambers to sort you out. Being recompressed ensures that the problem won't worsen to any permanent damage and also doesn't mean you can never dive again. Again it is never too late to seek advice, and I have treated divers some time after the problem has occurred and had very good results. So call your local unit first, get some good hyperbaric advice and don't just assume you will be fine and it'll pass.

> "The pain in her hands began to wear off after about four hours but she noticed that she had a red blotchy rash coming up on her cheeks and chin."

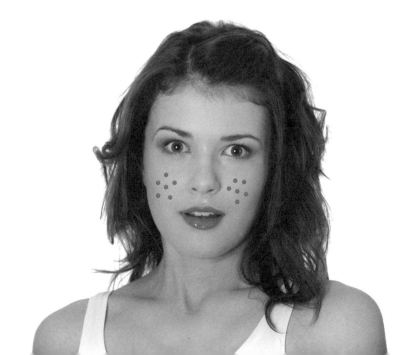

TYPE II – NEUROLOGICAL

Earlier this year, I had a bend in the Maldives where I was working and had to go into the chamber three times. My left hand and forearm were numb and I could not feel the difference during the sensation test. After the treatment, the hyperbaric doctor told me to stay out of the water for two weeks. I thought it was a bit short but he guaranteed me it was fine. As I am diving instructor and could lose my job if I stay out of the water too long, I waited two weeks and then did a very shallow dive to 16m on Nitrox.

I was fine. At the beginning I was feeling very tired for doing practically nothing compared to what I am used to doing, but unfortunately I hurt my lower back. Three months later, I finished my contract and stopped diving. I have had some treatment (acupuncture) for my back and feel much better and will soon be off to work as an instructor in Asia.

Do you think I should visit a hyperbaric doctor to do some tests before I go back in the water? Also, I would like to know if my body is weaker after the bend and should I stop taking contraceptive pills?

This is a real point of debate amongst diving docs: when should you go back in after treatment for a bend?

In the UK, the regulations from the HSE state that after a neurological bend you should wait 28 days before returning to diving, but these guidelines are really meant for full time commercial divers. In some navies they will let you back in after only seven days with a bend like yours, but again, here the expectation is that these naval divers are young and at the peak of their fitness. We generally say six weeks off diving, but there is a degree of flexibility: we wouldn't tell a poor old unbent diver to cancel their trip of a lifetime if it was five and a half weeks away. But the bottom line in your case is that two weeks off after a Type II hit in a non-naval diver is too short a time.

Four weeks would have been better.

There is another factor here concerning the realities of life. All too often a doc will dispense completely unworkable advice: "Oh, just take two weeks off work and you'll be fine." "Just ignore your child and it'll learn to behave." That sort of stuff. So there may well be issues in your contract there, the roll on effects of taking time off as well, that may affect a decision to go back in. As I said, there has to be flexibility.

Do you need to be checked over before you go in again? No, however having had a bend before it might be needed for insurance purposes. Finally, only come off the Pill if you want to have a baby, as in your case there is no reason you cannot dive on it.

My buddy and I got back from a week holiday in Sharm where we did four dives in two days. Whilst we've just completed our Advanced Open Water course, we don't have many dives under our belts and have never dived at sea or from a boat. Since we don't have 'sea legs' we took some seasickness medication but, although we followed the instructions, they didn't help. My buddy was ill five times that first day and I was ill once. We drank plenty of fluids to ward off dehydration etc. and following the advice of our instructor, switched to Stugeron for the second day which worked a treat.

The second day's dives were to 22m. On the first dive, my buddy lost her mask, panicked and made a gradual ascent. She has a buoyancy problem, having not perfected the one quick press on the inflation hose, and if she's not near the bottom she's usually above me. I saw her lose her mask and went to her aid. By then, we were near the surface and she couldn't descend so we didn't do a safety stop.

"She has a buoyancy problem, having not perfected the one quick press on the inflation hose, and if she's not near the bottom she's usually above me."

My buddy again made an early ascent (gradual, not rapid) on the afternoon dive. The problem this time was that her reg had flooded with sea water. Once more, we didn't do a safety stop. The following day we got up at midnight to go to Cairo by bus (we didn't fly because of the dives), and arrived back to our hotel at midnight the next day on a very bumpy road. We were really tired as we didn't get much sleep.

Since the boat dives, we're both feeling as though we're still on the boat and it's bobbing up and down. Could it be due to not

having really had a good night's sleep during the week? The flight home took seven hours because of a mess up at Sharm airport and whilst we did the exercises they advise on planes, we still feel slightly disorientated. Could you advise what this could be?

I think with two bounce dives and now disorientation, you have to consider this might be inner-ear DCS. This is where nitrogen bubbles manifest in the vestibular canals, causing havoc with your balance. If the ascents were just slightly faster than normal, and you were not dehydrated, and the bottom times were of a normal length, then it may well not be a hit, but you can't be sure until a dive doc has a look at you. It will be a tough call to differentiate this from, say, a middle ear over-expansion injury, but a good doc will know what they're doing.

To shoot from the hip, I would guess that if your buddy is only feeling like she's on the boat still, and you have that AND disorientation, then my Law of Inequality will reign. That is, the panicking diver shooting to the top gets hit less than the cool one dragged up with them. C'est la vie.

I am just back from two weeks diving in St Lucia. Great first week with eight dives over four days but after doing two dives in one day during the second week (both about 14m for 40-45 minutes), I felt extremely tired, my neck, shoulders, arms and under my ribcage ached, and I had some slight tingling in my fingers. The next morning I spoke to the dive instructor and he immediately put me on oxygen for one hour and phoned DAN. The local doctor carried out various tests, all of which were okay. He did not think I had DCS.

Three years ago I had a micro-discectomy on L4/L5. One consequence of this is constant pins and needles in my right foot, which I combat by taking 500mg of Gabapentin three times a day. A side effect of this is tiredness. This was the first time diving whilst on medication. My specialist said that whilst there should be no problem diving (his wife dives), I should try a different drug because of the tiredness. I reduced the dosage over the course of my holiday and my last dose was the day before my final two dives. I have not started the new drug yet.

I was not feeling 100% before I went away and the doctor thought that my symptoms could be viral. He also thought that

"I think with two bounce dives and now disorientation, you have to consider this might be inner-ear DCS."

it could be dehydration: from cold London to hot and sticky St Lucia; a long boat trip in the sun the day before; eight dives in the first week etc. I had been drinking plenty of water but perhaps not replenishing salts and very little alcohol was drunk. He prescribed some of those rehydration sachets and told me to rest for the remainder of the holiday.

The tingling soon went but all the aches and tiredness still continue even though I've been back in the UK for four days. I am wondering whether a visit to my GP is called for.

Hmm, a complex mesh of interwoven symptoms, overlaid with curve balls and red herrings, resulting in a big slice from the pie of confusion and doubt. Here are some thoughts. The Gabapentin decreases the tingling but makes you tired. So by stopping it you'd think your tingling would increase but you would feel less tired. After the diving, and since your return, you still feel tired but the tingling has gone too. And your previous tingling was in your foot, not your hand. Dehydration can predispose to a bend as you have less fluid to take away all that nitrogen.

Yes, viral illnesses can make you tired and mimic any symptoms, but they usually run for 7 to 10 days, and you have these problems after a two week holiday and four days back. Should you see your GP for something that could be dive related? Probably not. They wouldn't have a clue and would tell you to come back in a week, so you can catch something off someone else in the waiting room.

Here's my advice; and remember the mantra. If it wasn't there before diving, and it is there now, always assume it's a bend until proved otherwise. So, best you see the doc at your local chamber for full assessment for DCI, as that can only be treated by recompression. If it's not a bend then post viral/change of meds/holiday fatigue will get better.

"If it wasn't there before diving, and it is there now, always assume it's a bend until proved otherwise. So, best you see the doc at your local chamber for full assessment for DCI..."

About 10 minutes after surfacing from a dive in Roatan recently, I started to feel light-headed and when I got off the boat I felt very dizzy. I was put on oxygen (about 40 minutes after surfacing) and taken to see a dive doctor who put me on oxygen again for another 30 minutes. I then had an hour break in which I felt 99% better, apart from a slight soreness in the elbow.

I went into a recompression chamber for two hours, 15 minutes and felt fine afterwards. The following afternoon, I started to feel light-headed again and slightly spaced out. In the following week I saw the doctor twice and she told me that it was just a result of the treatment and it would pass. I haven't dived since and I still feel the same.

A two hour plus recompression is not really adequate if you have been diagnosed as having a bend. The fact that you had these symptoms before treatment and they were still there afterwards means you need retreatment.

At our chamber we use a standard Royal Navy Table 62 for the first treatment. This is a minimum of four and a half hours and is accepted as the minimum needed for the first recompression. We would refer to you as having a 'partially treated bend' because there was only one treatment and it was very short. You need to see a dive doctor for assessment and then start all over again if your symptoms warrant it.

The lesson here is that in various chambers over the world you may well come across different treatment tables, but if you are going into the pot then you may as well go in properly. If you don't then you will have to on your return to the UK anyway, and I'll tell you from experience it can be a bit boring the second time around.

I was doing my Rescue Diver course in Sharm, and on one exercise, although I was only under for approximately 12-15 minutes, had to descend and ascend three times. Later that afternoon, I took part in a dive during which the instructors illustrated some novice diver mistakes / antics and during which I was responsible for leading the dive. This dive was very tiring, even though it was short, and was to a maximum depth of 20m.

About half an hour after this dive I began to feel exhausted and faint in the 47°C heat. I attempted to rehydrate and immediately felt better. An hour or so after returning to the shore I felt extremely dizzy but again, sitting indoors and drinking water helped considerably. The dive instructors (and I) thought I had heat exhaustion or sunstroke, but the following morning I woke up feeling pretty ropey with tingling fingers and a dull pain in my elbow. The dive doc in Sharm treated me with oxygen and after a positive result, put me in the chamber for two hours. I was asked to return twice to check that none of my symptoms had reoccurred and I received no further treatment because I was fine.

"The dive instructors (and I) thought I had heat exhaustion or sunstroke, but the following morning I woke up feeling pretty ropey with tingling fingers and a dull pain in my elbow."

I want to start my DM course in Thailand soon but have noticed that my elbow (the one which hurt in Sharm) is painful if I press on it. It is a different kind of uncomfortable feeling than I think I remember from Sharm, but I just wondered if that is something I should be concerned about.

I've been in 45°C, and it's hot. 47 has to be the hottest time ever out there. That and all those up and down shenanigans will easily equal a bend. You got better with the treatment, but now the pain is back. Well in my experience, if you press something hard enough it will hurt later. It doesn't mean the bend is back. But in these cases always see a dive doc just to make sure.

Three weeks ago, I had Type II DCS (bubble in the brain). I was treated with five hours in the chamber and have fully recovered. Are there any rules regarding alcohol consumption post DCS? I had five pints on Saturday and have a bit of a sore shoulder now. I did wake up lying in a strange position, it is getting better and it isn't sore when standing, but I'm a bit paranoid after the whole bends incident.

Only five pints. That's an aperitif, in the diving world, mate. But be calm, there are no rules about drinking alcohol after a full recovery from a bend. You are allowed to. The only rule is about drinking the five before you dive. A tad foolhardy that would be.

As for the other problem: you are three weeks away from full DCS recovery. Sleep funny on your shoulder? Wake with pain there? Mmm, I'll go with it being bed trauma rather than a recurrence.

I have been experiencing balance, coordination problems, and tremors since my last dive. It was six weeks ago now, but I had an uncontrolled rapid ascent. The maximum depth was 21m and I lost control around 14m. I emptied my BCD and breathed out, but still came up so fast that my mask was ripped off my head. The dive operation in Malaysia said I was fine and to stop complaining. That night I had itchy skin. They told me not to worry. 20 hours after the dive, I flew. The next day I was staggering and had pain in my arms. I went to hospital in Korea, where I live. They told me not to worry; it's not dive related. Now I have neurological problems that I've never had before. Could it be related to the rapid ascent? What should I do?

"Are there any rules regarding alcohol consumption post DCS? I had five pints on Saturday and have a bit of a sore shoulder now."

This may seem like one of those no-brainers but I wanted to highlight the sort of advice that is sometimes dished out by those 'in the know' when overseas. I'd like to say I made this up but unfortunately it is genuine, unadulterated, and all too representative of the overseas cases we see at LDC and MDC. I hardly need point out the salient features that would have me hollering down the phone but this poor diver has illustrated perfectly the dangers of leaving decompression illness untreated. We have naturally urged her not to dive again until she's been seen by a competent dive doc, but the salutary lesson is never be fobbed off by a dive school eager to absolve themselves of any blame.

We have just returned from a trip to Tobago. We did a night dive with two inexperienced Germans on their third dive of the day. One of them lost his fin, his torch, and after a bit of a panic, ran out of air. His buddy gave him his alternate, but they were taken in a down current to 33m (from 15m). The dive guide and another diver went down and brought them to the surface. The two Germans were given oxygen at the dive centre, but declined treatment at the decompression chamber, due in part to the dive doc not being able to find the key. Two days later one told me he had pins and needles and the other had had bleeding from his ears.

Will they be OK? Would a bend sort itself out if you leave it long enough, or are you asking for problems next time you dive?

I love this. They turned down treatment on account of the doc losing the key to the chamber room. Yeah right. It sounds like someone persuaded them not to get un-bent because of the hassle of going to the locksmith. Ear bleed bloke was OK, but Herr Tingle did need treatment. The consequences of diving again, still symptomatic of DCS, are worsening the problem. Not clever.

On occasions it can just improve in time, but nitrogen bubbles are curious things. If they were totally asymptomatic, without treatment four weeks later, they could dive, maybe, but best to see a dive doc for a check up before risking it. In my experience though, on close questioning, there are always some symptoms left, and late treatment can be warranted if they want to dive again.

I have recently returned from a four day liveaboard trip in the Similan islands. Upon returning to shore, I felt a tingling sensation in my left toe and right thumb. These symptoms

"One of them lost his fin, his torch, and after a bit of a panic, ran out of air. His buddy gave him his alternate, but they were taken in a down current to 33m (from 15m)."

developed sporadically in various parts of my body (elbow, hand, knee etc). I went straight to the SSS chamber in Phuket where I was assessed by the doctor and had two Table 6 treatments followed by two Table 5 treatments. I flew home around 85 hours after my final treatment.

There was no apparent cause for the bend: I was diving with an instructor throughout the trip and well within the limits of my computer. I still have a few tingles in my left hand, but was discharged by the doctor with no firm confirmation that I even had the bends; the treatment was precautionary.

In order to satisfy my insurance company I have to have a medical before I return to diving. Can you tell me what kind?

An interesting story here. No provocative dives, but symptoms that were still resistant to an awful lot of recompression. Two Table 6s, or 62s in the UK Navy definition, is quite a lot for minor tingling in a toe and a thumb. We would normally do one only, with more follow up shorter treatments, until all the symptoms have gone, or there is no difference in tingling from one treatment to the next (the so-called plateau). But I would say that if you did improve in the pot, and your residual symptoms are way less than what you started with, then this is most likely to be a bend, so you need to put that on your medical form. Your insurance company is right; you do need to have a check up before diving again. It's a straightforward 'Fit to Dive' medical where we look closely at your nervous system.

A couple of other issues here. Although you stayed well within limits, and your computer made no noises at you on the dive, we are all physiologically different, and dive tables etc. are only a guide. It is possible to pop out of that bell curve and be the rare case at either extreme. Also, bear in mind other factors that can increase on-gassing, or decrease off-gassing. Dehydration and diarrhoea are common examples, and these can easily occur on a boat in the hot sun in a far-flung destination.

"Although you stayed well within limits, and your computer made no noises at you on the dive, we are all physiologically different, and dive tables etc are only a guide."

EVERYTHING ELSE YOU WANTED TO KNOW ABOUT DCI

Can DCI result from freediving in 4-5m of water? I was lobstering for 10 days in Australia last August and only had a real issue after this first day of freediving. Upon return to the dock, I almost fell over from dizziness and sight difficulties, and had to lie down for a couple of hours before I could walk around again.

The following nine days went mostly well, particularly with the use of Scuba, but on occasion with freediving some dizziness at the surface would occur whenever I failed to release a little of my held breath on the way up. It seems that even a held breath may force some nitrogen into the blood stream, but I cannot find this to be a factor in any of the literature that I've researched since.

This is an interesting one. In the 1950s, DCI after freediving was thought to be impossible for two reasons: the amount of nitrogen contained in one breath was not considered sufficient to cause symptoms, and dives were too short to allow the nitrogen to dissolve into the blood. We now know that it is indeed possible.

Studies were carried out in the 1960s on pearl divers in French Polynesia, who dive to 30m or more 40 to 60 times a day (each dive lasting about two minutes with a three to four minute surface interval). These divers showed a high rate of 'Taravana' (literally meaning 'to fall crazily'): a range of symptoms varying from vertigo and impaired vision to loss of consciousness and paralysis, consistent with DCI. Interestingly, divers on neighbouring islands performed similar profile dives but with surface intervals of 12 to 15 minutes. Taravana there was almost unknown.

Your symptoms seem to have come on severely after the first day. US Navy tables at 10m on air give a bottom time of over six hours, so at maximum depths of 5m, you would have to be underwater for a huge amount of time, breathing compressed gas, to put you at risk

"Can DCI result from freediving in 4-5m of water? I was lobstering for 10 days in Australia last August and only had a real issue after this first day of freediving."

of DCI. On single breaths, even with multiple dives, you would not accumulate enough nitrogen after one day to induce DCI.

I suspect that another issue may have been the culprit here, possibly an ear barotrauma from repetitive equalising.

Recently we were having discussions at my dive club on the dangers of freediving after Scuba. Some members seem to think there is no possible physical or medical problem with the recompression and rapid decompression associated with freediving, when you have a skin-full of dissolved gas. What is your advice?

Although there isn't much definite evidence on this, freediving soon after a Scuba dive could give rise to two problems. As you know, during a Scuba dive, tissue loading with inert gases occurs at different rates, with some tissues taking longer to release gas once the diver has ascended. Microbubbles which have expanded on ascent after a Scuba dive but have not been filtered out through the lungs can be recompressed by freediving, and potentially bypass the lung. They will then end up in the arterial circulation and predispose to arterial gas embolism.

Secondly, freediving is similar to bounce diving or sawtooth profiling, in that rapid decompression or ascents can reload the tissues or impede the diffusion of gas out of the body, thus increasing the risk of DCI. The actual amount of inert gas loading on a freedive is likely to be small so this effect is unlikely to be a big problem.

Nevertheless, the accepted wisdom is not to freedive at all until your computer has cleared. That way, you have the best available evidence that you are starting from as clean a slate as possible.

I bought a holiday home about 1,000m above sea level in Italy, and every summer for the past few years I've been diving for a week or so whilst staying there.

I retired last year and am going to live there for pretty much the whole year, but someone mentioned to me that there might be a problem with driving back to my villa after the diving because of the height gain. I didn't think it would be a problem but then I remembered buying one of those 'salads in a bag' in a shop at sea level after the diving, which I left on the passenger seat. On the way home the bag expanded so much that it burst and

> "Microbubbles which have expanded on ascent after a Scuba dive but have not been filtered out through the lungs can be recompressed by freediving, and potentially bypass the lung."

showered the whole car with bits of lettuce. Apart from nearly crashing I thought the whole incident rather amusing but it occurred to me that this might be happening to my lungs on the way up. So, is it safe for me to continue driving down to the sea for a couple of dives then going back home to 1,000m every day?

Exploding bags of salad are a somewhat unusual diving hazard but it's a very good illustration of expanding gases and Boyle's Law. We at LDC and MDC have been considering this long and hard, and have done some digging around, however there don't seem to be any specific tables or hard and fast recommendations for this scenario.

In essence what you are doing here is the equivalent of flying after diving, and as such you really ought to be leaving a good 24 hours after your final dive before driving home. In naval rescue situations, the usual ceiling on flying immediately after diving is 300m, so you are well in excess of this. The potential for bubble expansion precipitating a bend is well known even with moderate altitude increases and stories of divers developing bends whilst driving across the hills between Sharm and Dahab after diving are common.

If you really must go home each day, maximise your safety margins and minimise your nitrogen load, by using Nitrox on air tables, leaving it as long as possible after diving before ascending, allowing regular no-diving days to allow yourself to off-gas, and keeping your depths shallow and times well within the limits. I have to say I could not possibly recommend this course of action as it does pose a significant risk of getting bent. If you can afford it I would almost consider getting your own recompression chamber built in a bespoke annexe so that you can leap in as soon as you get home.

I'm a bit of an exercise freak and train with weights most days for at least two hours. Some of the lads at the gym are divers and were saying that you shouldn't exercise when you dive as it might trigger the bends. Is this true?

Good question. These days kids are ballooning in weight, gyms are big business and everyone is being admonished from all sides for not doing enough exercise. Diving can be a physically demanding sport: those tanks don't carry themselves and unexpected currents

"Exploding bags of salad are a somewhat unusual diving hazard"

can put a sudden strain on the fittest of finners. As you say though, there are concerns that exercise can increase the chance of DCI. How to balance the two?

Like a good gag, it's all in the timing. Vigorous exercise is thought to produce micronuclei, ie the beginnings of very tiny bubbles, due to blood being agitated and warmed, and shearing of tissues with movement. These micronuclei can turn into bigger bubbles or act as 'seeds' around which bubbles can form. And more bubbles means a higher risk of DCI. Luckily, about 98% of micronuclei vanish within six hours, so the advice is to leave it at least this long after exercising before diving.

The other issue is gas absorption: if you've been for a workout just before a dive then your heart will still be pounding, pushing the blood round your body at an accelerated rate when you're in the water, which will increase the amount of nitrogen in your tissues.

Another (admittedly preliminary) study has shown that exercise 24 hours prior to diving might actually reduce the chance of DCI and the cause of this phenomenon is being investigated. So a workout 24 hours beforehand might be protective, but you should reduce the duration and intensity of any exercise closer to a dive. The other aspect is dehydration, so remember to tank up on fluids too.

During a dive, the idea is to minimise your inert gas absorption. Flapping around like an untrained seal will increase your nitrogen uptake and make bends more likely. On the ascent, however, there is now good evidence that light exercise will accelerate off-gassing because of the increased blood-flow mentioned above, and can therefore reduce DCI risk. By light I mean leisurely finning, rather than hanging motionless on the shot line. Heavy exercise is more likely to produce more bubbles though, so don't start any 200m races with your buddy at the safety stop.

What about after a dive? The same suggestions apply: strenuous gym sessions could cause more micronuclei to form and combine with the extra gas that might be liberated from muscles as the blood flow to them increases. Any post-dive workout should be gentle and at least six hours after the dive to allow sufficient time to off-gas and avoid micronuclei issues.

"Diving can be a physically demanding sport: those tanks don't carry themselves and unexpected currents can put a sudden strain on the fittest of finners."

Are there any tests for decompression illness?

Experiments have been made on Doppler ultrasound and transthoracic echocardiography (both basically refinements of the gel-on-tummy baby scan) to pick up microbubbles. The bottom line is that although both can detect the little bleeders (microbubbles, not babies), some are too small for the current top-end devices to pick up, and the idea of a test is to exclude DCI with as near to 100% certainty as possible. A non-invasive optical method has been developed which has higher resolution, so this has potential, but as yet it is still some way off the affordable market.

Progress is being made, but for the time being at least, we will have to put our faith in good old fashioned clinical acumen. Which is no bad thing: I'd hate to be replaced by a machine.

Do you use different recompression tables when treating a diver with DCI, depending on what depth they got symptoms, or which gas they have been using? If someone has been diving on a rebreather or Trimix, does that change things?

Basically, the answer is no. Diving physicians select from a range of treatment tables, but the choice is rarely influenced by depth or gas mix; more by the clinical picture and severity of the symptoms. There are several different sets of tables in use, some developed by the military, some by commercial or sport diving organisations, and they do vary depending on which particular gas bubble model they are based on. The primary purposes of recompression, though, are threefold: to compress gas bubbles to relieve local pressure and restart blood flow; to allow enough time for bubbles to redissolve and be breathed out; to increase blood oxygen content and oxygen delivery to damaged tissues.

The protocol for achieving these three aims is largely independent of the depth and gas mix used in the accident as a Royal Navy Table 62 is usually deep and long enough (maximum of 18m for at least five hours) to achieve success. Over the years, countless divers have been guinea pigs to the fine tuning of the commonly used tables and the protocols that have evolved are tried and tested in all sorts of diving accident situations. Some macabre research has been performed recently on rats (unlucky creatures). They were exposed to Trimix in a hyperbaric chamber, decompressed rapidly to induce DCI, then treated with either oxygen or Heliox (50% helium and 50% oxygen). The control group (the really unlucky ones) were not

"Over the years, countless divers have been guinea pigs to the fine tuning of the commonly used tables and the protocols that have evolved are tried and tested in all sorts of diving accident situations."

treated at all. 40% of the control rats died, none of the treated ones did, and the rate of recovery was the same whether they were treated with oxygen or Heliox. So in this model there's no advantage to using Heliox to treat Trimix DCI over good old oxygen.

Sometimes, when DCI symptoms are very severe or not responding to the usual tables, deeper ones are used, and in these cases we often do use Heliox. This is because there's too much danger of the 100% oxygen having a toxic effect at the depth of these tables, so a 50% oxygen and 50% helium mix is used. Theoretically, diving on a closed-circuit rebreather where the PPO2 is kept constant reduces the amount of nitrogen absorbed thus lessening DCI risk, but if you were to get a hit using one, well, forget about what the risk was because you've got a hit so the treatment and tables would be exactly the same. It's a complex subject, as you'd imagine, but I hope that gives you a flavour.

Hi, I am only 14 years old and have been diving with PADI for about three years. I've nearly clocked up 50 dives and have started diving up to four times a week. I'm not quite old enough to do Nitrox but when I am I would like to know what would be the best gas for me to use, considering I could be diving at this rate for another 30 odd years and am interested in one day becoming a technical diver.

In theory Nitrox is always a safer gas to use. Less nitrogen, less chance of micro (or 'normal') bubbles, and thus DCS. And if you are doing a lot of diving daily, you feel less knackered as well.

However, the thing is not to get too obsessive about what you breathe. An average of four a week is way under that of a full on air swigging, four a day Sharm instructor. And they're all normal aren't they. Aren't they? So if you want, go for the Nitrox, but don't not dive if it's not available. Anyway, if you get into techie stuff and deep depths, you'll be on Trimix or Heliox anyway and only using oxygen enriched air for long, shallow deco stops.

As a paramedic who dives, I've heard that it's important not to administer Entonox to a diver who might have DCS. Please could you clarify the medical/technical reasons for this? What about if the diver is not showing any signs of DCS, but needs pain relief?

Entonox, which goes by the more colloquial names of 'laughing gas', 'gas & air' and 'phlogisticated nitrous air' (thank its discoverer for that

last one), is a 50:50 mix of nitrous oxide and oxygen. Priestley, an English chemist, first synthesised it in 1775 and was so impressed with himself he wrote: "I have now discovered an air five or six times as good as common air... nothing I ever did has surprised me more, or is more satisfactory." This was probably due to the fact that it smells and tastes sweet, and induces a pleasing euphoria together with 'slight hallucinations'. It soon became the anaesthetic of choice for dentists, but nowadays its main proponents are (para)medics who use it for emergency on-site pain relief, midwives who administer it to women in labour to stop them screaming, and Mr. T who occasionally injects it into his engine to escape the clutches of Colonel Decker in The A Team. And the odd blissed-out hippy at a psychedelic music festival.

The reason it's not given to divers with suspected DCI is that nitrous oxide is a highly soluble gas, so it will increase the diver's inert gas load and worsen any decompression illness present. Also, it can cause expansion of trapped gas in the body (eg in sinuses, middle ears etc.), and so should be avoided in anyone who has dived recently. If you have a diver in pain for another obvious reason and can exclude DCS and gas-trapping confidently (eg they've just trodden on a sea urchin and not dived), then by all means it can be used. Its half-life is short, but general advice is that you should not dive (or drive) for 12-24 hours after using Entonox. But don't tell that to Bosco Albert (Bad Attitude) Baracus…

Am I right in thinking that treatment for DCS is on the NHS, or do some chambers bill the diver afterwards?

If you are treated for decompression sickness in the UK then that is done on the NHS. It is considered an 'emergency treatment' and so is fully funded by our hard-earned taxes. Some chambers are within the grounds of NHS hospitals and some are located at privately owned hospitals or buildings, but it doesn't matter where they are as the treatments are paid for by the Health Authority that sits over the area your GP works in.

Problems arise if a diver is not registered with a GP, but this is unlikely if you are born and live in the UK, as you probably have at least been for your childhood shots. However, this is not always the case with, for example, expats. The rules are that anyone working in the UK is entitled to register on the NHS once they have worked for six months over here, so cover yourself with insurance if you still have time left to do. Effectively no chamber should ever bill a patient in the UK, so don't worry about cost when it comes to DCS.

"I have now discovered an air five or six times as good as common air... nothing I ever did has surprised me more, or is more satisfactory."

Can you recommend a good provider of annual multi-trip travel insurance that will provide decent cover for Scuba diving?

In my experience most year round insurance from the main advertised providers will need a Scuba top-up premium. It is worth noting what depths they will cover you to, though. Most will do it to the limits of your training, ie 18m for Open Water and 30m if you have the Advanced. Again, check that you are covered for recompression abroad in case you have a bend, but all companies do cover this in reality.

However, what may be worth noting is that in the UK, some Health Authorities are now refusing to pay for any recompression treatment if the diver is deemed non-emergency. They are now asking the chambers to ask the diver to bill it against their insurance. This could cause problems as some companies will not cover you once your feet touch the tarmac at the airport since you are now deemed under NHS care for any problem caused whilst travelling.

A 'non-emergency bend' though is an oxymoron in my mind as they all are. But then again, I don't write the cheques to the chambers for the costs of recompression.

I guess the lesson here is if you do have any tingle or joint pain, in fact anything abnormal after diving, don't just hope it will go away: call your local unit as soon as you can as you may be footing the bill yourself.

I am currently doing a massage practitioner training course. In May, we are spending a week on a liveaboard in the Red Sea. I'd like to practice my massage on my friends, but are there any contra-indications for massage after diving?

Easy Gents, settle down, and form an orderly queue.

What a sweet surprise that would be after the night dive each evening. No, there's no real issues here. All I suggest is for you to avoid hot oils and towels for anyone immediately after a dive, just simple massage, nothing Thai, Swedish or Hot Rock. And watch yourself, too. Too much exercise post dive can affect off gassing, so only do as much massage as does not make you sweaty and breathless.

> "I guess the lesson here is if you do have any tingle or joint pain, in fact anything abnormal after diving, don't just hope it will go away..."

EARS, NOSE, THROAT AND EYE PROBLEMS

Like all of us, my first real fears regarding the realm of ENT developed whilst watching Star Trek II: The Wrath of Khan. Ever since then I've harboured a vague, subconscious fear that one day someone, somewhere will put small wriggly creatures into my ears and these will slowly eat my brain (whilst emitting high pitched squeaking sounds) until the agony makes me kill myself. Nobody wants that. Mind you, looking back, I'm not even sure that's what happened in the film, so I suppose my biggest fear now ought to be being made to pay by a wrathful Trekkie for my inaccuracy.

Speaking of inaccuracy, I wish that when I learned to dive, I'd known then what I know now. Well, obviously, it would've saved a lot of time and money since I wouldn't have actually needed to learn anything because I'd already know how to dive. But with regard to ENT, it would've saved a lot of time getting my ears syringed in a Thai hospital. I'd had a hard time equalising, you see, and, trying to force it, had filled my middle ears (that can't be right, can it? Sounds too much like Middle Earth); had filled my Middle Earths with gunk, probably consisting of blood, mucus and, I don't know what else, wheelbarrows, probably. Not much you can do about that other than wait for it to go away and try and ignore the fact it sounds like you're hearing things through syrup.

Well, I know that now (and so will you, if you didn't already, after reading this chapter), but I didn't then. Coincidentally, neither did the medical staff at the hospital, so they charged me 200 Baht to syringe my ears with lukewarm water. I don't think they even put the syringe properly into my ear; just squirted it vaguely at the side of my head. Even at the time I remember thinking "surely this can't work", but then I thought "ah, but have faith. Yes, maybe faith is all you need for any medicine to work", and then I added, vaguely: "placebo effect etc." and so I filled my very soul with a firm belief that this was a process that was definitely going to work.

It didn't work.

Tip: If you can blow smoke rings out of your ears, it's best to get them checked by a dive doc before you get back in the water, even if you are JBS Haldane.

By the way, I shoe-horned eyes into this section on the strength that last time I dived with a cold on massive quantities of pseudoephedrine, I'm fairly sure that I was equalising through my left eye.

EQUALISING AND MIDDLE EAR

I am keen to do a PADI course, but found it very difficult to equalise my ears on the try-dives I did. As a result, my enjoyment was seriously marred by the considerable pain, even though I certainly wasn't down very deep.

I have a similar problem on planes and have been told that having my adenoids out as a child may have something to do it. Is there anything I can do to alleviate this problem and, if I decide to ignore the pain, am I likely to suffer any damage to my ears from doing a diving course?

This problem is a frequent occurrence in those who are just taking up diving. As you descend and put your body's air-spaces under increased pressure, the air within them is compressed and you need to add air to them (or 'equalise' the pressure with the outside environment, to put it another way) in order to maintain the same volume as normal. The most common way to do this is by blowing gently against a pinched nose.

You are getting the ear pain because you are not equalising your middle ears adequately and as most qualified divers know, if the air in your middle ear contracts, it pulls in the ear drum and causes the pain you describe. The reason it occurs most frequently on your first pool dives is that the Eustachian tube, which links the middle ear up to the nasal area through which the air is pushed, has been lying under used and dormant for a while.

Normally, this tube is rarely used as we do not experience pressure differences of any significant degree. Unless you are a pilot or a miner, the tube lies closed and dormant. So when you suddenly don a BC, leap into a pool and blow hard onto your closed nose you can't really expect instant trouble free equalisation. I always tell divers to 'exercise' their Eustachian tube if they have not been diving for a while or it is the first time. Just blow gently onto your closed nose up to 10 times a day for five or six days before you dive.

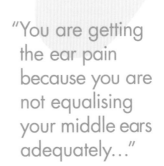

"You are getting the ear pain because you are not equalising your middle ears adequately..."

What you should never do, though, is dive deeper through the pain. Always ascend until the pain goes and then try equalising again before continuing your descent. After a certain point, if you try to descend through the pain, the pressure will cause the Eustachian tube to close entirely and there's no way you'll get any air through it until you ascend. This kind of pressure can cause permanent problems, such as a ruptured round or oval window (the interface between the middle and inner ear), causing tinnitus, deafness, and even long lasting balance problems.

Simple things you should try include avoiding alcohol, tobacco and dairy products before you dive, as they all increase mucus production. Keep water out of your mask for the same reason. Never try to dive with a cold or any sinus blockage.

What you also say about not even being able to equalise on aeroplanes worries me a bit, though. There are conditions, collectively called Eustachian Tube Dysfunction (ETD), where an abnormal Eustachian tube means that you will always have trouble equalising. This is only really diagnosable by an ENT consultant with CT or MRI scanning, but if it is the cause then sometimes it can be corrected surgically allowing you to dive again.

So try practising equalising and see if that helps you get down to the bottom of the pool without any pain, but if not, stop where you are, surface and get a referral to a consultant ENT surgeon.

I have managed to get a cold, which started yesterday as a sore throat. This has now gone but left a blocked up nose. Do you think I will be okay to dive by next Tuesday?

You could be lucky here. If the cold has come and gone through that sore throat, swallowing razor blades, choking on a porcupine phase, leaving just a stuffed up nose, then it could clear in time for diving. Only you will be able to tell on the day. The easiest way of telling is to stick your finger up your nose. If it comes out wet and mucousy, don't dive. If it's dry then off you go into the blue.

The problem with trying to dive with a cold, is that when you equalise, instead of air going up the Eustachian tube, it's snot instead. This will fill the middle ear, and stay there for a good six weeks. Your hearing will be dulled and you'll hear every footfall echo in your head when you walk. Some people think this is a reasonable trade off for a certain dive experience. Others do not.

> "Simple things you should try include avoiding alcohol, tobacco and dairy products before you dive, as they all increase mucus production."

Medication like Sudafed is an option at times, but I prefer to use this for the flight out there, and if I get a snotty reaction to sea water as it's not always enough for a cold.

I did a lot of diving about two and a half years ago and didn't have any problems. However, I've since had problems with my ears popping when flying (it took me an hour and a half of trying after one flight to try and pop them and it hurt when they did). On that basis would it be worth having a medical before going on a diving holiday this summer?

I think it would be a good idea. The cabin pressure in a plane does not vary that enormously from the ground. As the plane is pressurised during the flight, you have to pop your ears to the equivalent of say half an atmosphere, or about 5m of water. If you are having problems with a pressure change like this, then you sure as hell will if you dive any deeper than that. Something may well have happened in the last couple of years that made it harder for you to equalise, so rather than see me with middle ear barotrauma or a perforated eardrum after the dive, best pop in to help the poppin'.

I have just returned from a trip to Sharm, where one of our group had some sinus congestion at the beginning of the trip. They used Sudafed on the first day, and all was well, but the dive centre staff stated that under no circumstances whatsoever should Sudafed be used before diving.

What is the issue here?

A very common question. Funnily enough I was nearly arrested whilst innocently trying to buy Sudafed in New Zealand, for reasons which will become clear.

The first issue with using decongestants in general is that they may clear out your tubes and sinuses enough to get you to depth without a problem, but if they wear out whilst you're underwater, you may find yourself becoming stuffed-up with mucus, which could trap expanding air as you ascend. Fortunately, decongestants are available that act over a 12-hour period, so this problem can be avoided with a little sensible self-medication.

The active ingredient in Sudafed is something called pseudoephedrine. Its therapeutic effect occurs by stimulating receptors on the

"As the plane is pressurised during the flight, you have to pop your ears to the equivalent of say half an atmosphere..."

muscles of blood vessel walls, causing them to constrict. This means that the vessels leak less fluid, and so congestion in the sinuses and nasal passages is in theory reduced. The other handy benefit for us divers is that it also opens up the Eustachian tubes. All well and good, but as with most drugs the effects are not limited to the airways alone: the same receptors being stimulated elsewhere can cause the heart to race, blood pressure to rise, and generate anxiety, excitability and insomnia. Generally this would only occur with consumption of elephantine quantities, but nevertheless these side effects are what lead to its use being discouraged.

As far as diving with Sudafed goes, the usual caveats apply: there has been little rigorous scientific research on it and so many of the recommendations are based on anecdotal case reports and extrapolation. Some research on rats in the 60s suggested that sympathomimetics (the class of drug to which Sudafed belongs) can enhance oxygen toxicity. So taking Sudafed and diving on gas mixes with high partial pressures of oxygen (eg Nitrox) is not recommended.

The reason I was nearly arrested? Owing to its structural similarity to amphetamines, pseudoephedrine is a sought-after chemical precursor in the illegal manufacture of crystal meth – hence it was classified as a Class C controlled drug in NZ. I was diving with a group of friends and, unaware of its status, I tried to buy rather a lot of it...

Any hints on how to clear a blocked ear which is hanging around a week after diving?

Yes, you need to widen the diameter of your Eustachian tube. This can be achieved by using nasal sprays like Beconase or Otrivine which constrict the cell lining of the tube and so increases the bore. Or you can take Sudafed tablets orally which have the same effect. On a more non-druggy note, try inhaling steam with Eucalyptus as this can dislodge the blockage.

If you find you have difficulty equalising later on during your dive trips, it's probably due to the lengthy exposure of your Eustachian tubes to the marine environment. The constant process of equalising and unblocking the tubes can make them get a bit inflamed after a while making equalising more difficult.

What I tend to do is take one of the above nasal sprays with me on

"On a more non-druggy note, try inhaling steam with Eucalyptus as this can dislodge the blockage."

these trips. One puff up each nostril twice a day should sort it, but if it's just the odd dive here and there you don't need to bother.

I was diving out of Weymouth three weeks ago and had a fast descent to 34m, during which I failed to equalise properly. After four minutes at 34m we made a very slow ascent (19 minutes) and respected all stops. At the surface I had a nose bleed but continued diving for the rest of the weekend, experiencing only slight discomfort in my ears. They felt better under pressure, although I experienced no pain on the ascents.

Since the weekend I have had pain in both ears and the feeling that I need to equalise permanently as they still haven't cleared. Thinking I had an ear infection, my GP prescribed antibiotics, ear drops and recently a nose spray called Flixonase. These have made no difference to my current condition.

Can you help?

You are a lucky diver. A rapid descent to 34m without equalising properly can only mean one thing: barotrauma. And often this one event could affect your ears so much that you wouldn't be able to dive again for a while, so the fact that you were able to equalise for the rest of your dives means you got away lightly.

The reason you feel like your ears have yet to clear is that as you descend, if you cannot blow the necessary air through your Eustachian tube, the increasing negative pressure or vacuum as you get deeper will pull inwards on your ear drum and also the vessels lining the middle ear. Some thick exudate from these vessels will fill up your middle ear as well as your Eustachian tube to compensate, so that after the dive you feel bunged up like after a cold.

On top of this anyone having a look down your ear canal will see a bloody red ear drum as all the vessels have expanded and burst as they get sucked in with the negative pressure inside your ear. This redness is often mistaken for infection and the doc hands out some antibiotics thinking it will help. Well it won't as here time is the great healer. The Flixonase is a good call as it is an anti-inflammatory and anything that can help make the Eustachian tube wider will help.

"You are a lucky diver. A rapid descent to 34m without equalising properly can only mean one thing: barotrauma."

I also suggest Sudafed tablets as they have a small amount of an adrenaline-like substance which helps constrict the inflamed lining of your nasal and ear passages. However, be warned as we all know this is what got poor old Maradonna sent home from Italia 90, so if you are a professional athlete tell the judges that your performance enhancement is on my orders.

So, stay on the Flixonase, add Sudafed, and give it about a month or so to get better.

After a dive to 14m for 40 minutes, during which I had a very small cold, I carried out a one minute stop at 6m and then suffered a reverse block upon ascending (which hurt a lot until I reached the surface). Since then I've had continual tinnitus in the afflicted ear in the form of very faint 'interference' rather than ringing. My afflicted ear, and strangely, to a lesser extent, my 'good' ear were both initially sensitive to sudden changes of pressure caused by such things as car doors slamming, but this has now diminished greatly.

My GP referred me to a specialist who tested my hearing. This showed I had a slight loss of hearing in the high frequency range. The specialist decided that I must have ruptured my round window, and warned me against diving again. I asked him why I hadn't experienced any dizziness as a result of this (I understood that subsequent loss of perilymph fluid would result in vertigo) and why my 'good' ear was sensitive to sudden pressure changes, but he didn't know. What's your opinion?

I've carried out 30 dives since then, including several to 40m involving decompression stops of up to half an hour and my ears have not given me any problems.

This is a tricky one to deal with and one that probably needs referring to an ENT diving doc, rather than someone with little knowledge of hyperbarics who will just tell you that "you can never dive again".

Anyway, his automatic assumption that it is a round window problem is not strictly accurate as tinnitus can result from other damage during a reverse block. Generally, round window and cochlea (part of the inner ear) damage would give you a loud tinnitus whereas middle ear damage to the drum and the ossicles could cause a tinnitus of a lower volume like you seem to be experiencing. Also, it is the oval window that connects to the balance part of your inner ear and damage to this is what would cause dizziness and vertigo. So, before you think that you will never put on a BC again, get a second opinion from another ENT consultant.

Finally, if there is any vertigo or dizziness after a dive, a diagnosis of inner ear DCS should also be considered and prompt advice from your local hyperbaric chamber sought.

My son would like to take up Scuba diving but is concerned that because he had 'glue-ear' as a child and had grommets fitted for some time, he may have a problem with pressure. He is now 31 years old and has had no problems for many years and flying does not affect him.

If he can equalise well on planes, then it is likely that he will be fine whilst diving.

Grommets were placed in their thousands into kid's ears a few decades ago. Many of those who had them now dive perfectly well. Glue ear or Chronic Secretory Otitis Media [CSOM] is a problem where mucus builds up in the middle ear in youngsters, resulting in poor hearing which affects learning. The grommet is a short plastic tube put across the ear drum that allows air to flush through from the outside, pushing all the gunk out of the Eustachian tube.

They normally fall out of the drum a few years later by which time the problem seems to be over, but a grommet would be a real issue if it was still in place in any way at all as it would let the whole ocean into the middle ear. Great for equalising, but terrible for infection and consequent deafness, so let an expert have a look-see first to make sure there's no grommet and that everything's healed over, and he should be OK to dive.

> "Glue ear or Chronic Secretory Otitis Media [CSOM] is a problem where mucous builds up in the middle ear in youngsters, resulting in poor hearing which affects learning."

My husband has just had a 'modified radical mastoidectomy', and he has not yet completed PADI Open Water qualification. Will he be able to dive?

The short answer to this is no, I'm afraid. I'll explain. Orientation first: everyone know where the mastoid is? Put your fingers behind your earlobe and the hard bone you can feel is our culprit. The mastoid contains air cells which are connected indirectly to our friend the middle ear. This means that infections in one can often spread to the other. Lots of gooey middle ear infections can lead to an overgrowth of the skin of the eardrum, which goes by the lovely name of a cholesteatoma, and if this growth is left unchecked it can increase in size and destroy the surrounding delicate hearing bones of the middle ear.

The 'modified radical mastoidectomy' is a very long complicated name for what is, in essence, removal of infected mastoid bone. The theory goes thus: a cavity is created in the ear which is open to the outside world and this makes ear diseases such as cholesteatoma safer by allowing an easy passage of disease out of the body. Now, the 'radical' mastoidectomy is not some politically extremist form of surgery, it refers to removal of the eardrum and two of the tiny bones in the middle ear that conduct sound, in addition to removal of the infected mastoid. This is only done in the most severe cases as it often leaves the poor patient with damaged hearing. In the 'modified' version, the bones and the eardrum are saved, which preserves hearing as much as possible. The issue with both these procedures and diving is this: because the mastoid is now connected to the outside world, it is much more susceptible to infection and water can flood straight in, hugely increasing the risk of vertigo. As you would imagine, a sudden unheralded attack of dizziness is not ideal underwater, so the view of most doctors is that diving is unsafe in these circumstances. Vented earplugs theoretically can stop water entering the ear, but these can be unreliable and any leakage could be disastrous. I think your husband would be best off sticking to above water pursuits from now on.

I've heard a lot about 'reverse squeeze' but what does this term mean exactly? It sounds awful and I'd like to know how to avoid ever experiencing it if possible.

When we talk about 'squeeze' we mean the contraction of gas in a confined space, as pressure increases on descent. This is most often felt in the middle ear, or the sinuses in the forehead and cheeks. But gas can also get trapped in these spaces on the ascent, where it expands (hence 'reverse squeeze'), causing barotrauma which is often more serious: most divers can't get past 2 or 3m with a squeeze on descent, but a reverse squeeze can occur at much deeper depths, risking a far greater pressure change on the ascent. The classic culprit for this used to be short-acting pseudoephedrine (Sudafed): it would widen up the Eustachian tube enough to allow descent, but as it wore off during the dive the congestion returned causing gas to become trapped at depth. Long-acting decongestants have largely eliminated this risk, but to be on the safe side you should avoid diving with any congestion, particularly if you've had a middle ear problem recently.

"When we talk about 'squeeze' we mean the contraction of gas in a confined space, as pressure increases on descent."

For the past nine months I have had problems with pressure in my ears (popping/squeaking/squelching), tinnitus and difficulties with my balance. I have visited an ENT specialist on three occasions and recently had an MRI scan (which was clear). He has diagnosed me with labyrinthitis and says there is nothing more he can do.

Three months before having these problems I had done a number of dives (30 to 40), some of which were deep (40 to 55m) and had no problems at all afterwards. I have been told that there is no way it is connected but can't help but think it must have something to do with it.

What do you think?

I think I've gotta go with the ENT team here.

Three months after diving is too long a gap for any ear problems to appear if they were diving related, be they middle ear barotraumas or even inner ear DCS.

If the problem you describe had been either immediate, or even up to a week after, then I would have suspected diving as the cause. The only other explanation would be that you didn't realise until three months later that you had a problem. But a popping/squeaking/squelching sound in your ears is pretty recognisable from day one, unless you were the sound engineer on a porno shoot.

I will say though, that in my experience labyrinthitis is normally associated with dizziness and vertigo. It's an inner ear problem: inflammation in the balance centre, often caused by a virus. Popping and squeaking is more likely to be middle ear related. So this could be one of those chuck-away diagnoses when they can think of nothing else. I reckon you ought to get your scan results and seek a second opinion from a middle ear specialising ENT surgeon.

I am currently training to be a Navy Clearance diver in Australia, but have huge issues with equalising my left ear. When I equalise on the surface using the old Valsalva technique my ears are usually both rather slow according to medical specialists. My left ear in particular always comes second and usually needs a head tilt to get going. If I have any sort of cold then equalising is usually impossible and just recently had a grade 4 in both ears whilst coming close to actually rupturing one ear drum.

"…a popping/squeaking/squelching sound in your ears is pretty recognisable from day one, unless you were the sound engineer on a porno shoot."

I had my adenoids out when I was four due to serious and constant ear infections. I have tried diving on a steady diet of Sudafed, Logicin, Sinutab etc. but these have other side effects. Is there a surgical solution to the problem? My course mates seem to be able to equalise by just wriggling their jaws, yawning etc. which is something I cannot do. I also have trouble on planes, but this has improved over the years with frequency (when I was younger I would actually lose hearing for hours after a flight).

Even I can have sympathy for an Okker. Bad luck, mate. This sounds like a classic case of Eustachian tube dysfunction, from childhood where they whipped out your adenoids, through to the inability to always pop your ears on a plane. The other telltale sign is just about managing it normally, but add any cold or mucousness, you fail miserably.

The grading system is basically a way of us docs describing to each other how bad the barotrauma is, by looking at the eardrum. The most common system has 6 grades, confusingly numbered 0-5. Grade 0 is the least serious – someone with symptoms but nothing abnormal when you peer into their lughole. A poor grade 6-er has a perforated eardrum. In between are various levels of bruising, bulging and blueness.

Now for you, this is serious. A career is at stake. A naval diver responsible for getting rid of bombs etc., so you must see the best. I assume there has to be a top Naval ENT doctor with specialism in diving issues, not just a civvy ENT pretending to be one. See if you can get referred to them for total assessment. This may involve MRI scans of the Eustachian tube, but it will give a clear picture of what is going on.

> "Now for you, this is serious. A career is at stake. A naval diver responsible for getting rid of bombs etc, so you must see the best."

If your tubes are exceptionally narrow or follow an odd course (thus preventing air from going in and out, hence problems equalising) then there are three possibilities. Try diving on all the decongestants you can get, though this may impinge on Nitrox usage. Quit the job. Or I have heard of a Japanese doc who uses laser to widen the bore of the tube, but this is experimental at the moment. Still, it could be worth a try if that's all that separates you from Naval Diving or a career topside.

I've just done the TDI extended range course and am diving to around 45 to 65m on air. I'm fully aware of the dangers of such

air dives following a huge amount of research and will be doing the advanced tri-mix course in a few weeks time.

However, I have noticed something rather strange when I go beyond 45m and breathe in (which I have to do from time to time): I hear a very loud beat in my head. If I clear my ears with a small blow, the sound disappears (this happens even if I'm level and not descending or ascending). Once I ascend, it stops. I've just done a couple of 30m dives and no beat in my head. It has only started since I've done deep dives. I've done over 300 dives above 40m and never heard it before.

The sound is like a propeller: thud, thud, thud. It sounds like it's my heart beat or pulse, but really loud, and it gets louder the deeper I go. Is this narcosis, O2 toxicity, my Eustachian tube pressing on a vein due to the increased pressure (as my buddy thinks), or something else entirely?

From your description of the sound, it can only really be an awareness of your pulse. Quite why this should have arisen now and not on previous dives is anyone's guess, but with increasing depth your Eustachian tubes are likely to be compressed nearer to the blood vessels that are causing the sound, and so I can see some merit in your buddy's explanation. It tends to be louder with exertion (as your blood is being pumped around with more force), which would also tie in with deeper diving. If you have any middle ear congestion, then the sound will get louder too, as the congestion conducts sound much better than air.

The main thing to say is that a lot of people get this from time to time, non-divers as well as divers, and it is simply a heightened awareness of the big arteries pulsing away in the neck. It is, basically, nothing to worry about.

My partner recently suffered great pain in the ears during a training descent at 7m. The dive was aborted.

She consulted her GP who diagnosed a small hole, severe swelling and inflammation with water in the middle ear. He advised not to dive before a further check up, but said she would be OK to fly to the Maldives in three weeks and continue diving thereafter. He also prescribed antibiotics and Ibuprofen for the pain, however we are worried that this kind of injury may result in never being able to dive again.

It sounds like she either didn't or couldn't equalise on the way down to 7m.

Once you get too deep the Eustachian tube will close down on itself and no matter how hard you try you will not get any air through it into the middle ear, hence the ruptured eardrum and all the gunk in it. She should have ascended a bit and taken it more slowly. She'll probably be fine in three weeks to fly but before she dives she really needs to have a doc look in the ear, as recovery times can be affected by things like infection (hence the antibiotics).

Eardrums can heal themselves quickly and easily, sometimes within a few days, but you need to have definite proof that all is healed before diving as a perforated eardrum increases the chance of getting an infection as the seawater flows into the middle ear.

If the drum has healed she really must get the whole equalisation process right. She could use the Pro-Ear mask in future to take some of the strain. And if she finds there are still problems on descent then she should abort the dive immediately and seek an ENT opinion on her return. Sometimes, these sorts of injuries can result in a permanently perforated eardrum, which requires grafting. A small piece of skin is taken from behind the ear and placed over the drum and sewn into place. This takes a while to 'take', and when it does it should be as strong as before, but she would be unlucky if this were the case.

My 15 year-old son has been advised by BUPA, that due to bad eardrum scarring caused by infections and three sets of grommets when he was young, he should not Scuba dive.

Would a Pro-Ear mask help?

If your son has had all these ear problems when younger, then there is a chance that equalising will be more difficult. However, I have seen many divers with scarred drums equalise OK as the drum can still move a bit. Also, in the equalising process, if he can push air up the Eustachian tube easily, the drum won't have to move as the air equalises the shrinking gas volume effectively, so no drum movement is required.

The Pro-Ear mask is a neat way of helping ear problems with diving, and I know a few instructors use them routinely now to prevent ear infections. A cup sits over the whole ear, so the equalising interface,

"A cup sits over the whole ear, so the equalising interface, instead of being across the drum, is across a chunky piece of plastic."

instead of being across the drum, is across a chunky piece of plastic. The space is equalised by a sweet tube running from the mask face space to the ear cups. It can't 100% guarantee that no water will enter the ear canal though, and for this reason you must make sure he sees a dive doc before diving to check there's no hole in the eardrum.

So here's the plan. See your local dive doc, preferably with ear experience. If they feel it's not as bad as all that, give it a go diving normally. But at the first sign of trouble, try the Pro-Ear mask.

Following what seemed to be an infection, I went to a specialist who saw something pulsating in my ear; I have now had a CT and MRI scan and there is some soft tissue in the middle ear and mastoid. No one thinks it's a tumour or anything recognisable but I am having a tympanoplasty soon, to find out what it is and hopefully remove it.

How will this affect my diving?

Good call on having the op. As regards a return to the deep, it depends very much on what they find.

If there is anything that will affect your balance or cause permanent dizziness then you may have to give up the sport as it will cause disorientation underwater. However if all is well post op then all you have to worry about is the eardrum healing. Once it has healed fully you should be OK to return to diving. How long this takes depends on how much they have to open it. Ask the ENT team afterwards. I'd say no flying or swimming for six weeks is a good idea. If your Eustachian tube remains in full function, your drum is healed, and there's no residual balance dysfunction, then you will be fine to dive afterwards.

OUTER EAR

Every time I dive in plankton rich water, I end up with an ear infection despite using fresh water to rinse my ears on surfacing, trying Swim Ear and using other treatments. The infection in the outer ear is always painful and keeps me out of the water for a few days, which is unpleasant and inconvenient.

It has been suggested by an instructor friend that I use a mixture of 5% acetic acid in propylene glycol to 'oil' the ears and prevent infection.

Where do I get this stuff from and do you think it would work?

This is an all too frequent problem for those on extended diving holidays and one which happens to me each time I go away, so I will give you a few tips on how to avoid what we call 'otitis externa' or 'OE' next time you dive.

Firstly though, you can't blame the poor old plankton all the time as this is far more frequently caused by water borne bacteria that are plentiful the closer you dive to major coastal conurbations and areas where the tidal flow is poor. So as a consequence you have to be really on your guard in the Mediterranean, especially around Southern Spain and Italy. Likewise, in some developing countries the sewage outfall from a hotel or resort is often only yards off the shore and onto the reef where people dive.

The key to outer ear infection is in the prevention, and your instructor's cocktail of vinegar and propylene glycol acts in very much the same way as Swim Ear, in that it breaks down the surface tension of the water that is left in your ear canal after a dive so it can run out more easily when you shake your head. As well as this, the alcohol component helps in evaporating any water left in there, which means that any bacteria are expelled so the infection can't take a hold.

"The key to outer ear infection is in the prevention... cocktail of vinegar and propylene glycol..."

The consequences of OE are that although it's not going to cause you any long term harm, the fact that you are off diving is enough to make this minor problem a major irritation. I always take antibiotic ear drops with me as well to use after a day's diving and I've showered off. These can give the peace of mind that if there are any bacteria that have managed to hang on in the ear canal then they will be killed off by the antibiotic before they can cause OE. My preferred drops are called Gentisone as there is a small amount of steroid in the drops, so if OE has taken a hold the steroid can reduce the inflammation which is the main cause of the pain in this condition. These are prescription only drops so ask your GP for a scrip, which will have to be a private one as you are taking them just in case.

So my suggestion is Swim Ear after each dive and a couple of the antibiotic drops at the end of the day and that should see you well on your next trip. If this doesn't work then try the Pro-ear mask made by Oceanic. This seals around the outer ear preventing water from getting inside. It's equalised by tubes running to the ear cups from the mask itself. Just make sure you don't dive behind a muppet who kicks it off your face and bear in mind that even without that, it's not guaranteed 100% to keep water out of the ear.

A final point here is that if OE has set in then only drops will work for it. I have seen a lot of people treated with oral antibiotic tablets for this problem, which don't work as they are not concentrated in the tissues of the ear canal in high enough doses to be of any real use. If OE does not clear up quickly then insist that your GP does an ear swab to culture any bacteria as there are some rarer bacterial causes such as Pseudomonas which may need a far stronger antibiotic to treat it.

By the way: if you want to be sure an infection is OE and not OM (otitis media, or a middle ear infection), the easiest way to find out is by pulling on your ear lobe. Does it hurt? Then you're looking at an outer ear infection. Otherwise, you'll need to look elsewhere.

I have problems equalizing and someone suggested I get my ears syringed by the nurse before I go away diving, to remove all the wax. Would this be wise? I do also get bad headaches, sometimes daily for a week at a stretch. This has happened about three times this year. Would this suggest I have problems with my sinuses and would a nasal pump be recommended to try and clear them before I go?

Getting your ears unwaxed is a good idea, but it won't really affect equalizing. Wax is in the outer ear canal. Equalizing is all about the middle ear. If you have a lot of wax, it can affect the process of getting all the sea water out of the canal, as some can get trapped, but it seems that you don't really know if there's any there or not. Get the nurse to have a look in the ears and syringe as necessary.

These headaches are interesting. Here's a very basic rule of thumb. If they are frontal they could be sinus, which will be a problem diving, so see a dive doc before you go. If they are in your temples, think migraine. Anywhere else then it's stress or neck problems radiating to your noggin.

It's never a good idea to dive if you do have a splitting headache though, so find the cause and try to stop them.

I've heard from some friends that vented earplugs can help stop infections and make equalising easier, but when I mentioned this to another friend who is a GP, she thought it sounded like a bad idea. What's your view?

"If the person you are talking to doesn't appear to be listening, be patient. It may simply be that he has a small piece of fluff in his ear". So spoke Winnie the Pooh. Our favourite bear was obviously not an earplug-wearing diver. Earplugs and pressure don't mix well in my opinion. The idea of vented earplugs is that a narrow passage through the plug allows air to move in and out, whilst stopping water entering the ear canal. In theory this reduces the risk of ear infections and makes equalising easier. Much anecdotal evidence from divers seems to support these assertions, but there are potential problems: if the vent becomes blocked with wax or other debris, you suddenly have a closed off air space which could lead to barotrauma. If this occurs on a dive, the manufacturers recommend you take the plug out, but the sudden influx of cold water could then lead to vertigo, nausea and vomiting. I'd suggest it's probably best to get to the root of the ear problem and sort that out, rather than relying on earplugs.

I have ear eczema. Will this affect me diving?

Yes it well might. If you have a condition that inflames your outer ear canal, ie the bit you put your pen in whilst you think, then this can make you more prone to outer ear infections if you dive in mucky water.

"Earplugs and pressure don't mix well in my opinion."

So here's what you do: logistically, seeing the doc before every dive to see the state of the canal is too difficult, so you have to assume you always have it. Before each dive I would suggest you use a barrier cream with a bit of steroid in it to protect your ear from contact with potential water borne bugs. Try Betnovate ointment. And I mean ointment and not the cream as the latter is too flimsy.

At the end of every diving day, put in a couple of Gentisone ear drops after your shower or bath. This is good stuff and will beat any bug that's slipped through the cordon.

If you try this combo then you should stay clear of otitis externa, which can ruin a dive trip.

I've recently taken up diving and went to get myself checked over with a doc to be on the safe side. Lucky I did. She told me she couldn't see my eardrums with her telescope. I thought she was talking about wax (I've always been a waxy man) but she said there were 'growths' in my ear that were blocking the canal. I've always surfed and skin dived but never had ear problems from it. What are these growths and do they mean I can't dive?

I suspect these growths are exostoses; a fine, juicy term for bony growths that appear in the ear canals after long term exposure to water (or air, chemicals, fingers: anything, in fact, that causes prolonged irritation). They're commonly spotted in surfer-type dudes or grizzled commercial divers, but only rarely enlarge to the point that they obstruct the ear canal. I'm surprised your hearing has not been impaired – but perhaps it has and you've put this down to too many gigs and all that bleached blonde hair in the way. They're entirely benign (ie non-cancerous), but if they grow too much they can predispose the sufferer to ear infections and in the worst case stop them equalising.

Before you dive, I'd suggest you're reviewed by an ENT doc as they can be removed which would make your diving a whole lot easier.

"I suspect these growths are exostoses; a fine, juicy term for bony growths that appear in the ear canals... They're commonly spotted in surfer-type dudes…"

INNER EAR

I have been having problems with what I think is vertigo. Every time I dive in cold water I feel nauseous and last weekend I was violently sick during and after both of my dives. It didn't happen abroad (when the visibility was good and I was not wearing a hood) and it doesn't happen in the swimming pool. It seems to be worse when I am ascending up a slope. It has been suggested that I should flood my hood with water at about 1m on the descent and that this may help if it is an ear problem. Any suggestions?

Vertigo means many different things to different people. Depending on your tastes, a histrionic drone or a heartfelt chorus of Irish rock courtesy of U2; a serene cinematic exploration of obsession, courtesy of Alfred Hitchcock; or a genus of tiny land snails. Even in the medical sense the term is ripe for confusion. True vertigo is defined as 'the sensation of spinning or rotating while the body is actually stationary with respect to the surroundings.' Not quite the same as the jelly-legged feeling as you peer over the railings of the Empire State Building; more the whirling dizziness experienced on the bathroom floor after an over-exuberant binge drinking session (so I've been told).

Numerous causes for vertigo exist; those specific to diving include narcosis, sea-sickness, hangovers, DCI, contaminated gas mixes, hyperventilation, and equalisation problems (not necessarily in that order). I suspect in this case that the vertigo is due to the sudden exposure of the ear to cold water. This can occur in other situations such as having your ears syringed (in the medical world we call it 'caloric stimulation'). If the ears are exposed unequally (for example if one ear is completely bunged up with wax), for a few seconds only, it can confuse the brain and cause vertigo and nausea. Once the water warms up, the effect usually goes away. So you should get your ears checked out for any blockage such as wax, and if it persists, give your ears a good soak before you descend to see if this will alleviate the effect.

"Vertigo means many different things to different people. Depending on your tastes, a histrionic drone or a heartfelt chorus of Irish rock courtesy of U2..."

What is the maximum hearing loss you can pass a HSE diver's exam with? I am a commercial diver, and I work and live in Croatia. After the war I suffered some hearing loss (from noise) and want to check that I can pass.

The HSE rules are that your hearing should be good enough to permit no loss greater than that of the normal spoken voice. There is a range there of course, from the shouty bloke on the train with a mobile, to the softly spoken priest at confessional in a quiet church. My rule of thumb is a 30 to 40 decibel loss is OK. Make sure you get an audiogram each year at your HSE renewal, as you don't want diving over a period of time to tend you towards full deafness. If it were you may have to pull out of commercial diving.

I was doing my Open Water course last week. I had trouble equalising on my first dive and had to push really hard to pop my ears. At about 3m, I suddenly got dizzy. Everything was whirling around so I came up quickly. It seemed to settle on its own, so I did three more dives, all to about 7m, and had no problems on those. A day later though the vertigo came back, much worse than before, and I had loud roaring and ringing noises in both ears. Now every time I cough or get up or turn my head too quickly, I get very bad vertigo, feeling sick and very unsteady. Also, my hearing seems to be good on some days and bad on others. What should I do?

This sounds to me like a classic case of inner ear barotrauma. The key pointers are the persistence of your symptoms, their association with positional change, and the fluctuating hearing loss. I suspect that there's been a rupture of the cochlea, what we call a 'perilymph fistula', and each time you strain or move, there's fluid leaking out, causing your symptoms. You should see an ENT specialist as soon as you can to get investigated properly, but I can make a few suggestions here. What you need to do is steer clear of any situations that increase the pressure in your head. This means avoiding sneezing, coughing, lifting, sexual activity, equalising... basically anything physically strenuous. Ideally, bed rest is advised, in a quiet environment, to allow the fistula to heal. This can take several months. I'm sorry to report that in many cases there is permanent loss of some hearing, although the tinnitus tends to improve as the brain gets used to it. Quite often vertigo will persist too, and it would be difficult to sanction future diving in these circumstances.

"This means avoiding sneezing, coughing, lifting, sexual activity, equalising… basically anything physically strenuous."

I have been told that a young woman who is a very good swimmer and qualified lifeguard at a municipal swimming pool, would very much like to learn dive with Scuba, but has been advised that because of deafness, which causes her to have to wear a hearing aid (presumably not while swimming), she would not be able to descend more than a very few metres. Is it deafness that prevents diving, or only that certain conditions involving deafness may do so?

It very much depends on the condition that causes the lack of hearing. In a nutshell any cause that includes tinnitus and vertigo, such as Ménière's disease, may be a problem. Likewise an auditory nerve tumour that is untreated could also be an issue. If it is also a condition that involves destruction of the ear drum or middle ear, then there would be a situation where the inflow of water or inability to equalise would prevent diving. Some deafness, though, is a simple affair present from birth and in these situations she may well be fine to dive.

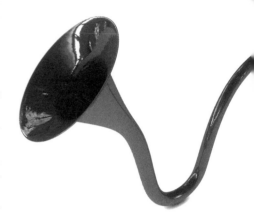

There are issues of communication underwater that should be addressed. She should always stay close to her buddy and even think of a way of being attracted in case of emergency, that doesn't involve sound. Also, think about situations on ascent where a boat is coming in, she has to always come up with a hearing buddy so she can be protected from not hearing the props on ascent.

So don't worry about underwater hearing aids and depths, but get advice on the exact nature of her deafness as she could well be fine to dive.

> "It very much depends on the condition that causes the lack of hearing."

I'm waiting for a cochlear implant. Will I still be able to go diving with it? Currently I don't dive beyond 30m and have no problem equalising or any other problem with my ears.

Hope to hear from you soon.

And I hope you can hear from me soon too. There are a few issues here: firstly, there are some docs that don't let divers with deafness on one side dive, because if you were to frag your other ear, you would be in a terrible situation. However it seems you have been given the OK, and are diving merrily, so it would be a cold heart that stopped you now.

So, can you dive with this little gizmo that cures nerve deafness? First a little history, as some of this is great 'eccentric scientist' stuff. Apparently the lengthily named Count Alessandro Giuseppe Antonio Anastasio Volta (from whom we get the well known electrical unit) was the first to discover that sound could be perceived by directly stimulating the auditory system. This he did by sticking a couple of metal rods in his own ears and connecting them to a 50 volt circuit. He experienced a "jolt" and a noise like "a thick boiling soup" (presumably his brain curdling). Nearly two centuries later some adventurous surgeons zapped an exposed acoustic nerve, whose owner heard sounds like "a roulette wheel" and "a cricket".

These macabre experiments laid the groundwork for the cochlear implant, or 'bionic ear'. Essentially it's a surgically implanted electronic device which directly stimulates auditory nerves. External parts (including a microphone and speech processor) transmit sound signals to an internal receiver (implanted in bone behind the ear) and thence into the cochlea (the hearing bit of the inner ear) via electrodes. Not your average hearing aid, which is basically an amplifier. The results are pretty impressive, especially in those who have grown up with the implants and whose brains have presumably learned to 'hear' in a different way. Older recipients are often not as enamoured with the devices; one described a human voice as sounding like 'a croaking Dalek with laryngitis'.

As far as diving goes, it all depends on the manufacturer. It's rather like pacemakers, you can use them but only those that churn them out know the mechanical limitations with depth. You have to ask your ENT surgeon to find that out for you. Once fitted, they sit in your inner ear and interface with the middle ear. Oh, and they cost a fortune too. So you must make sure that if there were a dive problem, that you did not burst your ear drum, letting water flood in, and potentially affecting it in the inner ear. Again, this is a worst case scenario, and as you can pop your ears fine, it should not happen, but it might be an idea to wear the Pro-Ear mask, as this could build in a safety factor.

Finally, I would leave it a couple of months before diving, if all the above is OK.

About 12 years ago, I woke in the middle of the night with the feeling that the bedroom was spinning violently. After this incident I experienced a lot of dizzy spells and, after several visits to various doctors, was told that I had probably had a

"Count Alessandro Giuseppe Antonio Anastasio Volta... was the first to discover that sound could be perceived by directly stimulating the auditory system. This he did by sticking a couple of metal rods in his own ears and connecting them to a 50 volt circuit."

bad ear infection. The dizzy spells subsided but ever since I have had problems with my balance if I go on a reasonably long boat journey. When I get off the boat I still feel as if I am on it (ie the floor and objects around me seem to be moving up and down like the swell on the water) for a number of hours afterwards (usually until I have had a good night's sleep). When I mentioned this to my GP he said I have a "delicate" balancing mechanism, which is easily unbalanced. I have also spoken to friends and have been told (rightly or wrongly) that there is a "pea-shaped" lump behind your ear, which is what affects our balance. I can feel one behind my right ear but not behind my left, which is the ear that I had the infection in. Could the infection have damaged this balancing mechanism and if so will it affect me when I am diving?

Also, for some time now I have been experiencing pain in my left ear. It is not like an earache as it is not totally inside the ear. When I experience pain it hurts to touch around the entrance to my ear and also around the back of my ear. Sometimes the pain is also accompanied by a slight sore throat. I have spoken to my GP but he said he couldn't see anything wrong. However, on the occasion that I did go diving, and also in the swimming pool, I did experience some discomfort. I have put it down to the coldness of the water against my eardrum but am wondering if it is anything more serious.

The coming off the boat issue is completely normal. Part of the ears are the organs responsible for you feeling steady; they're called the 'semi-circular canals' and a fluid called perilymph whooshes around inside them to tell you which angle you are at. After a boat trip, the nerves that this liquid is connected to continue to think they should be getting messages of movement. You aren't of course, but the brain hasn't figured that out yet so you still feel as though you are moving up and down. Don't let that stop you diving.

As for the pea sized lump that controls your balance your friends tell you about. You are rubbing the wrong pea-sized thing. The mastoid has little to do with balance and a lot to do with where a muscle attaches to your skull, so no worries there.

As for the penultimate issue about the ear pain, if your doc says all looks fine but you have this nagging pain around your ear it could well be a neuralgia. Go to see an ENT surgeon if your GP is offering you little help.

Finally, your dive in the pool pain was probably due to not equalising properly. All in all you will probably be fit to dive, just get seen first by your local dive doctor.

I became partially deaf as a result of German measles at the age of 11. I have been diving for the last two years and as yet had no effect on my hearing. Is it possible if I continue to dive my hearing may worsen?

I intend doing my diving instructors course but is it possible that my GP will not give me a clear medical?

I don't see a problem here. The only way you could worsen your hearing is by blowing your middle ear on a descent, but as you know divers do not suffer a serial decrease in hearing just because they dive.

It may be wise to get an audiogram before you do the IDC for medico-legal reasons, just in case your employers in the future send you down with a bunch of muppets who somehow cause you to blow said ear. At least you would have a baseline measurement in case of future litigation. The audiogram is part of the HSE medical you need to have to pass your IDC in the UK, but this is not necessarily required in other parts if the world.

SINUSES

On my last two diving trips I found that on surfacing, there was some mucus coming out from my nose, which, on the first occasion, was brownish yellow in colour and on the second occasion was red with blood. Apart from this I did not suffer from any other apparent problem or discomfort. What is the cause of this phenomenon? Is it dangerous?

I think that in your case you will be fine. Having thick coloured mucus come from your nose after a dive is quite a common occurrence for a lot of divers and is a combination of the contents of the sinus being pushed out on ascent, and a reaction in your nose to the salt water that may have been in contact with it in your mask during the dive.

Most divers would agree that we are not a pretty sight a few moments after surfacing, due to this snot effect, so don't worry on that account.

Where problems do arise though is if you dive and have a case of sinusitis at the same time. I assume you didn't as you said you had no pain, but those that do will either experience extreme pain on descent as they cannot equalise the sinuses due to a blocked sinal canal, or when they ascend, the inflamed sinal lining can act as a valve and block the air that needs to escape. This results in a sinal barotrauma which feels like a hot poker being stuck into your forehead.

My call in your case is that you may have had a sinal infection in the past but had yet to clear all the gunk from your sinuses, and the blood was a result of trying to equalise too hard and popping a nasal capillary.

So the conclusion here is: don't dive with active sinusitis but get some antibiotics sorted quickly.

"Having thick coloured mucus come from your nose after a dive is quite a common occurrence for a lot of divers…"

Finally, we still aren't really sure what a sinus is for yet medically, one theory is that it makes our skulls lighter. Good news, as it means we don't all need necks like an All Black prop forward.

During the safety stop at the end of a dive to 30m recently, I developed a dull ache in my left cheek, and my upper left teeth and gums felt numb. This persisted during the surface interval (two hours), but went away on my next (and last) dive, only coming back during ascent. Over the next two days the sensation (or lack of) hung around, and on the flight home it got worse; nothing unbearable, but it's still there three days after I've returned to the UK. I had no colds or congestion prior to the diving, but I'm wondering whether it's a sinus issue, and why this would affect my teeth. And will my teeth stop feeling numb?

You've hit the nail on the head, this has all the hallmarks of a sinus barotrauma. There are a couple of big air-filled spaces in the cheeks, called the maxillary sinuses. Running in very close proximity is the infra-orbital nerve, which wends its way through a canal under the eye ('infra-orbital') on each side. It supplies the sensation to the upper teeth, gums and upper lip, and also part of the nose and lower eyelid. I'd guess that the air in the left sinus couldn't find its way out on your ascent, and put some pressure on this nerve as you came up. By now the trapped gas would have probably oozed its way out, so I doubt there is any ongoing barotrauma occurring, but a 'bruised' nerve can sometimes take quite a while to recover. It could be worth a trial of decongestants or steroid nose spray to accelerate the healing but I expect the sensation will return spontaneously over the next week or so. If not, then a trip to the ENT docs for a CT scan of the sinuses may be on the cards.

Years ago, whilst performing a mask removal on a Red Sea orientation dive, salt water got into my nose and the subsequent inflammation meant that I managed only seven dives in the whole week. The holiday ended with a visit to a dive doctor in Sharm after a reverse block in my nose and a resultant sinus blow out. On returning to the UK, I consulted a specialist in hyperbaric medicine, who put me on a course of Beconase and anti-inflammatories.

Five months later I returned to diving, and although I suffered minor discomfort between my eyes and in my front teeth, there were no recurrences of what had happened in Egypt. Last

"I'm wondering whether it's a sinus issue, and why this would affect my teeth. And will my teeth stop feeling numb?"

year, however things started to escalate during my divemaster training and I also felt discomfort when I flew, so I went back to the specialist for X-rays. Their diagnosis was polyps and they referred me to an ENT specialist at our local hospital. He used a probe to establish where the polyps were and found none. His diagnosis was that the sinus linings were getting inflamed during a dive or flight and not settling as most other people's would. He told me to use Sudafed and Beconase before a dive and if that didn't work, give up diving.

I took a year off and tried again last week. The pain was excruciating even with the Sudafed and half a bottle of spray up my nose. I really don't want to give up diving and would like to actually finish my DM course at some point. With the discomfort that I feel when I fly I would like to know what else (if anything) I can do or if there are any operations that can be done to get rid of this problem once and for all.

It seems that you have done the rounds of experts but still not come up with a solution to your problem. If a GP, a diving doctor and a regular ENT surgeon haven't nailed it yet then there's only one place left you can go to. That would be an ENT surgeon who specialises in diving medicine.

However my thoughts here are that a plain X-ray is considered a fairly rough tool in trying to diagnose sinus problems. A far more accurate and sensitive method is to use either CT or MRI scanning. This is because things like polyps which can block the flow of air in and out of the sinus are made of soft tissue, which can be very hard to visualise in an X-ray.

So what would an ENT surgeon consider?

Well the most probable diagnosis is that of a very chronic inflammation that has built up since your incident in the Red Sea which has almost closed off the sinal canals that drain the sinuses. Using steroid nasal sprays will only work in the short term as soon the tissue that you are trying to get rid of the inflammation in becomes 'refactory' to it. This means you have to use more and more of the medication to have the same desired effect. Sometimes a cure can be effected in problems like yours by having a sinal washout and scraping away all the inflamed lining to the sinuses. But all this would be a decision that the ENT surgeon would make after consultation with you.

I've been suffering from (mild) chronic sinusitis. I have been referred to an ENT specialist but have to wait for two months. Will my sinus condition affect me in the early part of the Open Water Course (ie pool-based work)? I don't expect to finish the rest until the summer when I'm somewhere hot and sunny (with no sinus problems). I have been swimming recently and haven't suffered any discomfort.

As I am the Prince of Sinus Suffering, I can help you here. You should be fine for the pool based dives. In reality, a 3m dive is not going to really need you to equalise that area, and you can get down to that depth without any pain.

If there is any aggro there, have a toot of Otrivine to help in the pool, but before you hit the 18m depths, do make sure that ENT doc has had a look at you. Sometimes polyps in the sinuses can affect equalizing and cause your problem, likewise the structure of your nose where the sinal canals empty into. These could cause problems with diving in the future, and it's best to get it sorted first, rather than enjoy the agony of a sinus squeeze.

I was doing my Rescue Diver class recently and during a descent of about 3m-4m, I felt a sharp pinch over my left eye. I went up then tried to descend again and the pain was less severe. The whole dive was only to about 6.5m for 15 minutes. On surfacing I had blood in my mask. My DM said it was not a big deal and if I felt okay I could continue. I did three more dives of similar depth and time. There was no pain on subsequent dives, but the bloody nose continued. It tended to stop about five minutes after surfacing, however I had blood coming up in my throat the next day.

I was referred to an ENT department where I had a CT revealing a 1.5mm polyp in the left frontal sinus, with no other abnormality or fluid. MRI revealed the same findings. The specialist was not sure what caused the bleeding, but the radiologist who was familiar with diving felt it was due to having mucus in the sinus and trauma from the dive. I have never had any problems before even at 35m. Any thoughts?

Polyps in the nose or sinuses can lead to excessive mucus production, and we all know what a bunged up nose or sinus means for equalising. 1.5mm is pretty small for a polyp, but if one has been found in the left frontal sinus (the site of your initial pain) then it's quite possible that this is what bled. Mucus and congestion often build up in the sinuses with repetitive diving, and the more forceful equalising that results can also cause bleeding. Blood in the throat the next day, without any other obvious source, is commonly swallowed blood from the previous nose or sinus bleed. It should all settle down spontaneously but if the bleeding occurs on future dives then you may need to have something done to the polyp. It's a bit of an eye-watering procedure though, so hold off if you can.

NOSE

Why do new divers, especially those who have equalisation problems, tend to experience nose bleeds? Is there any way to avoid this? Are there any likely complications that may arise if the new diver were to make a repetitive dive the same day?

From my experience the answer to this falls into two common reasons.

Firstly, the novice diver, I agree, does seem to get a blood filled mask more often than someone with a 100 or so dives under their weight belt. This is because of late and violent equalising. Suddenly, at 6 or 7m they realise they haven't equalised yet, and the deeper they are the harder it is. If you haven't equalised by now you won't unless you ascend a bit. But the first timer is unlikely to call up the group and will try harder and harder to blow some air up the Eustachian tube. By doing this the pressure on the nasal mucosa lining the septum of the nose is enough to blow some capillaries, and hence the bleed. So remember here, if your kit works on the surface-check it will as you go down. Equalise a little and often: don't leave it late and have to blast it hard.

The other common reason for a big bleed is a sinus squeeze. Novices may not be able to call when not to dive if they are a bit stuffy in the nose. If you cannot equalise your sinuses then the negative pressure in these bony cavities will suck the lining off the sinal walls and cause the blood vessels to swell up and explode. The sinus will then equalise, not with air but with the red stuff. Then as you ascend the little air inside still expands, and forces the blood out of the sinus, through the nose and into your mask. So at about 5-10m you notice a red fluid level ascend towards your eyes. Not nice for the new diver.

The moral here is don't dive with a cold, and if you get searing pain in your forehead on descent, call it a day.

Should you dive again that day?

> "The novice diver, I agree, does seem to get a blood filled mask more often than someone with a 100 or so dives under their weight belt."

If the bleed is minor and due to leaving it until too late to equalise, then you should be fine for the afternoon. But if you've had a major bleed, I would leave it, inhale some eucalyptus to open up the sinal canals, and try again tomorrow.

Is it generally permissible to use Beconase nasal spray prior to (days and immediately before) a dive? Has it been shown to affect your susceptibility to DCI? I have had some difficulty in pressure-balancing my ears, mostly after swimming-pool chlorine-related nasal inflammation, which has lasted a week and a half.

The active ingedient in Beconase is a corticosteroid, beclomethasone dipropionate, 50mg per spray.

There's no real problem in using Beconase in the days going up to a dive if as you say you have a chlorine-induced bunged-up nose. I would far rather you did this than risked a middle ear barotrauma, which would ensue if you couldn't get any air up your Eustachian tubes. If it is just a chlorine thing then hopefully when you dive in fresh or sea water it shouldn't be needed before a dive.

But there are divers who get this super mucus reaction even when going into sea water which then poses a bit of a dilemma. Do you avoid using them before a dive as the effects may wear off underwater and risk a reverse block on ascent, or do you just never dive at all as you get snotty during a dive? Well, I would take option three where careful use of these sort of products can make equalisation possible for a range of sufferers and the real risk of a medication that is supposed to last for 12 hours (ie it's used twice a day in normal hay fever cases) running out just as you ascend is really pretty remote if you last for 40 minutes underwater and have had a toot an hour before going in.

And it won't predispose you to DCI, even if you fell into the Beconase vat at the factory and swallowed the whole lot. So dive on in there, just tell your buddy what it is before they hear you snorting away on the boat.

Can I dive with a broken nose?

Funny thing, nose trauma. You can break it and all is fine. Or you can break it and it can be a disaster. It's all about where the septum lies. That's the bit in the middle that stops you from picking the right

"Funny thing, nose trauma. You can break it and all is fine. Or you can break it and it can be a disaster."

nostril when your finger's in the left side. If the septum is left straight then you could well be fine. If the break has thrown it off to one side then you are going to have one hell of a time equalizing. The septal deviation will prevent you from blowing air up that side's Eustachian tube, ergo a full on screaming ear pain on descent.

So I advise you get your doc to have a look up your nose and make sure everything is in the right place. If it is, I think you will be OK.

A patient has approached me asking for a medical to go diving whilst on holiday. Three years ago he had ligation of his external carotid artery as an emergency procedure following severe left sided epistaxis. Is this a contra-indication to diving (either relative or absolute)? The paperwork he wanted me to fill in for him was American and had no helpline for doctors to phone.

Ligation of the external carotid is obviously performed only where all else has failed to stem the bleed from epistaxis, as we docs like to call a nose bleed.

It is a permanent procedure that stops the blood flow directly to Little's area on the nasal septum where all the blood comes from on a bleed.

This should prove to be no problem with Scuba diving at all. Blood flow remains to the head and brain through the internal carotid so there should be no risk of any faints or light headedness underwater.

Last February I collapsed at home and was rushed to hospital. I was diagnosed as suffering bacterial meningitis and septicaemia and have spent the last six months or so off work recuperating. The illness itself was apparently triggered by a severe infection in my left ear. My consultant says I have a problem in my left nostril that is interfering with the passage of air into my 'tubes' and will operate later this year to remove some cartilage that is partly obstructing my airway. This problem may well have exacerbated the ear infection.

I did my PADI Open Water course last October and haven't dived since. I am really keen to get back into it but with my recent history and the nasal op coming up I wondered what your views might be?

Poor you. To get that sort of problem due to a simple nose anatomical fault is really unlucky. I think you should stay away from diving until it's all sorted out. And then leave it a good three to six months after the nose op before you try to equalise on a dive.

If this problem is enough to cause you meningitis and a near death experience, then getting it sorted is your main priority. It must be along the Eustachian tube axis for the nose to affect your middle ear and cause an infection, and this is precisely the one you need for equalising. This could risk causing another infection if you ended up blowing bacteria into the middle ear on a dive. And if that happened you know what happens next. Yup, intensive care and needles in your spine. So leave it for now. Get the nose op and take it from there.

"Yup, intensive care and needles in your spine. So leave it for now. Get the nose op and take it from there."

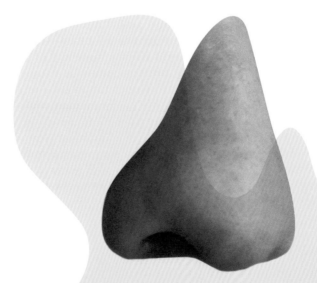

EYE PROBLEMS

I am currently a Divemaster Trainee who wears contact lenses. I went for a check up recently and was told off for wearing my contacts whilst both swimming and diving, due to the high levels of bacteria and particularly 'flesh-eating protozoa'. I was warned that if a protozoa such as this got into contact with my contacts that I could lose my sight overnight. I was so stunned at the time that I didn't think to ask any further questions.

As many student divers also wear contacts, should I warn them not to, and is the bacteria/protozoa problem also valid in the sea, or is it confined to swimming pools?

I have spoken to a selection of optometrists and ophthalmic surgeons and the good news is that it should be fine to dive in contacts. Sure, there are situations in swimming pools where there are bacteria that could infect your eyes but this is not as common as you think.

What they suggest is that you use softer lenses and after diving in the pool wash them thoroughly before replacing them. If you develop any redness in your eyes afterwards then go and see your doctor to rule out any conjunctivitis or other infections. Don't worry about flesh eating bacteria as that's alarmist nonsense. The Ebola virus is the flesh eater you are worried about, and at the moment the only way you will get that is to eat some bush meat in the rainforest of Central Africa, and not by doing a try dive in your local baths.

I don't think you should worry about using lenses in the sea, either. Again, stick to soft and if you get any reaction because of the salt water then perhaps it's time to try a prescription lens mask. Getting a prescription lens for a mask is easy to do nowadays. They can be pricey, but if you got two it would be really good as there's no accounting for who will drop a tank on your kit on the first day of a liveaboard.

If your sight is particularly bad, then kitting up without your lenses can

"…use softer lenses and after diving in the pool wash them thoroughly before replacing them."

be difficult and that is where mistakes could happen. So in all, I reckon it's probably up to you, but it's probably best not to just leave yourself blind.

I rather foolishly managed to get a mask squeeze. The whites of my eyes have been very red for a week now and are now starting to itch and weep tears. How long does this take to clear up? My vision and balance is fine, but I look like a zombie.

Right, mask squeeze: the negative pressure of the tight fitting mask sucks your eyeballs out and pops the blood vessels. Result: subconjunctival haemorrhage, or red eyes. This normally looks worse than it is, and clears in a week. But if you are now itching and weeping, chances are that you may have some allergy in there now as well. Best try Opticrom eye drops for a day or so. If that nails it then continue for a week longer. If not then see a doc ASAP to rule out infection.

I have been prescribed timolol maleate by my eye doctor to equalise my eye pressure. Is glaucoma a contraindication to diving?

Diving does not exert any more pressure on your eyes so diving with a glaucoma is acceptable. There are two things you should look out for though. Firstly, mask squeeze (where insufficient air is in your mask) and secondly, the fact that very rarely the eye drops you are using can have a wider effect on your body. Timolol is a beta blocker and in theory could reduce your heart rate enough that your tolerance to exercise is affected. So, if you have noticed this as an effect, you should see a local diving doctor to have a fitness check in order to avoid discovering that you get short of breath on a dive where a lot of exertion is needed.

We are on a diving holiday in Sharm and my poor daughter has got suncream lotion in her eyes. She has bathed them in cold water but they are still burning after about two hours. Is there anything I can do?

Poor little thing. It takes ages to persuade kids to apply this stuff, and when they finally get the point, this happens.

In these situations, when the water doesn't get rid of all the pain, use steroid eye drops. Predsol is one brand I like, but it's scrip only, so either go prepared, or run like hell to a pharmacy if there's one close. Two to three drops three hourly will keep the tears at bay.

> "The negative pressure of the tight fitting mask sucks your eyeballs out and pops the blood vessels."

Will my son be able to Scuba dive with a prosthetic left eye?

Poor lad. Of course he can. A prosthetic eye is a solid object. As we all know (and he will learn from training), solids and liquids are not compressible at diving depths. Only air is. So nothing will actually happen to the eye on a dive. However, what he must watch out for is mask squeeze. This is where the compression of the air inside trapped inside the mask causes a vacuum on descent and pulls at anything within the mask. Obviously a false eye could be pulled from the socket into the mask if this happened.

He must make sure he has a loose fitting mask (you can tell when divers' masks are on too tight as they leave an imprint on their face for half an hour after the dive), and knows how to equalise it by blowing out through his nose as he descends.

I have a keratoconus: a thinning of the cornea in my left eye. It hasn't stopped me from diving so far, but since I'm considering going pro I would like to know if a keratoconus is really a no-no condition which excludes diving. Mine is so far stabilized and does not require surgery.

A friend rang me recently in a state of hysteria. She'd been all set to get laser surgery for short-sightedness but was declined on the basis of the same thing: keratoconus. Since the laser basically slices off layers of cornea, you can't really go ahead if it's too thin to start with. Apparently she used to rub her eyes constantly, which has worn the corneas away over time. In extreme cases, the cornea becomes so thin that it ruptures, fluid-filled swellings form on the surface, and a corneal transplant is required urgently to avoid loss of the eye.

Diving-wise, the condition itself is not affected by pressure or depth changes. The risk is largely down to mask squeeze. If the cornea is sufficiently thin, and a negative pressure builds up in the air-filled mask space, then theoretically this could lead to rupture through the weakest point of the cornea. The current method of dealing with this is to use rigid but gas-permeable contact lenses. Gas-permeable lenses avoid the problem of bubbles becoming trapped between the lens and eye, whilst strengthening the cornea to stop it rupturing. The time course of keratoconus is variable: some are stable indefinitely while others progress rapidly or get unpredictable exacerbations, so if you're considering turning pro then it will be important for you to keep a close eye on the condition (a pun punishable by sustained flogging).

"...the compression of the air inside trapped inside the mask causes a vacuum on descent and pulls at anything within the mask. Obviously a false eye could be pulled from the socket into the mask if this happened."

My partner has just been diagnosed with a partially detached retina; apparently there are several layers at the back of the eye, and over a small area these have separated and a small bubble of liquid has managed to get in between. Is this something he can dive with?

Well, if it were me, I would be checking out the batfish schools on the Ras and the Camel Bar in Sharm. A liquid-filled retinal detachment will not be affected by diving as the eye, its contents, and this problem are incompressible during diving, so it won't worsen. The thing you have to watch out for though is any over exertion that will enlarge it. An increase in the pressure of the eyeball can be caused by straining when exercising, such as putting on a tanked up BCD or lifting your buddy out of the water in an emergency.

So, as diving is always unpredictable, your husband should wait until it is lasered back to normality or do the most basic of dives where a problem could never be encountered. So as four metre diving surrounded by three year-old snorkelers on the house reef can be a bit tedious by the second day, I would stop off at the one-stop-laser shop to get it fixed quickly before you go.

I have a type of glaucoma which caused high pressure in my eye and resulted in an operation which built in a drainage channel to relieve the pressure. There is a permanent stitch in the eye to prevent this from healing but no other signs. I have noticed pain in my eye when flying, although this could be caused by the dry air.

Can I dive?

This is a very difficult one.

The key thing is mask squeeze. When you descend to depth, the air in your mask contracts and this may cause problems if you've had the operation as there is a chance that the negative pressure could affect your eye, but there are ways to prevent this by blowing air into your mask on descent. The pressure at depth should not be a problem as you only dive for a short while and if you can equalise the pressure in your mask then it shouldn't be any different to normal atmospheric pressure on land.

My only other concern is that of infection if you have an open stitch exposed to the elements, but the sea is no more polluted than bath water at times. However, if you do experience any redness in the eye after diving, then you may need to start antibiotics very quickly.

I am considering having laser surgery to correct my vision, but before I do would like to know what duration to remain out of the water, with relation to both infection and any pressure-related problems.

Here's the deal with diving and eye surgery. It's not a case of compression or the eye bursting at depth. It's a solid with some jelly like stuff in the middle, so it won't be affected by pressure. It's all about the abrasion to your cornea, and the chances of infection getting into the scratches. The main nasty is called 'acanthamoeba'. Get it and you can lose your sight in a few days. And the main way it is contracted is by swimming or diving and getting into contact with it in the water, be it in pools or the ocean.

So, when your eye-doc gives you the all-clear to swim, then in theory you are fine to dive as well. I always used to say at least six weeks though. When you dive, hang that mask loose and watch out for any squeeze.

I had an orbital floor fracture repair about four months ago to cover a hole that was around 2cm in diameter, and in excess of 50% of the orbital floor. The material used was titanium mesh.

A complication arising from the initial trauma, however, was that it was not possible to correctly reposition a portion of the eye tissue at the back of the orbit. This tissue remains trapped behind the titanium sheet and in the maxillary sinus. It has been decided that any further operation would be too risky to my sight. Can you please advise as to if there would be any contraindications for my diving.

Blimey that's a big hole. The orbit is the cavity in the skull which accommodates the eye. Orbital floor fractures commonly result from blunt objects (fists, car dashboards, balls) impacting on the eye socket, which then breaks. Over 80% occur in males (funny that). What actually happens is that the object in question, say a well-aimed punch from the gloved fist of Joe Calzaghe, squishes the incompressible eyeball inwards. The rapid increase in pressure in the socket then causes it to 'blow out' at its weakest point, the floor. The fatty tissue around the eye then drops through the hole, often pulling a couple of eye muscles with it, resulting in double vision. And a rapid lie-down.

"What actually happens is that the object in question, say a well-aimed punch from the gloved fist of Joe Calzaghe, squishes the incompressible eyeball inwards."

In a victim without visual disturbances, where the fracture covers less than 50% of the floor, and where there's no trapped fatty or muscle tissue, one option is to leave the area alone and treat with steroids and antibiotics. In your case however, surgery was undertaken, repositioning the disrupted bony fragments and patching up the fracture with a mesh. One issue with this type of repair and diving is whether there is any possibility of trapped gas within the tissues. I would assume that any gas introduced would by now have diffused safely away, but it would be worth checking with your eye surgeons to guarantee this. A second issue is whether the tissue trapped in the maxillary sinus will obstruct your ability to equalise, or make that area more susceptible to barotrauma. I would imagine that as long as the sinus can drain normally you would be OK on that score.

Otherwise you should be fine once you're fully recovered.

ARTICLE – DIVING AND VERTIGO

I went diving once with a guy called Jeff. Nice divemaster but the ravages of time had begun to affect him more than he liked. To deflect from his grey hair and increasing obesity he had a story he would tell divers before they went in with him. It happened a few years earlier when he took four British Army lads on a straightforward wall dive, but with a drop off to 200m. Before the dive they had teased him about how slow and fat he was and how they were at the peak of their fitness. "You'll slow us down, you should give this game up and retire mate" they'd said. Jeff took them down to 30m, but one of them looked down for too long, got a dizzy spell which fast became a panic attack and then went to bolt for the surface. Jeff pinned him to the wall, the others floated and watched, and he slowly brought him up in a controlled ascent. Back on the shore they all quietly stowed their gear in a hired jeep and drove off back to their hotel. He never saw them again, despite it being the first dive of a five day package.

"Vertigo, that's what he had" said Jeff, but Jeff was wrong. All he had was a sensation of a fear of heights brought on by the long drop and then a panic attack. If it had been vertigo, Jeff would have been dragged up too. Vertigo is where the brain cannot interpret vestibular signals from the inner ear balance centre. The inner ear is the third part of the whole ear organ system and lies beneath the middle ear which is the bit you have to equalise. Most often with vertigo, there is a mismatch between the signals from the left and right sides of this inner ear which the brain cannot interpret. This results in the classic symptoms of a feeling of rotation, either of your surroundings or yourself, and believe me can be one of the most terrifying situations underwater.

I was nearing the end of a perfect dive in the Red Sea: maximum visibility, huge batfish schools and warm 3mm shortie sort of water. I ascended what must have been a couple of metres to go over a coral head when it hit me. With no warning everything in my field of vision started to rotate, and not just slowly, but at 100rpm. On top of this I had a ringing in my ears, known as tinnitus, coupled with a horrible feeling of nausea. Vomiting was not far off.

I was experiencing one of the commoner causes of vertigo whilst diving: alternobaric vertigo, or ABV for short. What happens here is that on ascent, the middle ears don't clear the expanding air equally, the pressure across the inner ear is not equal and the poor old brain can't cope with the asymmetric messages. End result: vertigo. One study in Sweden has calculated this as probably causing over 60% of the cases of vertigo in all divers that experience it. It also seems to be more frequent in experienced divers, and perhaps the resulting disorientation and vomiting can explain some of the deaths in this group. Bolting to the surface will only make it worse as it increases the asymmetric pressure difference. The way to cope with this is to grab on to a rock and make that point the centre of your field of vision, so the nausea is lessened as you look at a fixed non-rotating point. Then you must try to descend a little so the middle ear air compresses a bit and takes the pressure off your balance centre. Normally all will be fine in 30 seconds, but it can go on for up to 10 minutes. What I now do is tell any buddy I dive with that this could happen and not to try to drag me topside as this will only worsen it. Also, try to figure a sign for ABV as waving your hand by your ear makes most people think you are having equalisation problems and again they may try to take you up slowly, which will only make the problem worse.

So, this is an unequal response to the same stimulus. The other main cause of vertigo is an unequal stimulus to each balance centre. Here a common cause is what we call 'transient vertigo due to differential caloric stimulation'. It may sound complex but it's really very straightforward: it's all in the temperature of the water entering your ears. If cold water enters one ear canal and not the other, you can end up with vertigo. The causes of this are wearing a poor fitting diving hood or even having a lump of ear wax on one side and not the other, so the cold water hits one ear drum and not the other. But a rare cause is having a severe case of swimmer's ear. The bony outgrowths in the ear canal called exostoses can get so bad as to make colder water enter one ear canal more slowly than the other. So if you have a case of cold water vertigo but you are not wearing a hood, always get your ear canals checked by your doctor.

One of the harder to treat causes of vertigo with diving though, is an inner ear bend. Fortunately, this is rare but you would have a

"...it's all in the temperature of the water entering your ears. If cold water enters one ear canal and not the other, you can end up with vertigo."

clue to its origin as it can occur after a long bottom time coupled with a rapid ascent, especially if you have been diving on Heliox. This vertigo, unlike ABV, would last a lot longer, it would be present back on shore or the dive boat, and it would have started after the decompression stops. The only treatment for this is recompression at your nearest chamber, but if it happens some distance away, then do all the usual things on the way: 100% oxygen, lie down and plenty of non-alcoholic fluids.

But what can you do about the fear of heights (or depths as it's underwater), so you don't end up pinned to a rock by an old DM called Jeff? Well, don't look down is the simple answer, but the devil on our shoulders always makes us do that. So my tip is to find a cleaner shrimp. You need to quickly focus on something in a level plane of vision to your depth, but just staring at a rock won't fix it. You need to engage the brain away from the thoughts of the abyss beneath you a little bit more. A cleaner shrimp is just easy enough to find but not that easy, and when you do find one they're interesting enough to keep you otherwise occupied for those crucial moments before you could completely lose it. Trust me... it works.

"You need to quickly focus on something in a level plane of vision to your depth, but just staring at a rock won't fix it."

CARDIOVASCULAR SYSTEM

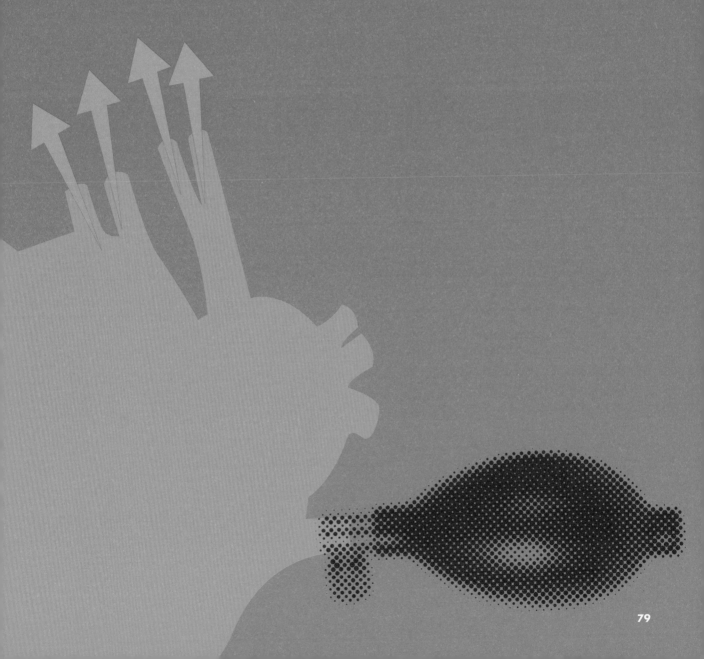

INTRO

Hard to find anything amusing to say about the cardiovascular system, which is one of the reasons that cancer doesn't have its own category in this book. As much as anything though, this chapter goes to show how much the attitude in diving medicine has changed from the olde approache of finding reasons to keep people out of the water, to the new one of finding ways to get them in. Except in Australia, where they're still not sure whether it's safe for bald people to dive or not.

Personally, I feel a bit squeamish about most things in this section. Maybe it's because the whole concept of pumps and tubes seems so 19th Century. Surely we should have kept with the times a bit more and evolved a way to get gases and materials to and from our cells by radio waves via satellite or something. Posh people could refuse to send their kids to local schools on the grounds that "half of the children there still use haemoglobin, for God's sake". Your entire physical wellbeing could be controlled at the touch of an iPhone. I suppose it already is.

This section will answer many questions you were too afraid to ask, such as "what is a PFO?" and "heart attacks: good thing or bad?" When I was seven years old, the girl that lived two doors down told me that you shouldn't pick moles because they're the ends of veins. There's no further information on that in here, though. I'll get The Shaman on to it for the next edition.

Tip: If you're reading this book and using the surgeon's elbow to lean it against whilst they perform a triple bypass operation on you, it's probably best to go and get a proper dive medical before jumping back into the water.

BLOOD AND PRESSURE

I am going diving soon in Oban. I started on Ramipril 2.5mg increasing to 10mg. I have been on the 10mg for just over a week and take it at bedtime. Last week, after taking the first 10mg dose, I woke up regurgitating acid and felt very dizzy with strange feelings down the left side of my face. Since then, at the weekend, I felt nauseous and dizzy. Will it be safe for me to dive or will I have to wait until I have been taking the medication a little longer?

Whoa, this sounds like quite a side effect, and I hope you have gotten rid of it by now. If not, go see your regular GP for an immediate assessment of your blood pressure. When you increase a dose like that there are chances it can drop your BP too much, hence the nausea and dizziness. Strange feelings on one side of your face really need a neurological assessment, to make sure there's no strokey sort of thing going on. So, assuming this is still present, do NOT dive.

If it does settle and it's simply a transient problem with the dose increase and now gone, this is what you do: high blood pressure needs to be assessed by a dive doc before diving. You need an ECG to make sure there's no damage to the heart, and a general once over, but these meds are dive friendly, with few side effects unlike the dreaded beta blockers or diuretics. I reckon your chances are decent, as long as all this side effect malarkey has gone for good.

During a full and very comprehensive annual medical from my GP, it transpires I currently have mild hypertension. Under normal everyday conditions he stated he would monitor my blood pressure again in six months time. Unfortunately, there are no limits relating to hypertension levels within the guidelines for the PADI medical declaration form to help my GP assess my condition with regard to diving.

The guidelines are fairly straightforward as regards high blood pressure and diving. In the UK, if you are an established diver with a BP of under 160/100 you are allowed to dive, but if you are new to the sport and you have a BP of over 150/90 then you need to see a medical referee first.

Now, before you get too worried you need to understand something. The pressure that your doctor checks is a variable thing. It may be high when he or she checks it, but it may be low later when you are at home. So in my practice, I never go on a single reading that I take. I always suggest that a patient with borderline high BP either buys a machine to check it themselves at home on a regular basis (which I think is a far more accurate way), or even better, has a 24 hour BP monitor. This gives the most accurate reading for your BP and quite often shows that it was normal anyway. However, if it is raised enough to stop you diving then hypertension is very easy to treat and can be under control within a week or two with a choice of medication that won't interfere with diving. So, get it properly checked first and then get it controlled and you'll be diving sooner than you might think.

I take warfarin 7mg daily and have done for six years. I was diagnosed with primary phospholipid antibody syndrome. My INR target is 3.5mg Would I be able to complete an Open Water dive course?

The deal with taking warfarin has changed. At one time there was a total ban due to the risk that any spinal bend could be worsened by the warfarin causing a bleed on top of a hit into the spine. End result: potential paralysis, as opposed to a bit of tingling. For those unacquainted with warfarin, it's what we used to use to kill rats with. It thins the blood and after the rodents had eaten cheese flavoured warfarin they would bleed to death if they banged their little heads on your neck when they were jumping to bite when cornered. Or so my mother used to tell me.

We use it to thin the blood if it's more clottable. You have that condition. However the powers that be have looked well into this subject and decided that if you can manage a dive profile so well that a bend is unlikely then you would be fine to dive.

So, we now have a depth limit to warfarin takers of about 20m to 25m. In a perfect world, I would advise you use Nitrox on air tables as that would slot in that extra safety factor and totally minimise a hit risk.

"For those unacquainted with warfarin, it's what we used to use to kill rats with."

You need to get clearance from a dive doc as is usual, and I would add that it's best to get your clotting or INR checked the week before you go to make sure you are not too thin on the blood side. If that's fine then you should be safe enough, but remember this: you of all people cannot risk a 'bend denial' as it could leave you in a wheelchair for a while. Report any odd symptoms like tingling, numbness or weakness ASAP to a doctor who knows. They won't be found in A&E but via your local divers' medical help line.

In October last year I experienced unusual chest pains and was checked out in hospital. I underwent a range of tests including an exercise ECG on the treadmill. My problems were diagnosed as stress/anxiety as all the tests came back clear, and no medication was prescribed. My own GP checked me out after and said my BP was raised (145/95) and prescribed propranolol as this would help both BP and anxiety. After this, I must say I felt awful and eventually in December I managed to persuade him to stop the medication and let me settle down.

My BP when checked by the nurse last week was 130/90. My GP has agreed to let me go diving again but seems insistent that we get the 90 down to 80 and I believe he will be prescribing more drugs next time I see him. Please could you comment on whether my BP is high and if so what medication is OK to take when diving. Diving is important to me in enabling me to cope with stress.

So, diving makes you less stressed, and the problem was stress in the first place. Sounds like we need to re-open Mr Cousteau's Sudanese underwater world for you. Your BP is actually OK to dive with, anything below 160/100 in an existing diver can be considered fine. If you are going to go onto meds, my recommendation is any drug ending in '-sartan'.

My dear wife (49 years of age) uses atenolol for high blood pressure which she hopes to come off from as we are going to Egypt soon on a liveaboard. Can you suggest any other alternatives?

Dear wife, yes I agree they can be expensive. Atenolol is a beta-blocker which has a risk of causing a build up of fluid in the lungs if she were to exercise more than she was used to. This is called 'pulmonary oedema' and results when the heart, which is slowed by the medication, fails to cope with the amount of blood returning to it, which then oozes out of the capillaries of the lungs into the tissues of the lungs itself. You can recognise someone with this as they are classically short of breath and cough up frothy blood stained sputum, rather like the head of a glass of strawberry Cresta, if you can remember popular 1970's soft drinks. Atenolol is the most commonly used of the anti-hypertensives as it's cheap and pretty effective, but I've got to advise that she try a non beta-blocker, and the best of these for a diver is probably losartan. So try to get her medication switched afore she goes.

I am a 51 year male and my LDL cholesterol is a little high. My Doctor has just put me on a daily dose 20mg of statins to try to get the level down. My blood pressure is normal and I am otherwise healthy. Is there anything he or I should be aware of that would inhibit my taking diving lessons?

This is going to get more and more common, as NHS GPs are paid to put people onto these sorts of meds at the soonest instance, but as long as you are not a coronary risk, and it sounds like you're not, then you are fine to dive.

I am a BSAC diving instructor and yesterday a friend's wife asked if she could learn to dive whilst taking amlodipine to control high blood pressure.

Amlodipine will probably be fine but I think a 'sartan' would be better. Either way, I suggest she gets a check up before diving. The doc will make sure all is well with the BP, but make sure she doesn't rush to the surgery and arrive late and hassled as the BP will be sky high. Get there early and chill in the waiting room with an old copy of Readers Digest to keep the pressure low before the doc gets out his sphygmomanometer.

That's a blood pressure cuff to the rest of us.

I have always been a blood donor and still want to carry on giving blood, but I'm not sure (and no one can tell me), how long I have to wait before going diving again after donating.

This is a very good question and oddly one that I have never been asked before, though there is an obvious relation between the two. However, do rest assured. When you go to give blood, the transfusion service always do a haemoglobin test to make sure that your blood is not too thin or anaemic, and also to make sure that taking it won't leave you in that state either. So you won't be left in a state where the thinness of your blood would increase the chances of a bend or exhaustion if you had to exert yourself during a dive.

About 45% of blood is composed of cells (mainly red blood cells, which contain the haemoglobin that carries oxygen) and the remaining 55% is fluid ('plasma', which transports dissolved gases and proteins). Each time they take an armful of your vintage claret, your circulating volume drops by about half a litre (470mls to be precise). The average human has a total blood volume of about five litres, so we're talking less than 10% of that with each donation. The body responds by moving fluid from the tissues into the circulation, so that the volume loss is replaced within 24 hours (quicker if you drink lots of fluid). It takes up to eight weeks to replace all the cells that have been removed though, so the concentration of red cells takes this long to recover and this is what governs your fitness to dive again. A hormone called 'erythropoetin' or EPO, a favourite of Tour de France cyclists, is released which makes the bone marrow step up production of the red cells.

The consequences of this on diving are several. In the first 24 hours after a donation, you are more prone to fainting due to the reduction in your circulating volume and hence your blood pressure. This is why you are force-fed tea, biscuits and preferably Guinness afterwards. In essence, you are dehydrated. Divers get notoriously dehydrated anyway, through immersion, breathing dry compressed gas, being cold/shivering etc, so I would certainly advise no diving within 24 hours, and preferably about a week to be on the safe side. There is no evidence that donating blood increases your susceptibility to narcosis or oxygen toxicity. Nitrogen is dissolved in the plasma, and for various reasons the plasma volume and delivery of blood to the tissues increases after a donation. Theoretically then, the risk of DCI might increase slightly, but so many other factors are involved that the effect is probably tiny and not worth worrying about.

I would like some advice on the suitability of medication I have been prescribed for high blood pressure. This is purely for my own peace of mind. The brand name of the medication is Diovan; the chemical name is valsartan. The prescribed dose is 80mg.

Well you can rock the house as you have got the right medication there in one. The 'sartans' are the best ones to take. They are from a group called A2RI's (don't ask what that's short for as it's too boring and the reason why I spent most of my pharmacology lectures

> "...you are more prone to fainting due to the reduction in your circulating volume and hence your blood pressure. This is why you are force fed tea, biscuits and preferably Guinness afterwards."

either asleep or in the pub), which block the angiotensin receptor itself, not the enzyme, and do not seem to cause side-effects such as a dry-cough (not the best when breathing dry, compressed air) associated with the old ACE inhibitors like perindopril. Any diver though with high blood pressure, controlled or not will need to get a fit to dive cert before going in deep as the doctor has to check for 'end organ damage'. This is not where you may have scraped your love pump on a urinal but something more complex to do with eyes and kidneys.

I've just been diagnosed with chronic lymphocytic leukaemia (CLL). My haemoglobin is 12.1, platelets 86 and white blood cell count 91. The consultant has advised me to start chemotherapy shortly but I had planned to try Scuba diving before all this. Is diving still a possibility? I am aware my comparatively low platelet count would be a problem if I were to cut myself, but are there any other implications?

Very sorry to hear of your diagnosis. The leukaemias are a group of disorders, basically cancers, of the blood or bone marrow. What distinguishes them is the rapid proliferation of abnormal white blood cells. In the acute form, many immature non-functional cells overcrowd the bone marrow, making it unable to produce healthy cells, and so treatment needs to be immediate. The chronic type takes much longer, but still results in the presence of many abnormal cells in the blood. It tends to affect an older age group, and sometimes is monitored for a time to determine when treatment will be most effective.

Despite the fact there are excessive numbers of cells in the blood, the symptoms result from the lack of normal, functioning ones. Platelets are crucial to blood clotting, so for divers the low count can lead to easy bruising, prolonged bleeding from cuts or scrapes, or in the worst case, a spinal DCI. White cells are an important line of immune defense, making a leukaemia sufferer more prone to picking up infections, and to those infections being much worse than usual. Finally, the depletion of red blood cells, so important for carrying oxygen around the body, renders the patient anaemic and often breathless with poor exercise tolerance as a result.

Treatments for all leukaemias have improved vastly over recent years, but as a disease it still shortens lifespan. With CLL, however, some patients may require no treatment if their disease progression is sufficiently slow. I'm never one to give a blanket "no" to anyone,

"I am aware my comparatively low platelet count would be a problem if I were to cut myself, but are there any other implications?"

as I believe in assessing on a case-by-case basis, and it is possible that you could dive, based on your current condition and symptoms. Once chemotherapy has started, however, your chances would be much slimmer, due to the side effects of the agents used.

I would like to know if Adalat and perindopril are OK to dive with. Also, are any diuretics acceptable?

Yes. Yes. Maybe.

Alright I'll expand on the brief answer. The first two are drugs used most commonly for high blood pressure. For any budding pharmacists out there, they are a calcium antagonist (Adalat, or nifedipine) and an angiotensin converting enzyme (ACE) inhibitor, respectively. They lower BP by dilating blood vessels and blocking an enzyme that causes blood pressure to rise via fluid balance. So the key thing here is that if your blood pressure is controlled by these meds, then you should be fine to dive. You will need a dive medical as well as the doc needs to do an ECG of your heart to check for any abnormalities that long term high BP can cause, notably left ventricular hypertrophy. If you have this then diving could cause problems.

Now to diuretics. They do what they say. Cause diuresis: medical for peeing. The theory is that if you pee out all this fluid, there's less in the system, so your BP decreases. The only problem with diving here is that you can dehydrate a tad on these tablets, so increasing the risk of DCS. I think best leave these alone if you want to dive a lot.

My employer is calling me from Hawaii. She wants to Scuba dive for the first time but she is being treated for high blood pressure. She is in otherwise good health, only an abnormal eye exam recently related to the high BP. There were other references to blood pressure on the dive website, but nothing specifically related to an angiotensin receptor blocker. Can you advise whether she should dive? She is in her early 40s.

I'm trying to get my head round this. Your boss is in Hawaii, needs a medical question answered, and instead of asking the dive shop's dive doc, calls you. I hope you don't have to wipe her… Anyway, she will need to get seen before diving, to check what the hypertension has done to her, but the good news is that the meds she is taking are the best with diving, so she should be OK to learn. Hey, you could even do her PADI exam for her too.

"Your boss is in Hawaii, needs a medical question answered, and instead of asking the dive shop's dive doc, calls you. I hope you don't have to wipe her…"

My husband has been on medication since he received a kidney transplant in late 1999.

He currently takes: 1000mg of mycophenolate mofetil three times daily; 2mg Tacrolimus twice daily; 5mg amlodipine once daily; 3mg prednisolone once daily; 1mg doxazosin once daily; and 100mg metoprolol Tartrate twice daily.

He is in good health and is not overweight, but can he dive?

A successful kidney transplant where the donor kidney has taken, the blood urea and electrolyte balance is all fine and the side effects of the medication are not causing any debilitation is no bar to diving. However looking at the meds he is on, one rears its ugly head: metoprolol. This is a beta-blocker and can cause fluid on the lungs if the dive were to turn strenuous.

Now here's the rub. The metoprolol is to keep his blood pressure down, vital after this sort of operation. In non-renal transplant divers there are other choices of BP tablet, but this may not be the case if he's got someone else's kidney. I think the best option is to go back to the specialist, see if there's another alternate to metoprolol that is not a beta-blocker, eg a calcium antagonist, and if that's the case then switch. But if his specialist says it can only be metoprolol then I think that he may have to steer clear of sub-aqua pursuits.

And finally, whilst on the subject of try-dives, I have just done a medical on a young girl keen to learn to dive after a similar initial experience. Only she was very nearly put off it for life after her session. Why? Well they only went and took her cave diving didn't they after a 20 minute pool session. Makes you realise where all the cowboys have gone.

My wife (and diving buddy) has recently received the results of a blood test, which shows that she is quite badly anaemic. Apparently (according to second hand reports), a normal blood iron reading is between 20(ish) and 200(ish) (I cannot recall the precise ranges); she has a reading of four. Moreover, she has been anaemic for at least several months now, having been turned away from donating blood on two consecutive occasions, despite eating more iron rich foods. She has since refused to accept a prescription for iron tablets on the grounds that they make her uncomfortable.

"A successful kidney transplant… is no bar to diving. However looking at the meds he is on, one rears its ugly head: metoprolol."

I am very concerned that this presents a danger vis a vis diving for her and thus for the both of us, and am reluctant to go diving with her again until I get some reassurance. Am I being unreasonable, or do I have grounds for legitimate concern? We are only at an early stage of our training and are still limited to pool training, but we are aiming to become open water qualified in about four weeks time. Should we delay this until my wife's blood-iron count normalizes?

Grounds for legitimate concern? Grounds for divorce, mate.

If your wife is badly anaemic caused by a lack of iron, and then won't take the prescribed iron tablets as they makes her uncomfortable (in which case she risks death), then that is pretty dopey.

Iron builds haemoglobin (Hb). Hb carries oxygen molecules to the tissues. Oxygen is the fuel for the cells in the body. The oxygen also creates diffusion gradients to help get rid of nitrogen. So you can see its importance to the diver. Anaemic people also get short of breath, and become faint and excessively tired with the simplest of tasks. And look rather pale and ghostly.

So here's the plan. If her Hb is that low, ask your GP if he can refer her for a quick transfusion. That's the quickest way to get better. Otherwise she will have to eat more spinach than 10 Popeyes. If it is a borderline low then iron tablets will have to do. Sure, they can make you uncomfortable, but that's only really constipation. And the best way to treat that? Traditional Egyptian cooking.

I am a 47 year-old male and dive regularly throughout the year. I take 2.5mg of Tritace (ramipril) and 20mg Lipitor (atorvastatin) each day. I am fairly fit, work out three or four times a week (weight training), and I have never smoked. I am considering using a supplement to assist with my weight training called Pro Test and to quote the sales pitch it "boosts natural hormone production, increases muscle gains, increases strength, lowers oestrogen & stimulates luteinising hormone production. It contains Tribulus terrestris, protodioscin, concentrated extract of the herb Avena Sativa & diindolylmethane". It describes itself as an "endocrine support system offering natural testosterone elevation".

I don't know if this is all rubbish but a number of people including instructors at the gym I use say it is quite effective at building

up muscle and strength. I'm not a hardcore bodybuilder or anything but I just like to keep fit and have a good physique (a bit vain, I guess) and at my age a bit of help would be welcome. But I don't want it to affect my diving so I would value your opinion.

The first bit about the blood pressure pills and cholesterol lowering meds is fine. If your BP is under control then you are OK to dive.

As for the muscle bulking supplements. The reality is that we don't dope test yet in diving, and I am sure that anything sold is probably fairly benign, so it should be fine with diving. My only reservation is that history has proven that these supplements don't often either contain or say what they will do on the tin.

Be careful you don't grow breasts and have your nads disappear.

I'm taking the alpha-blocker Omnic MR (400mg once daily), to help with a prostate problem. As a result, I occasionally get dizzy if I stand up too quickly and my heart races if I do any anaerobic exercise. Although these symptoms are easing, and I have been diving with no problems, I am a bit worried whether I should be diving or not.

Also known as tamsulosin, this alpha-blocker, as well as being a drug that can reduce the size of the prostate, is also a blood pressure lowering medication. It may take a while to get used to the side effects of this drop in pressure as your prostate shrinks, but things will level out later.

You need to get a pressure check to compare standing versus lying to see if there is too much of a drop. If there is then it may be worth trying another med, or even going for the prostate reducing operation.

"Be careful you don't grow breasts and have your nads disappear."

VALVES AND HOLES

I am very keen on doing a Divemaster Internship but have only dived once in my life. During some travelling a few years ago, I was prevented from diving on the Great Barrier Reef as I was born with a hole in my heart (atrial septal defect) even though this was corrected when I was two years old. I think I still have a murmur (I don't know much about it really) but I don't think it is a problem. I am a fit and healthy 32 year-old, I can exercise and have never had any problems with it. I go to hospital every two years for a check-up, but if I am considering diving, would you recommend that I have a diving medical done by a specialist?

Not many people realise that we are all born with a hole in the heart. It lies between the top two chambers, called the atria. When we're curled up in the womb, it's the presence of this hole that allows oxygenated blood to pass from the placenta through the foetal heart and round the body, bypassing the lungs (which are full of amniotic fluid and therefore not much use). At birth, what's supposed to happen is that the hole closes; the blood then gets directed around the lungs to pick up its oxygen, before being pumped around the body. This hole is called the foramen ovale (because it's oval-shaped), and sometimes it doesn't fully seal over, resulting in a 'patent' or permanently open hole: the PFO, of which you may have heard. So a PFO is one type of atrial septal defect (ASD); there are others, of all sorts of shapes and sizes, and I suspect yours must have been rather large if it needed to be operated on at two years of age.

To understand why ASD is a problem, a little explaining is required. The right and left sides of the heart are normally separate. The left side of the heart pumps blood around the entire body, and so the pressure is much higher than on the right, which just pumps blood to the lungs. If you have a hole between the two sides, then the right side of the heart becomes exposed to the higher pressure of the left, which in time will overload it. This is called a 'left to right shunt'. Fluid will then accumulate in the lungs causing breathlessness, and ultimately the heart will fail. If the ASD is small, this process may take many years, but a large hole can cause heart failure in childhood.

These days the hole is easily closed with an umbrella-like device which is threaded through a groin vein into the heart, and deployed on either side of the ASD (or PFO for that matter). After a few months, enough scar tissue will form to occlude the defect completely, and separate the two sides of the heart again. So, at the ripe old age of 32, if you are able to exercise without any symptoms, the heart should be normal to all intents and purposes. An echo test to put some numbers on the heart function would be useful, but I anticipate it will show a ticker that's perfectly capable of diving.

I had a 'hole in the heart' (VSD), which was patched at about eight months old and I wish to know what steps I need to take (if any) before embarking on deeper diving. I went for checkups at Great Ormond Street hospital until the age of 14 when I was cleared for a normal/active life.

I am now 28 and a cardiologist that I know who consults from Guy's Hospital has agreed to see me and give me an echocardiogram once he has received a referral letter from my GP. Is this necessary after such a long period of time?

A VSD, or ventriculo-septal defect, is where a hole between the two ventricles still exists after birth and is picked up on listening to the heart sounds when you are a baby.

A quick echocardiogram, a small op and it's fixed. Well in your case anyway. The potential problem with holes in the heart is that if they shunt blood from the right to the left side, nitrogen bubbles from the venous circulation can get into the arterial circulation, avoiding exhalation and causing the bends. But your luck is in. Those with a VSD tend to shunt blood the other way, from left to right, so the understanding is that divers with a small untreated VSD should be fine to dive. However, blood shunted from left to right with each beat of the heart can, in periods of exercise, potentially put too much blood back into the heart/lung circulation and block it up causing pressure on both those organs. I would advise a diver with an untreated VSD to see a doc for an exercise test to make sure this doesn't happen.

In your case, as it was treated at birth you have been given the all clear, but with the offer of a free echocardiogram, well, how can you turn that down? I would have it just to make really sure that all is well. If there is still a tiny fault then you should be OK, bigger hole and get the exercise test done, but I reckon your chances are near enough 100% that you shouldn't lose any sleep over it.

I am an active bodybuilder currently weighing 17 stone of mainly solid muscle mass. I am also a re-breather diver regularly diving to 80+ metres on Trimix, using a VR3 that I have set to 30% conservatism. I am unable to drop this below 30% without feeling unwell once out of the water, while all of my dive buddies can run theirs on 10% or less.

I have previously had two bends from what were textbook dives and am now wondering if my muscle mass is affecting the rate at which my body off-gasses, thus causing me to retain nitrogen even after my computer says I am clear to surface. What do you think?

"Mainly solid muscle mass". Love it. Get you, in front of the mirror at the gym, ducky.

Well here's some news for you, muscle is pretty darn well perfused with blood. It'll on-gas and off-gas equally well, so no joy as an excuse there. But feeling odd out of the water after a long dive: it's your body craving steroids. OK, sorry, you will find me and beat me up, so no more jokes.

I think you need a PFO check. Two unexplained hits with normal profiles points towards that hole in the heart that pushes bubbles across to the arterial circulation, bypassing the lungs. I suggest you contact your local pot and see if they can arrange it for you.

I have just had something called aortic valve incompetence diagnosed after a long fever. Can I carry on diving?

This problem is not what we call an 'absolute contraindication' to diving like aortic stenosis where the valve stays tightly shut limiting the flow of blood out of the heart to the body, but it is a 'relative contraindication', which means your diving future depends on how loose and floppy the valve is.

At its worst, this condition means that blood exiting the heart falls back into the chamber, slowing down the new blood filling the chamber up for the next beat. This can cause a back pressure on

"I am an active bodybuilder currently weighing 17 stone of mainly solid muscle mass."

new oxygenated blood arriving to the heart, which results in a build-up in the lungs making you short of breath. You can see why this could be incompatible with diving. However, if the problem is only minor and the valve stops most of the blood from coming back into the heart, then you may well be fit to dive.

The best thing to do is discuss it with a cardiologist, make sure you have regular echocardiograms (ultrasounds of the heart), and if you get any symptoms of shortness of breath, see your doctor quickly.

I have a maximum of two migraines per year, with aura and transient sensory loss of right hand and wrist. I've never needed prophylaxis medication. I do approx 80 dives a year as a BSAC instructor and am Trimix qualified. In the past year I have had two DCI events. The first was after two 30m dives in Malta, may have been brought on by post-dive exercise (climbing steep steps with kit at the dive site), involved the shoulder joints and necessitated recompression treatment. The second was to 30m in Ireland, a non-aggressive profile but dehydration may have been a factor in a skin bend on the stomach. I am now concerned about PFO and would appreciate your advice on the issue.

Yes, you do need a PFO check, and definitely before you do another dive. The frequency and profiles of the hits plus history of migraine all point PFOwards. But just as every diver with a PFO doesn't always get a bend, not every migraine is symptomatic of a PFO. The easiest way of checking for a PFO is for a dive doc to refer you to a cardiologist with experience in these tests. Or you could ask your NHS GP, and join the queue behind all the 'more needy' cases.

I was born with a congenital heart condition which included aortic stenosis, and various other problems. This was operated on in 1977 and the stenosis removed. Although the procedure was successful, I have a leaky valve (the left ventricle) and so I have a systolic murmur. The hospital tells me that the heart is 20% overworking.

The consultant I saw thought that my stenosis would reoccur by the time I was 18, but it hasn't as yet. I have annual checkups at the Royal Brompton National Heart and Lung hospital, which includes a full range of appropriate tests. They have not objected to any activity that I have discussed with them in the past. I

don't undertake super-strenuous exercise such as marathons etc., but I have been to a gym in the past and I regularly play football.

Please let me know if there is already a good reason why I will fail a diving medical.

Bad news I am afraid. Although your stenosis (closure of the main valve that regulates the oxygenated blood going out of the heart) is fixed, the other valve will cause you problems. This is the mitral valve and sits between the left atrium and ventricle. When the ventricle contracts, whooshing blood out of the heart, this valve stops the blowback of blood into the atrium and lungs. If it is faulty and leaks, you get a back pressure into the lungs. Blood will pool there and affect your ability to oxygenate the red stuff. This is pulmonary oedema and can be fatal for the diver. Frothy sputum on ascent, blood in the spit, the works. Add the fact that your heart is already overworking anyway and sadly you won't get into a dive doc's door, let alone pass the medical.

I recently returned from a liveaboard trip to Red Sea. After my second dive, I experienced quite bad bruising and blotchiness to the stomach area, and pain and redness on the fatty areas of my thighs. After a few hours this went down, I did another dive, and the same thing happened, this time I also experienced some glassiness in my eyes. I was diving well within the limits, had no fast ascents etc., did all my recommended stops and more, and was diving to a depth of approx 28m. I was OK diving the next day, although I did switch to diving on Nitrox, but later on in the week the same thing happened.

I have had these symptoms before on previous liveaboard trips, but it has never happened so quickly. I have always put it down to not drinking enough water and general tiredness, as I never sleep well on these trips. I was diving in the UK a couple of weekends before I went on holiday and never had a problem. In all my diving career I have never experienced a fast ascent or missed any deco stops, I always ascend very slowly and I consider myself to be fit and very active.

The thinking hat doesn't have to be on that long to figure this one out. An obvious skin bend, normal profiles, and even getting it when diving on Nitrox. And getting it often too. We have to consider that little 'ole hole in the heart called the PFO. A patent foramen ovale,

> "I experienced quite bad bruising and blotchiness to the stomach area, and pain and redness on the fatty areas of my thighs."

the remnant of us being a baby in our mother's womb, where blood circulates in a different fashion. A PFO in divers means that nitrogen returning towards the lungs in the venous blood passes through the hole on the way through the heart and ends up back in the arterial circulation. Skin bends, with that classic mottled marbled look, is a common consequence. So you need transthoracic echocardiography to rule this out, and if it's a positive result, you should have it closed before diving, unless you go for the ultra-cautious approach. By this I mean Nitrox only, computer set to air tables, 18m max, one dive a day. I suggest the former.

I have just been released from a five hour recompression treatment following a dive yesterday. The dive followed a normal profile without any issues and in fact took five minutes to ascend to 5m where I did a six minute stop for extra precaution.

20 minutes after surfacing I developed pain in my back and stomach that I couldn't locate and which was quickly followed by a mottled rash covering the same area. My legs gave out when I tried to move them and I experienced pins and needle sensations through my whole body. I took emergency O2 and drank water before ending up in A&E. The first time I had the bends, I was in hospital for three days of recompression following an uncontrolled ascent, however I am now three stone lighter and followed a perfect profile, which seems unfair.

The diving doctor who saw me suggested I should give up diving as no reason could be given for this bend. I have been following an extreme diet of 600 calories and four litres of water a day where your body goes into ketosis, and wondered if this might be the main reason I got a hit.

Hmm, tricky one here. Is a diet that tends you towards ketosis likely to bring on DCS, despite the increased amounts of fluids taken at the same time? I can see it causing cramps, see your body finding it harder to find energy to dive, and see odd osmotic issues causing increased cell fluid retention and so less ability to off-gas, but it may well be a red herring. With a second mystery hit, and with skin DCS to boot, I think you need to look up the PFO route for the reason. If this is confirmed, then closing the hole would allow you to return to diving. So some good news as I think the other doc is being over cautious with a total ban at this stage. If you turn out to be PFO negative, let's have a rethink.

"20 minutes after surfacing I developed pain in my back and stomach that I couldn't locate and which was quickly followed by a mottled rash covering the same area."

A point to note here, I think it's best not to go onto fad diets if you are diving a lot. Eat less, move more. An easy mantra.

I have recently undergone treatment for a bend for the second time this year. As with the first one, I have been advised not to dive for six weeks and after that I should be OK. The doctor has said he is not worried about a PFO or other susceptibility, but I would like to clarify.

The first bend occurred while using a new drysuit that had a shoulder instead of cuff dump (and which was also adjustable and inadvertently closed). I had dived to about 24m, and when it came time to ascend, my buddy and I both lost control. Part of the problem was that my buddy's faster ascent stopped me from realising my own situation. I brought it under control 1m from the surface, started to go back down to 5m for a safety stop, then changed my mind at about 3m and came up. I safely drove home from Chepstow to Poole, but felt ill that evening and next morning had a pain in my elbow. My buddies with faster ascents had no problems.

The second bend occurred on a shallow dive, with a maximum depth at 9m and most of the dive at 5-7m for about 50 minutes. At the end of my ascent I dropped my SMB reel, which I went down to 5m again for. I was shocked when the doctor described it as a 'guaranteed' bend, and this statement has provoked the same surprise from a number of very experienced divers and instructors, who reinforced my original view that, while not recommended, such dives are very common particularly with regard to tying off anchors and stuff. My symptoms in this case occurred straight away and included itching skin, generally feeling unwell and a lack of mental alertness. Stupidly, I denied this for 24 hours and was treated the following day.

Should I be concerned about a PFO? I have been referred for a six week follow up consultation with an independent doctor in Ringwood, but I'm moving to Essex in three weeks and they have told me that there is no one I can be referred to in London instead.

"Utter bollocks. Of course there are doctors in London who can assess you post treatment and pre-return to diving. There're about five or six including myself."

The last bit first. Utter bollocks. Of course there are doctors in London who can assess you post treatment and pre-return to diving. There're about five or six including myself. Whoever told you that should hang their head in shame.

Now, was it a guaranteed bend? Well itching, and feeling dull and drowsy are bends symptoms. You got this straight after a dive and I assume you got better in the pot, so it must have been. There are other causes of itching and dullness but it would be freaky if, say, you suddenly got eczema and Alzheimer's straight after a dive. So, we gotta say it was a hit. Now that's two for you, and the last one after a shallow dive with a tiny bounce. If it were me I would be hammering on the door of the cardiologist already. I think you have to find out whether you have a PFO for peace of mind and for the future, as you seem to be more than the once a year on holidays sort of diver. So, see a dive doc and get referred for an echocardiogram to look for this hole, and if it's there, get it fixed.

"So, see a dive doc and get referred for an echocardiogram to look for this hole, and if it's there, get it fixed."

ARTERIES, VEINS AND CAPILLARIES

I have heard about the sad death of a young girl from a clot in her legs and lungs after a long haul flight from Australia, and as I am flying to and from there next month to dive the Great Barrier Reef, I would like to know what I can do to prevent this and if diving increases the chances of these clots forming.

What happened to this girl was sadly preventable and also becoming more frequent as flights get longer and seats get more cramped. It even has a name now: 'Economy Class Syndrome'.

She suffered a blood clot in the deep venous system of her calf. This is called a Deep Venous Thrombosis, or DVT. If part of this clot dislodges, it travels up the venous system back to the heart, through the right side of the heart and to the lungs. This is what can kill you, because if a big enough piece of the clot gets to the lungs, it will cause a blockage of the blood supply there or a 'pulmonary embolus'. Recent research has shown that up to one in four people that get a DVT have been on a long haul flight in the last few weeks. You can see that this is an incredible statistic as a lot of the smaller DVTs go undiagnosed as they don't cause the classic symptoms of swelling of the calf with redness and pain in the same area.

The reason that air travel can cause this problem is due to several factors. Firstly, for a clot to form, the blood needs to be very slow moving. This occurs in-flight as passengers sit in a cramped position with their knees bent. This can restrict the flow back of the blood and help a clot form. The next problem is with dehydration. It is said that you should drink a litre of fluid every three hours on a flight, but what is normally given out, ie alcohol can actually dehydrate you more as it makes you need to urinate more often. As you now have less circulating fluid volume, the chances of clot formation are a lot higher. Finally, the swelling in your lower legs due to the position you sit in also causes the veins to constrict. Other factors that will increase the risk are being on the contraceptive pill, obesity and smoking.

"What happened to this girl was sadly preventable and also becoming more frequent as flights get longer and seats get more cramped. It even has a name now: 'Economy Class Syndrome'."

The general in-flight recommendations are to keep your toes moving by regularly going for a walk up and down the aisle, and also keeping well hydrated. I would also suggest that anyone who is high risk (and by that I mean overweight, Pill-taking smokers who have a family history of clots forming), take a dose of 75mg of aspirin before they fly, as this might thin the blood to help stop the DVT forming, although the evidence for this is controversial. However if you suffer from stomach ulceration or allergy to aspirin then there is a shot of a blood thinning agent called heparin available.

If you experience tender calf swelling or chest pain and shortness of breath after a flight, seek medical attention immediately.

There is little evidence to suggest that diving would increase the chances of in-flight clot formation on your return home, but again as most divers seem to spend their 24 hours pre-flight, non-diving time in a state of post alcohol dehydration, then it is doubly important to make sure you have enough fluids with you to drink during the flight back.

"...most divers seem to spend their 24 hours pre-flight, non-diving time in a state of post alcohol dehydration, then it is doubly important to make sure you have enough fluids with you to drink during the flight back."

I am 54 years old and have been diving for some six years now. Most of this is in either tropical waters or temperate areas with water temperatures of 18°C or more. Two years ago I underwent varicose vein surgery to both legs and vessels were removed from both lower limbs. The only discomfort I now suffer is the occasional cramp, which happens during the night.

I have just returned from Western Australia and among others, we enjoyed the inaugural dive on the HMAS Perth in Albany. The water temperature was 18°C and I was 'crippled' during the last 10 minutes of each dive, causing some concern to myself and diving buddies alike. The two layers of 5mm neoprene kept the rest of me quite warm enough in the water.

Is there any drug treatment that I can use to alleviate this inevitable consequence, or any physical treatment to be advised?

I assume that "crippled" was with the cramps you experience at other times. I think there are a few things you can do to make sure it doesn't happen again.

Cramps result after the build up of lactic acid, a by-product of the burning of elements other than the glucose that is the normal stuff the tissues need to give them energy. If you dive dehydrated or do

not eat properly beforehand then the chances of getting cramps are greatly increased. As we know, in diving, the muscles we use most are those in the legs when finning, so if you are going to cramp then the legs are probably where you'll get it. Also, keeping warm is important as cold legs and arms will result in cramps fairly soon into a dive if you have to fin a lot, so the lesson here is plenty of fluids (energy drinks may be the best for you), and perhaps a set of ergonomic fins so you use your leg muscles less.

If you do cramp underwater, depending on the situation your buddy could pull the muscle for you by flexing the leg But if it's a serious one just come up slowly and try the manoeuvre during a deco stop. The varicose vein surgery is a red herring as it doesn't necessarily contribute to cramp, but what you can use for any night cramps is a tablet called quinine sulphate. This is the same compound used as an anti-malarial and also found in tonic water. So if you're stuck for the tablets, a few bottles of this may help. Gin is optional.

I was wondering if there are any problems with diving if I have varicose veins?

I can't see any real issue here. Sure they're ugly, sure they may cause a bit of aching and discolouration, but as long as they're not really severe, you can dive. By severe, imagine great thick wriggly blue worms, trying to bust out from under the skin on your legs. If these are knocked or pricked on something spiky, the column of blood above them can dump out quicker than a Texan oil strike. The only way of taming this wildcat is to lie on your back and get a passerby to put pressure on the point of the bleed with your leg raised. But to let the varicosities get to that stage would be criminal, so as you are smart enough to take up diving, I assume the problem is a minor one. In fact, if you're wearing a full-length, nice, tight neoprene wettie, then the pressure might even act to improve the condition temporarily. And be a darn site more fashionable than one of those grotty NHS pressure stockings that seem to slip down to the ankle, especially in the elderly, obese, Richard and Judy-watching care home resident types. An image still burned into my brain from early years working voluntarily in old folks' homes. Ever been a bingo caller to people with Alzheimer's? The longest of all games.

"...darn site more fashionable than one of those grotty NHS pressure stockings that seem to slip down to the ankle, especially in the elderly, obese, Richard and Judy-watching care home resident types."

A few years ago, my partner suffered a DVT and recovered, becoming a dive instructor later that year and last dived in February.

We moved to Spain from the UK in April (very long drive) and in July, following a few long evening shifts on his feet, he suffered another bout of thrombosis, this time superficial, affecting a vein on the outer part of his leg. He was treated with Clexane and rest until the end of August and an ultrasound in September showed that the leg is clear of thrombosis. He still has discomfort in the leg but is desperate to get back in the water in the near future. Is it likely he will be able to dive again as a job? His doctors here do not really understand what Scuba is.

He is due to have a blood test next week to see if there is an underlying cause as to why a man of 42 should have suffered two bouts of thrombosis. We have already turned down a great job in Africa for fear it was in too remote a location and too soon, but would like some idea about how long it might be before he could safely dive again.

Two sets of clots in two different venous systems of the legs has got to be due to something. There is a chance it is bad luck, or the sheer standy-up-all-dayness of a shift, but before embarking on a career as an instructor, it is imperative that he has the triple blood test to look for proneness to clotting problems. If it is negative, then cool, all he has to do is make sure he is always hydrated and all should be OK. If it is positive, then he may be put on regular daily aspirin or clopidogrel, its less acidic cousin. If this is the case, then there is a good likelihood he will be allowed to instruct abroad at the very least, as medical rules are, frankly, slacker, but there could be issues in the UK.

Either way, for his own safety, I suggest it would be best to dive on Nitrox, and if doing repetitive dives, he should set his computer for air. Why? Well in cases of DCI, and also with microbubbles, it has been shown that a tiny clotting cascade tends to develop around the surface of the bubble. If you are prone to clotting, then this can be enhanced. So the best way of making sure there's no darn bubbles, is to O_2 it up with the Nitrox.

I have burgess disease. out of the 3 artery running down my calfs i have half remaining in one leg and almost two in the other i get intermittent claudication in feet and hands. does this mean i cant learn to dive

"Two sets of clots in two different venous systems of the legs has got to be due to something… before embarking on a career as an instructor, it is imperative that he has the triple blood test to look for proneness to clotting problems."

Honey, if I don't tell you, then no one will. The next book you read will not be the PADI Open Water course book; it has to be 'Ant and Bee Learn Basic Grammar and Spelling'. Capitalise your 'I's and caps after a full stop please. OK, that's enough pedantry.

It's called Buerger's disease, named after some German bloke no doubt as opposed to the acid-fuelled author of 'A Clockwork Orange', and is also known as thromboangiitis obliterans. It's a rare disease characterized by a combination of acute inflammation and thrombosis (clotting) of the arteries and veins in the hands and feet. The obstruction of blood vessels in the hands and feet reduces the availability of blood to the tissues, causes pain and eventually damages or destroys the tissue. It often leads to skin ulcerations and gangrene of fingers and toes. As you do have clogged up arteries in your legs, and you get this 'claudication', or angina, of the legs then it is a real issue with diving. If you were to fin at all, then you would get searing cramps and pains up your legs whilst at depth. This would result in the sight of you bent double in agony, desperately pulling the tip of a fin to release a cramp, but with no result as your blood supply would be so bad.

So, sad news I am afraid. But you could at least see the inside of a dive chamber, as hyperbaric oxygen has been trialled as a treatment for this condition. It doesn't work, but at least you can't smoke in there. And giving up smoking is the only real cure for Buerger's.

I received a blow to the head during a backward roll entry recently and after the dive, started to suffer headaches and trouble focussing while reading. The local A&E department checked me over and said it was post concussion syndrome, which would improve on its own.

After two months, the headaches were still quite bad so I made an appointment to see the A&E consultant. As a precautionary measure, having already had a skull X-ray, he arranged for me to have a head scan. The scan showed up what he thought might be an arterial angioma, which would have stopped me diving again. I was then referred to a consultant neurologist, who showed my scans to a senior consultant neurologist at Atkinson Morley. They both agreed that what I had was a small venous angioma which I'd had from birth and as I'd never suffered from fit or blackout they could see no reason why it should affect me in the future.

"Honey, if I don't tell you, then no one will. The next book you read will not be the PADI Open Water course book; it has to be 'Ant and Bee Learn Basic Grammar and Spelling'."

The consultant confirmed the post concussion syndrome headache would improve and that I could continue diving. As I am about to do an instructor course, I would like to know if the venous angioma would be a problem and whether it would affect a HSE medical.

I think that if you have two consultants from one of the world's top neurological hospitals agreeing that this angioma poses absolutely no risk of causing you any problems, then who am I to argue? The risk here is obviously that a lesion within the skull cavity could cause you to have a fit, but some are more fit inducing than others, and yours falls into the ultra-low risk category. It seems that the neurologists feel that it had absolutely no causal factor with your headache and was just a benign coincidental finding. However, I would ask you to ask them what the chances are that this angioma could increase in size. If it is 0% then you would be OK to instruct, however if there is a chance it could get bigger and pose a fit risk later, then you may well need regular MRI if you wanted to continue diving.

Finally, it was an interesting diagnosis you had there from A&E. Post Concussion Syndrome when concussion never happened, I assume, as you completed the dive. It must have been the August changeover.

A few years ago, I was hospitalised with Henoch-Schoenlein Purpura (HSP). It is a rare and sometimes recurring condition which causes blood vessels in the skin and kidneys to become inflamed. I have to take 2mg of Perindopril daily for life, to keep my blood pressure under control as high blood pressure increases the risk of long term kidney damage. I am in other respects a healthy, 42 year-old non-smoker.

After treatment I was cleared to dive and recently enjoyed a liveaboard holiday. I did four dives a day without incident, including several dives deeper than 30m and one to 60m. A few days ago I was diagnosed with a HSP flare-up and am taking 20mg of Prednisolone and 300mg of Ranitidine daily in addition to the Perindopril. These should halt and reverse the flare up and the quantity of Prednisolone will hopefully be reduced in two weeks. I am currently planning a two week dive holiday commencing next month. Can I still dive safely while taking this medication and should I follow any precautions?

Indeed, your problem is a rare one which characteristically starts off with a rash on the buttocks and upper thighs. It is also associated with pain in the joints known as arthralgia, problems with the gastrointestinal system which can lead to bloody diarrhoea, and most seriously, kidney damage which as you say is made worse by having a high blood pressure.

Thankfully, most people recover in time and do not end up on drugs forever. The fact that you've had a flare up and need the steroid tablets to control it normally wouldn't be too much of a problem if you weren't a diver, but steroids in very high doses can cause a degree of fluid retention in the body which could (rarely) manifest itself as fluid on the lungs (which we call pulmonary oedema). This would obviously cause you problems with breathing underwater as it affects the amount of oxygen you would absorb through the lungs with each breath. I suggest you discuss your steroid reduction with your consultant to see what dose you would be on when you go diving, and if it is low enough then you should be fine to dive.

The other situation here is that a flare up of HSP can cause a sudden haemorrhage of blood from your bowel, and this would be disastrous on a dive, so again your doctor should give you a clear indication of your particular risks and you shouldn't dive if there is a chance of it.

The medication you take for your blood pressure, Perindopril, will not cause any problems with diving but one of its side effects can be an irritating dry cough, which would be an annoyance to you with a reg in your mouth at 60m. So, if this side effect ever hits you, consider a medication switch or make sure your mouthpiece fits well with plenty of bite so it doesn't pop out of your mouth unexpectedly.

I've recently been diagnosed with something called Factor V Leiden after my sister had a DVT. The doctors told me it makes me more susceptible to DVT myself, but does it increase my risk of getting a bend?

Blood clotting is a complicated series of events involving a chain of 'factors', imaginatively referred to in Roman numerals from 1 to 12 (I – XII). So, when you slice open your unprotected scalp on a sharp bit of wreck (as I have done on several occasions, I REALLY must wear a hood), this cascade is triggered rather like someone pushing over the first domino in a line, and the end result is that the

> "Thankfully, most people recover in time and do not end up on drugs forever. The fact that you've had a flare up and need the steroid tablets to control it normally wouldn't be too much of a problem if you weren't a diver…"

blood thickens up and stops hosing from the wound. Some people, however, have faulty genes that make them more (or sometimes less) likely to clot. The commonest is Factor V Leiden, named after the town in the Netherlands where it was discovered in 1994. It is a mutant gene now known to be carried by about 5% of white Europeans.

Now, to my knowledge no diving related problem, bend or otherwise, has been directly attributed to Factor V Leiden, but there are a few issues to mention. You are more likely to develop a DVT on one of those long dehydrating plane flights to exotic dive locations, so get up and move around as much as possible and keep glugging the water. If you need to take anticoagulants for a clot, then these can increase your risk of bleeding due to barotrauma, so I would be very cautious about diving if you ever get put on Warfarin or one of the heparins. Also, tight-fitting dive gear and weight belts could conceivably reduce the flow of blood and make you more likely to clot at depth. You should plan your diving to try to minimise your risk of bubble formation and injury, as the clotting cascade could be triggered in response to either.

"You are more likely to develop a DVT on one of those long dehydrating plane flights to exotic dive locations..."

HEART ATTACKS AND ANGINA

I had a heart attack recently; apparently mild as it was quickly attended to. It has been reported as a clot in the right artery or in medical terms – acute inferior myocardial infarction. I was discharged from hospital after a nine minute treadmill test and am due to see a cardiologist later this month.

I received streptokinase on admission and am now on ramipril (5mg), simvastatin (20mg), atenolol (50mg) and aspirin (75mg). I have suffered no further pain since admission and am currently doing regular one-hour walks. On Saturday, I am meeting a hospital-trained fitness trainer to get a programme for further work.

I am hoping to travel to Hawaii by the end of next month and would like to do some diving. Is this sensible? I would not intend diving beyond 20m at this stage and am 61 years-old.

"I am hoping to travel to Hawaii by the end of next month and would like to do some diving. Is this sensible?"

Sorry to hear about your heart attack, but I guess the silver lining is that our medical advances mean that you can return to normal life a lot quicker than you could a few years ago.

As regards your return to the deep, there are a few criteria you have to satisfy first. There must be no remaining decreased blood supply to your cardiac muscle (this will come across as chest pain on exercise), but as your treadmill seemed to be alright then I assume that's OK. The reason for this is that we have to make sure you don't get another one underwater.

You are now not allowed to buddy with a novice diver either, but must team up with someone of DM standard at least. Before going back in you need to be passed fit by a diving doc who will probably impose a depth restriction on you, normally 20-25m. One of the reasons for this is that the deeper you go, the more resistance there is in your peripheral blood vessels due to the pressure, and the harder your heart has to work. You will need an annual medical, and you must never risk a dive where conditions could turn for the worse, resulting in an unexpected increased level of activity.

Sorry to lay it on like that, but that's the rules. You sound like you should be fine. See you on a one way drift in gentle tropical waters...

I wonder if you could give me some advice. I have a colleague wanting to take up Open Water, but he has angina. He is on beta blockers (Metoprolol) and carries a GTN spray. He also has a stent. Is he still able to dive?

Someone who has had angina, corrected with a stent (a small tube inserted into the coronary artery to keep it open) is often fine to dive. However your colleague's problem is that he has to have a GTN spray. This is an admission that he still gets the occasional attack of chest pain. He would then spray this under his tongue to help dilate the coronary arteries along with the other blood vessels. It would be hard to do this if he had an attack underwater. The other problem is the beta blockers. These are usually a bar to diving as they affect the heart's response to exercise and also can worsen breathing underwater. So, a double whammy there.

His only way out is if the GTN spray is cosmetic and he never needs it, or he does a full on exercise ECG to prove all is well. So, off to a cardiologist with diving experience.

A qualified SAA dive supervisor has just asked to dive with us. He's had a bypass, but says he never had a heart attack/ angina. His last medical is from January, 1999. The operation took place before that date. I know it's not much info, but in your opinion, is he fit to dive?

He probably will be if what he says is true. It's surprising that he had a bypass though having never had any cardiac symptoms. Something has to lead a man into the cardiologist to have either a coronary angiogram or a thallium scan that would show the necessary poor blood supply from the cardiac arteries to the heart muscles that then ends up as a bypass. So the fact he says he has never had any angina or even the teeniest heart attack makes we wonder.

However, if he is symptom free, and by that I mean he is not just sitting at home watching telly; beer in one hand, fag in the other saying, "there's no chest pain with me doc"; he has to prove that on exercise he gets no reduced blood supply to the heart, and this would need an exercise ECG or even better a thallium scan. He may well have had one of these after the operation and if fine, then let him dive with you as long as there hasn't been any symptom return.

Also note that some patients after this sort of op take beta blockers to decrease the workload on the heart, so if he is then he should not risk diving. It's also in his best interests that he gets certified as fit to dive with a proper diving doctor on a regular basis, in order to avoid any problems from insurance companies if anything were to happen.

I would like to do my Divemaster Course. I understand that I would need to have a HSE medical. Would my previous heart attack a few years ago prevent me from doing this? I have no chest pain and was taken off the cardiology consultant list after the first year following my heart attack. My BP is usually around 120/80 and resting pulse is 70. No oedema around my ankles or wet cough.

You are caught between a rock and a hard place here, so I hope the following makes sense:

A commercial diver, having had a heart attack, would normally be barred from diving. However, a non-commercial diver if they are controlled and fit, are fine to dive in your situation (as long as they pass the medical). So, is a DM a commercial diver? According to the HSE, they are as they all need to have the full HSE medical. But if you were getting the same level of qualification with BSAC you would not need a HSE and so would be OK. Confused? Yes, so am I.

For some reason BSAC divers, even the top instructors do not need to do a HSE but can self-cert themselves. Apparently it's because they are a club, and not a commercial organisation like PADI who do the DM course. I think your best bet is to contact the HSE and ask for an exemption and explain that you want to do the DM solely for yourself and would not be gainfully employed as a diver. If they get arsey about it, then try BSAC as it seems you would pass the basic medical for them.

I have high blood pressure for which I am prescribed Losartan Potassium 50mg daily, and which has been controlled for over

three years now because of my family history (my brother had a heart attack two months ago). My GP believes I may now have slight angina as I have been getting pains in my chest. He has arranged for an ECG and blood tests to be done, but suggests I have an exercise ECG done as well which I may have to wait months for at my NHS hospital.

In the meantime, he's prescribed a 400 microgram glyceryl trinitrate (GTN) spray to use if I get any pain and lipitor 10mg tablets (until the test results are known) as well as keeping on with the losartan. I also take a quarter of an aspirin a day.

I'm 56 and have never had any problems diving before. Can I keep it up?

"My GP believes I may now have slight angina as I have been getting pains in my chest… I'm 56 and have never had any problems diving before. Can I keep it up?"

Sorry mate, but the answer is no, you cannot dive at the moment. You need to have conclusive proof you have not got active angina. An exercise ECG, or even an angiogram is what you need to definitely rule out the problem. But with a relative who has had cardiac problems so recently, the pendulum swings against you.

So whilst this shadow of not knowing hangs over your head, you must not dive at all. If they give you the all clear though, then after a check for the high blood pressure, you may be fine. However if angina is diagnosed and all they say is keep up with the GTN spray when you need it, then you still can't dive. Here your only option is to get bypass surgery or angioplasty, which can effect a cure, and then after assessment you may be passed as fit to dive.

RHYTHM AND RATE

During the last two to three years, I have increasingly suffered with an irregular heartbeat. The frequency was such that I consulted my doctor soon after Christmas about the condition and was referred to a consultant who diagnosed atrial fibrillation after a 24 hour ECG. Initially, the irregular heartbeats occurred when I was at rest, but latterly came on during vigorous exercise as well. I do not experience any other symptoms like shortage of breath during an attack. I swim one kilometre in a local pool on most mornings without detrimental effect. A recent unmedicated ECG on a running machine conducted by the consultant did not bring on an attack even with my heart rate at 156.

In the middle of July, I am due to holiday in Cuba and plan to Scuba dive. My current medication is 25mg of metoprolol twice daily. With my current situation is it safe to dive or would I be a risk to myself and others?

This is an interesting question. Atrial fibrillation or AF is a condition where the heartbeat becomes irregular, but in an irregular sort of way. Unsurprisingly doctors describe the rhythm as 'irregularly irregular'. Diagnosing it is easy but what is harder is finding out why this has happened. It can be due to valve problems in the heart or even thyroid disorders, so it is important that your cardiologist has excluded the causes of the problem.

If no cause is found then it is known as 'lone atrial fibrillation' as it can occur with increasing age on its own. If it is this variety then you have to look at how often it occurs and what happens to your heart and lung function when it is happening. It seems that you are able to exercise well without it coming on but your consultant did not, it seems, check your lung function at the same time, as AF can (rarely) cause fluid build up in the lungs which would be catastrophic underwater.

The other thing that is a problem in your case, is that you are taking a medication known as a beta blocker. Metoprolol will slow your heart rate down, however it also affects your response to exercise (I see you were not on it during the ECG), again leading to a fluid build up in the lungs called pulmonary oedema. So, at this stage I would say that you are at risk and should not dive. There are other treatments for AF that are not beta blockers such as digoxin or disopyramide which it would be fine to dive on, but the medication switch is something you need to discuss with your consultant.

Also, to be able to dive you need to prove that the exercise test you do will never bring on a run of AF that would then bring on this pulmonary oedema. You also need an echocardiogram to exclude all other heart valve problems. So there's a bit of work to be done before you go, but with a non beta blocker, well controlled AF you should be fine in the end.

Lastly, it has been shown that AF can cause little clots to shoot off around the body called emboli. These are caused by the fact that the blood is not flowing normally around the heart chambers and can clot in the atria. Therefore is a good idea to take an aspirin daily to prevent these clots from forming.

I have recently been for a routine medical for my job. My doctor suspected that there may have been a problem so sent me for an ECG. The results for this came back and now he wants me to go for an 'echo' to see if I have an enlarged heart. Have you ever known anyone with an enlarged heart that would be safe to dive? I had a basic dive medical in April 2007 (ie blood pressure, ears, reflexes) and my blood pressure was 120/70 which I understand is OK for a 33 year-old male. My blood pressure was 136/80 on my last test three weeks ago.

Anyone remember Leonard Rossiter, the lecherous landlord in Rising Damp? Despite being exceedingly fit he died suddenly whilst waiting to go on stage. The cause – undiagnosed thickening of the heart muscle (or HOCM in medical speak). There are different forms of heart enlargement, but the principle can be explained by the old 'hot water heating' analogy. Imagine the water as blood, the pump as your heart, the pipes as your arteries and veins, and the water pressure as your blood pressure. If your pipes get furred up, then the pump has to work harder to keep up adequate water pressure, and to cope with this, your heart muscle enlarges. You might think this would make it a more effective pump, but in fact the reverse

"Have you ever known anyone with an enlarged heart that would be safe to dive?"

is true. The heart sits in a stiff sac, so any heart muscle growth occurs inwards, reducing the amount of space within it for blood and so less is pumped with each beat. Exercise capacity therefore drops, and any sudden strain on the heart can push it into failure. This sometimes explains those stories of young people suddenly dropping dead without warning: most recently one lad sprinting to try to set off a speed camera. Heart enlargement produces tell-tale signs on your ECG, which your doc is likely to have spotted, and hence you need a echo test to look closely at the chambers of the heart. It's this test that will determine your fitness to dive.

I had an ECG in December which indicated possible enlargement of the left ventricle. My GP has also detected a heart murmur. I am due to have an ultrasound of the heart in February which will give more info about what is wrong. If I do have an enlarged left ventricle in addition to the heart murmur, does this mean my diving career is over?

Left ventricular enlargement is not a bar to diving per se, but rather like the fading male porn star, it's all about the failure of the organ to pump properly. Bring out the fluffers I say.

A few things can cause the left ventricle to get bigger. High blood pressure and floppy or tight heart valves are but three of them. Now if the heart is compromised as it can't send the blood round the body properly, you can imagine the effects on the body demanding fuel as it dives. Likewise there can be effects on the ability to push out the blood returning from the venous side and the lungs. Pulmonary oedema or wet lungs that be, me hearties. So, it depends on how big the enlargement is, and how much it compromises the heart's function. As a ball park, 20% loss would be a problem and disqualify you. So get your cardiologist to check something called ejection fraction. A bit like our porn star on the wane. Well, just a misplaced consonant.

Three years ago, I was fitted with a cardiac pacemaker due to a slow heart rate causing dizzy spells and two blackouts. The pacemaker immediately stopped these symptoms. My cardiologist considered that I was safe to dive to 100ft, and gave me a copy of the manufacturer's test report detailing the results of hyperbaric tests on the device.

After a week of work as a diving instructor in the Middle East, I was sacked when I mentioned my pacemaker. The dive centre

"This sometimes explains those stories of young people suddenly dropping dead without warning: most recently one lad sprinting to try to set off a speed camera."

had consulted the naval hyperbaric specialist, who stated that I should not be diving at all, let alone instructing, despite any medical certification. I understand that the limitations are purely due to distortion of the titanium casing when subjected to pressure, but he suggested that temperature differences may also be a problem. The manufacturer has not replied to my emails on the subject, hence my career as an instructor is on hold. Can you help?

Yes, don't instruct, but you can dive. Sadly the rules are, in the UK at least, that an instructor can't teach if they have a pacemaker. If there was failure, which can happen but is very, very rare, your poor students would be left hovering around wondering why their man was floating off to the bottom of the ocean. Panic would set in, and as you have responsibility as an instructor, the lawyers would be after your estate.

As an individual diver, the rules are a bit more accommodating as the responsibility is on you. Since the problem that initially required the pacemaker has been cured by it, there's no worries there. The pacemaker maker(!) has OK-ed the pressure to 100ft, 30m, or four atmospheres. If that's what it will stand, then that's what it will stand, so you can dive to that depth. Temperature is not really an issue, as I assume you will suit up to keep reasonably warm, but for God's sake don't go naked ice-diving or boil yourself in a volcanic geyser as that would be into the realms of daft and the titanium might bend and affect the pacing.

On a tangent, I used to play cricket against a mate who had one. Fearing my extreme pace, he used to wear things to protect the machinery from the super-quickie. Ladies' sanitary towels were one of the oddest.

"If there was failure, which can happen but is very, very rare, your poor students would be left hovering around wondering why their man was floating off to the bottom of the ocean."

As well as diving, I also fly light aircraft (why do I choose expensive hobbies?) and my pilot's licence requires that I have an annual medical with an ECG. At the last medical it was discovered that I had Right Bundle Branch Block (RBBB). The Civil Aviation Authority then required me to be subjected to additional tests, namely, a stress ECG, an echocardiogram and a 24 hour monitor ECG. The results were deemed satisfactory and I get to keep my flying licence. It was my understanding from this, that the RBBB is of little consequence and shouldn't affect my health or life expectancy. I didn't think to ask the consultant if there is any problem diving with a RBBB.

The heart beats about 35 million times a year, so you'd expect it to have a fairly foolproof control system. In fact, the electrical wiring of the heart is quite simple. There are two 'nodes' and specialised bundles of conducting tissue (much like normal electrical cable) that pass 'current' through the heart muscle to make it contract. Electrical impulses begin at the sino-atrial (SA) node, which under normal conditions generates them roughly 60 to 100 times a minute. Each stimulus then passes to the atrioventricular (AV) node, and after a brief pause it splits and flows down the right and left 'bundles of His' (pronounced as in the snake noise). The end result is that the atria (top two chambers) of the heart contract first, emptying their blood into the ventricles (bottom two chambers), which squeeze the blood all around the body just afterwards. Clear as cocoa?

For a variety of reasons, the bundles of His can stop conducting impulses, which is unsurprisingly termed Bundle Branch Block (BBB). This can be left or right-sided, or rarely both (in which case all sorts of bad things happen and you end up with a pacemaker). In general, the left bundle does a lot more of the work than the right. Correspondingly, blockage of the left is far worse. Left BBB requires an evaluation of exercise tolerance, such as you've just had, so it's reassuring that the results were all OK. If the right bundle blocks then the left often takes over (with minimal fuss but regular demands for overtime pay). So in your case I have no qualms about your continuing to dive.

Recently, I experienced six days of ectopic heart beats. For the first few days they were extremely frequent, up to 10 a minute, gradually decreasing on the sixth day to an infrequent two or three an hour. I have never experienced anything like this before in my life. I have seen a cardiologist and all my blood tests have been normal. A 24 hour ECG monitor showed up a number of ectopics but at a rate low enough to be considered normal. An echocardiogram was also normal, and so no explanation could be given for the 'flare up'.

Do these ectopics have any impact on my ability to dive?

The 2.5 billion beats a heart generates in an average lifespan are by and large regular as clockwork, thanks to the sino-atrial node, a little clump of cells that act as a natural pacemaker. Occasionally though, another bit of the heart tries to muscle in and fire off its own contraction; an ectopic is the result. Basically they're extra beats out of sync with the regular heart rate. The vast majority are harmless and seen in many normal hearts, but if they occur too frequently or in long runs, they can indicate a diseased heart. Reassuringly in your case, the blood tests and echocardiogram were normal. Sometimes these ectopics can be due to excessive fatigue, caffeine, alcohol, nicotine or other drugs, so have a think if any of these factors are relevant. But if your cardiologist is happy that your heart is in good shape, then I think you'd be safe to dive again.

Earlier this year, I was admitted to hospital with a severe viral infection and kept in for four weeks. The virus was never identified but it caused me to become seriously ill and affected most of my organs. My blood potassium and sodium were extremely low and my kidneys started to fail, however with excellent nursing I have made a good recovery.

While I was in hospital, I developed atrial fibrillation with a pulse rate of 156. This has now been brought back to normal and I am taking amiodarone. I am told I have hypertrophic cardiomyopathy (HOCM) which must have been present all my life and only caused problems when the virus struck. I am still on warfarin but this will be stopped quite soon now. I have never had any previous illness and am a keen diver.

I am 70. Do you think I could dive again next year? I now have no atrial fibrillation and my pulse rate is 70.

You sound fit, fun and are obviously active. But sadly I have to be the bearer of sad news. I think diving is going to be beyond your medical capabilities.

Even if you are off the warfarin. Even though your pulse is a normal rate and not fibrillating (a kind of irregular irregularity in the pulse: imagine a monkey on a piano for the beat). The bottom line is that you have HOCM, and that can cause the heart to flip into an odd rhythm. This could cause a faint or collapse above the water. Imagine what would happen below.

I know you might think: "I've been diving all my life, never had a problem, until this darn virus did its worst". And I know you are also thinking: "the heart is fine without the virus, so why not just carry on, especially as the amiodarone has put me in the safe zone". And I know you are thinking: "if I went to some dive resort and just said I never had a problem, they would never know and let me dive anyway". But rules is rules.

"You sound fit, fun and are obviously active. But sadly I have to be the bearer of sad news. I think diving is going to be beyond your medical capabilities."

I am currently completing a UK Sport Diver Medical Form and have to ask you about two of the questions. For Question 1: I have a heart murmur that has been checked by an ECG and is normal. Will that be an issue?

Also, I had recurrent migraines at 14, they stopped after that and then three years ago I had recurrent migraines linked to the Pill I was taking: since changing my pill I have had no problems. Will this be a problem for Question 10?

You should be fine. Most murmurs are what they call a flow murmur. Just the sound of the blood rushing through the heart. An ECG won't necessarily show a murmur but it would show signs of heart changes if it were a pathological one.

Migraines are only a problem if you get one underwater. Searing headaches and visual distortion aren't a good combination with diving. But as you have resolved the problem by switching the Pill to another one, you will be fine as well.

"Searing headaches and visual distortion aren't good with diving."

STROKE

My father is an ex-military diver. He is now 68 years old, but has kept up recreational diving for many years since he left the Navy. He has always been pretty fit but six months ago he had a stroke. He suddenly lost the use of his leg and his speech went. The hospital have been putting him through rehab and he is doing really well; his speech is nearly back to normal and he can walk unaided now. I know how much he loves his diving and how good it would be for him to get back in the water, but is it safe?

I'm not usually partial to Americanisms but they have a vivid term for what we Limeys call a stroke – a 'brain attack'. It does evoke much more succinctly what is going on – a stroke is very similar to a 'heart attack' of the brain, where blockage or bleeding of a blood vessel in the brain causes damage and loss of function. It also emphasises the urgency of treatment: similarly to a heart attack again, clot busting drugs can be administered in certain strokes and can massively improve outcome. The precise symptoms of a stroke depend on the portion of the brain that is damaged, but like a phoenix from the ashes it has an amazing ability to recover and circumvent injured areas.

You don't mention whether your father's symptoms came on soon after diving, but a cerebral arterial gas embolism (CAGE) can look exactly like a stroke – in this case the cause is an escaped gas bubble blocking a blood vessel. Usually this is apparent during or immediately after surfacing and symptoms are sudden. Resuscitation and recompression are the important emergency treatments here.

It sounds as though your father's recovery is proceeding well. My concern though is whether he is at risk of a further stroke. Obviously the hospital will try to control his risk factors as much as possible (treating high blood pressure, diabetes, high cholesterol, stopping smoking – note again the parallels with heart attack), but the fact is that having had one stroke he is more likely to get another. Individual

> "...a stroke is very similar to a 'heart attack' of the brain, where blockage or bleeding of a blood vessel in the brain causes damage and loss of function."

assessment is important though: his general fitness and previous diving experience would count very much in his favour. If he regains full use of his leg and is able to hold a regulator comfortably in his mouth, then he might well be able to dive again. Is it safe? There is no 'yes' or 'no' answer to that, but if progress is good then the risks can be reduced to a potentially manageable level.

I would like advice on the resumption of diving following a subarachnoid haemorrhage (SAH). Four months ago I had an accident on my racing bike (bicycle) which was caused by the chain snapping. As a result, I went over the handle bars and struck the back of my head on the road (I was wearing a helmet at the time). I was unconscious for (I believe) a very short time. I was assisted on the road side by a passing doctor and rushed to A&E. Following a CT scan and assessment, it was considered that I had possibly suffered an SAH and was moved to the high dependency ward.

The following day I was given CT and formal angiography which showed a heavy bleed, although no aneurysm was detected. I did not undergo any surgery or clipping, nor did I require a coil to be inserted. I remained in hospital for 18 days before a final formal angiogram. This was negative and I was discharged the following day. I was prescribed Nimodipine for 21 days, together with pain relief as necessary.

My consultant advised rest for a few months but did not specify any restriction. I have returned to work and have resumed cycling and a normal life. I am an accountant.

Accountants do have the worst luck, don't they? This strikes a bit of a chord with me. Most days I bike into work along the canal and I've had several near misses. I memorably terrified a small child recently by rising from the swampy mire like some algae-draped lagoon dweller, having skidded in after a similar chain-snapping mishap.

A short anatomy lesson first: the brain is covered by three membranes, collectively called the meninges, the middle one being the arachnoid. So a subarachnoid haemorrhage means bleeding under this middle layer. Some bleeds are caused by head injury, others can be spontaneous (the so-called 'thunderclap' headache, a sudden 'most severe ever' pain developing over seconds to minutes). Most of these spontaneous occurrences are due to aneurysms (weak bulges) in the blood vessels of the brain, and if left they can rebleed at a later date. They are generally treated by clipping them off, or inserting little platinum coils which cause them to clot off and disappear.

But in your case the haemorrhage resulted from a bang on the head, and thorough investigations have not revealed any aneurysms which might potentially bleed again. So after this episode has fully settled (give it three months at least), and provided you have no complications, I would be happy for you to dive again.

I am 69 years old and have been diving for about 25 years. Two years ago I was discovered to have an aneurysm in my head. I was having very serious headaches. The investigations done by a neurosurgeon involved angiography to find the aneurysm and then it was treated with tiny metal coils (which form clots and block it off). The last of the coils let go of a clot which lodged itself up in my head, giving me a stroke. The net result was a total absence of short term memory. I had speech therapy for five weeks. I have slowly recovered my memory over the last 18 months. Apart from the memory I had no other symptoms.

The neurosurgeons are confident I can now dive without any problems. But my GP is not confident and suggests I get a diving doctor to decide. My wife however is still very concerned about 'diving pressure' on the site of the aneurysm.

Generally I do not go below about 25m and often much less. For the first time since the aneurysm we are going on holiday, somewhere sunny where I will find it hard to resist the urge to dive. What do you think?

I think you've been through a tough time over the last two years, particularly suffering a stroke after the coils, but it may be that the neurosurgeons are right. They are the doctors best placed to inform you of the potential risks. The main problems after surgery for cerebral aneurysms are bleeding, seizures and spasm of the blood vessels. As far as I'm aware, the risks of all three of these complications recede relatively quickly, and within six months are as low as they're going to be – which isn't necessarily zero, but is not appreciably high. There's no evidence that the water pressure experienced in diving has any direct effect on blood pressure in the brain, certainly no more than any other form of physical exertion. It's now two years on, and happily your recovery sounds full. If the neurosurgeons have excluded other aneurysms on your initial brain angiography and you are otherwise well then I think you should be allowed some sub-aqua shenanigans.

I am a diver who gave up smoking for three months, took to eating jelly beans instead and had to have a blood test which showed my blood sugars 'off the scale'. I stopped the sweets and went back to smoking (38 year habit) and a blood test a week later showed blood sugars as normal. I have not had a bad reading since then in four years, so consider myself a 'developing diabetic'.

Last Christmas I awoke to find myself blind in one eye, which lasted for approx 10 minutes. Doctors have diagnosed this as a mini stroke (TIA) and given me ECGs, carotid artery scans etc., all of which came out as 'normal' but a check on my eyes last week showed restricted blood vessels in the back of the eye due to 42 years of smoking. The mini stroke clinic consultant likened diving to flying as it involved a change of pressure and advised me not to dive for six weeks. However, I would like your opinion before the season starts. I have been diving in the pool all winter (down to 2m only) without any ill effects.

Well I think six weeks is about right after your TIA, provided you are fully back to normal, but from what you've said you are at quite high risk of a future problem. Smoking for that long (whether it's 38 or 42 years, it's still a very long time) will have furred up the pipes, caused significant lung damage and is likely to predispose you to high blood pressure. It's good to hear your carotids are hunky-dory but the other test you need is an echocardiogram. This looks at the four chambers and valves of the heart. Sometimes little bits of clot form on the valves or in the chambers, which can fly off and cause further TIA's or full-on strokes. While the pressure changes of diving don't cause strokes in themselves, vigorous exercise, tank lifting and forceful equalising manoeuvres can all raise arterial pressure in the head and increase the risk of a TIA or stroke. And of course, diabetes comes with its own set of dive-related issues. Basically I'd be pretty careful with the type of diving you do: try to keep depths and bottom times minimal and avoid situations where you are pushing your physical endurance. Pool diving is no substitute for the open water.

In February 1989 (I had not dived for about nine months prior to this) I had a sub-arachnoid haemorrhage due to a berry aneurysm which burst. Following a scan, I was found to have three such berry aneurysms. I had the one which burst clipped in March 1989, the next one clipped around August 1989, and the final one clipped around January 1992. After each craniotomy,

I was prescribed anti-epileptics as a precaution, but never had a fit. After the final op in 1992, I was given my driving license back after six months as I was symptom free.

I took up diving again when my children and partner were all keen to take the sport up, and obtained a medical from my GP. On the form, she ticked that she could find no medical conditions that she considered incompatible with diving, but next to this she wrote "but see below", and in the comments section she wrote "History of subarachnoid haemorrhage but no neurological sequelae. Aneurysms clipped so should not recur, but there must be some increased risk. Patient aware of this. Blood pressure normal – off treatment for six months". This was accepted by my local PADI club, and I have since completed over 30 dives with depths down to 36m.

I went to Malta over the Easter break, and they presented me with a medical form to fill in. I completed this truthfully, and made them aware of my past medical history, and they immediately called in a specialist hyperbaric doctor for his opinion. He was provided with the form from my GP, and he would not underwrite my fitness to dive. In his opinion, anyone who has had a craniotomy has an increased risk of having a fit, and is more susceptible to oxygen poisoning. He initially said he would advise me to limit my dives to 20m, but then said he could not take responsibility for saying I could dive at all.

I am now very confused and concerned as I was aiming to cross-qualify as a diving instructor for PADI in September. I was also hoping to dive with my family and help them to further train themselves. Please could you give me your opinion? I am not on any medication at all, and symptom free.

Ah poor you, not a lot to do in Malta if you don't dive. Unless you like falcons. I think you have been given the bum's rush here: to be passed as fit, then see an expert, who says yes to 20m, then changes his mind later.

"He initially said he would advise me to limit my dives to 20m, but then said he could not take responsibility for saying I could dive at all."

I think the deal with you, is that if all the berries have been clipped, you have not had a fit at all, and now it is 16 years later, then it is unlikely that you will have a fit this late. And as for previous craniotomy making you susceptible to an oxygen fit, well show me the evidence, I say. So in all I think you could have been passed as OK. These sort of haemorrhages are rare and are caused by a bleed into the brain from tiny defects in the inner brain circulation. The docs did the right thing, and found others, which they have now fixed, so it could be said you are safer to dive now then when you were merrily diving undiagnosed before the bleed.

I think for the future, it's best to see a dive doctor, proper and get the paperwork before you go to these sorts of destinations, or at least have a doc in the UK who can talk to the Malta doc, as you always have to be honest on the medical forms.

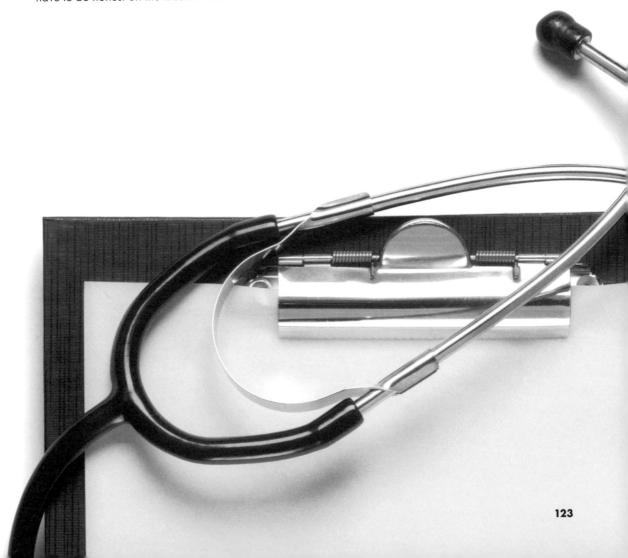

ARTICLE – DIVING AND HYPERTENSION

High blood pressure is one of the commonest conditions that affects divers throughout the world, but this is no great surprise really as it's one of the commoner conditions amongst the general population as well. As a diving doctor, I see the issues surrounding high blood pressure (hypertension) causing a lot of confusion amongst non-medically trained divers. Why can't I dive doc? How high can it be before I can't dive? Can I dive now I'm on tablets for it? Well, let's go for a stroll through the maze that is high blood pressure and diving.

Blood pressure is always quoted as two numbers and as a rough guide it is age +100 as the first number over anything from 60 to 100. An average BP for a 40 year-old would be 140/80.

The first number is called the systolic figure and represents how much work the heart has to do to push the blood around the body. The harder it has to work the higher the figure. What makes it have to work harder is often the state of the arteries through which the blood is flowing. If they are thickened and inelastic due to age or fatty deposits the heart has to push harder and the systolic figure rises.

The second figure is the diastolic blood pressure. This is the blood pressure between beats and seen as a more accurate resting blood pressure. Again a high number here indicates poor health and a bad arterial and venous system. The current guidelines say that any new diver with a BP above 150/90 shouldn't be allowed to dive, and any existing diver with a BP over 160/100 should quit diving until it's sorted out. Why? Well, it's not because of the BP itself as it's simply a number, but what the consequences of a high BP are.

In the short term, uncontrolled hypertension can increase your chances of having a stroke as the raised systolic pressure means the poor old heart is really pushing hard and so the fragile arteries

"The current guidelines say that any new diver with a BP above 150/90 shouldn't be allowed to dive, and any existing diver with a BP over 160/100 should quit diving until it's sorted out."

in the brain are at risk of bursting. This, if it were to happen underwater, would not only lead to a quick demise for the diver but also endanger their buddy. The long term dangers are more related to a persistently raised diastolic pressure. Disease of the kidneys and the blood vessels that supply the heart are a factor here, and this would cause problems to a diver as the risk of heart attack and heart failure are very much increased; once again leading to potentially fatal consequences underwater.

So you can see why the two don't really mix well. But one of the issues here is how can you tell who really has high blood pressure? Blood pressure varies throughout the day increasing when you are active and lowering gently at night time when you sleep. So, if you are 30 minutes late to see the doc, rush up three flights of stairs, straight onto the couch and have the cuff put on your arm. "Mmmm" he will say, "180/120, sorry you can't dive!" Would this be fair? Of course not. Blood pressure should never be assumed after one solitary reading if it is high. A lifetime's medication and being told never to dive should be a consequence of a whole series of readings and that is why I always insist on a test called '24 hour BP monitoring'. This is a small cuff attached to your upper arm at one end and a computer gizmo at the other. It gives a BP reading every 5 to 10 minutes. At the end of the 24 hour period, an average is worked out and a far better picture of whether you are truly hypertensive or not can be obtained. Quite often a person with an isolated high reading at their doctor's is found to be normal by this method, so avoiding all those tablets and allowing you to dive straight away. If you have only a slightly raised BP ie anything below 190/110, then always insist on a 24 hour monitor. But what if the reading is still too high? Well then, it's medication time for you and this is where it gets very interesting with diving.

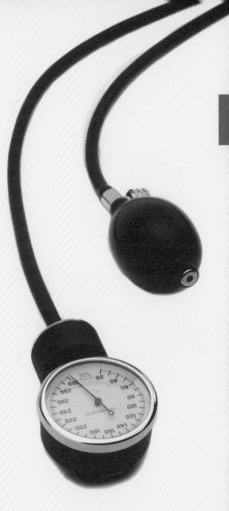

There are about six groups of different compounds that can be used to treat hypertension. Some are fine to dive on, but others aren't. Beta blockers, such as atenolol or propranolol, work well in reducing blood pressure, but the problem with diving is that they can cause constriction of the airways and also reduce the response of the heart to exercise. This can cause a back log of blood to the heart which collects in the lungs. Bad news if you are swimming against a really hard current towing a sick buddy, so stay off these if you want to dive safely.

Another commonly used medication is called a diuretic and basically makes you pee more often. This reduces your circulating blood volume, making it easier for your heart to function. Above water a few extra trips to the toilet may be OK but underwater it can reduce your ability to off gas your nitrogen. End result: a bend.

Instead, tablets I probably would recommend to divers are the ACE inhibitors. They've been around for a long time now, and are derived from a protein found in snake venom. They have few side effects relevant to diving except a dry cough. If this happens there is a theoretical risk of coughing out your regulator, so the next step is to try the ACE inhibitors brand new cousin, the A2RA.

Better known as Angiotensin 2 Receptor Antagonists, A2RA's are the perfect blood pressure tablet for a diver with hypertension, but like all good things in life there is a catch. It's one of the most expensive of them all, but for divers happy to spend their hard earned dollar on dive gear, it won't break the bank.

It is a well known fact that people will only remember six things from a lecture, a TV programme or a written article, but I'll make it easy with three this time: don't dive with untreated hypertension, the deep is the last place you want a stroke or heart attack; make sure the doc is right with the diagnosis; and take only ACE inhibitors or A2RIs for it. Oh, and there is a fourth: try losing some weight as this means you won't need the tablets at all. Simple really.

RESPIRATORY PROBLEMS

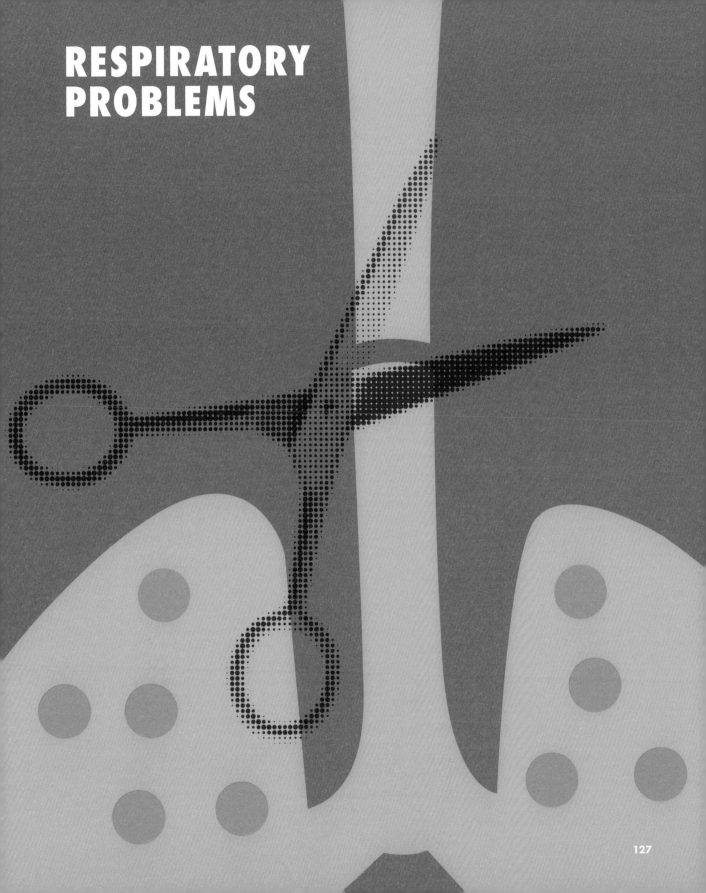

INTRO

I was on a boat with an American recently, who repeatedly told me that smoking was bad for your health. This is a bit like telling someone over and over again that three plus four equals seven and I'm not sure why he thought I might have missed the medical consensus on the subject. Perhaps it was because I was actually smoking at the time, but even if I hadn't been a smoker I would've lit one up just to annoy him. Several other people did.

I tried to out-bore him by telling him my granddad smoked 80 cigarettes a day and lived until he was 97. It's not true, obviously, but it is a very boring thing to say and demonstrates a suitable lack of understanding of statistics. And what time do you have to get up to be able to smoke 80 cigarettes in one day, anyway? Well, it quickly transpired that the American's dad had been an avid smoker until some sort of incident to do with throat cancer.

So, yes, smoking is bad. So is tuberculosis. And pneumonia. So are exploding lungs, collapsing lungs and anything in your lungs that isn't a gas. Quite a few gases are bad as well, so don't go around inhaling stuff just for the fun of it. Flowers are fine, though. Except for triffids, but they don't exist, so I wouldn't worry about that too much (just a bit).

One of the most popular parts of this section will be the lowdown on asthma. Statistics I've just made up show that 64% of would-be divers can't decide whether to tick 'yes' to asthma on their medical declaration or not, since most people have had a GP accuse them of having it at one time or another. I tried to contract it as a teenager in order to get out of PE so I could smoke instead, but it transpires you can't catch it from kissing. By kissing, I mean, looking at attractive girls out of the corner of my eye from the other side of the classroom.

Anyway, the medical consensus is that breathing is good. Keep it up.

Tip: Breathing is one of medical science's greatest accomplishments and is still recommended by over 78% of doctors as the best way to oxygenate haemoglobin. If you're having trouble getting the knack of it, it's probably best to give the emergency services a quick call rather than donning Scuba gear.

ASTHMA

I have mild asthma, mostly brought on by allergies to smoke and artificial fog. However, several years ago I did have an attack, which my school nurse put down to over exertion during a football training session. I also have problems equalising on aircraft, possibly due to sinus problems. I'm not sure I am the ideal contender for Scuba diving, but I am hoping you could give your opinion to settle the matter.

There is hope for you.

The bottom line is we doctors need to be able to guarantee that you have a zero percent chance of having an attack or onset of wheeziness underwater. The asthmatics who generally fail are those who get it easily on exercise or those in whom control is very poor. The reason the former flunk the test is that any dive can turn from a gentle fin around to heavy work if a strong counter current comes along. Likewise if you have to tow your ailing buddy 300m to the boat and you then get wheezy, it'll be curtains for you both.

So if there is any chance of exercise inducement then the doc will exercise test you and check on your lung function at timed intervals after the test. Pass this and you will be fit to dive. However I have a hunch that you will pass as I reckon you must have done a bit more exercise than the school nurse saw all those years ago.

The main danger with asthma is that if a diver suffers broncho-constriction whilst underwater, the expanding gas cannot be exhaled fully as the air passages are inflamed and so are blocked. This means that the tiny alveoli at the end of the lung tubes are ruptured by the expanded air, and so air bubbles pass into the arterial circulation causing the dreaded CAGE, or cerebral artery gas embolus. This can easily cause death.

This used to mean asthma was an automatic bar to diving, but as things have moved on, the evidence now is that a well controlled

"This means that the tiny alveoli at the end of the lung tubes are ruptured by the expanded air."

asthmatic has an equal chance of this as a smoker, and we let them dive. So in the UK at least we have relaxed our opinion.

Don't worry about the smoke and weird fog as a trigger as these should be rarely encountered underwater, but bear in mind that diesel fumes can swirl around from a boat engine. So if your diving doctor does pass you as fit then be sensible on the RIB.

The other issue of the equalisation is interesting. It doesn't bode well for you if you can't even do this on a plane, so your dive doc should check this as well by looking at your ear drums when you swallow and blow. But from what limited info you have given me I bet you have one of those allergic conditions where you bung up easily which makes your sinuses stuffed and the asthma-like condition too.

If you spent a bit of time with an allergist I bet they could sort you out. Good luck, but your first stop should be the diving doctor.

I was recently examined by a diving physician in Australia. When I mentioned that I had a mild asthmatic allergic reaction to cat's saliva and dust mite faeces, he signed me off as being permanently unfit to dive, especially as two of my grandparents developed asthma later in life. He also said that I should never have dived in the first place and that I was lucky to be alive due to the high risk of developing a reverse air embolism.

I have been in the tropics since October and have stopped using my inhalers due to there not being any of my particular allergens in the environment, and have not experienced any tightness in my chest since leaving the UK.

When I came to you in April last year, my peak flow was better than average and you gave me a clean bill of health for diving, using the same form that the Australian doctor used. I have since stopped diving until I can find out more about my condition and the risks that are involved.

I wonder if you could give me your opinion on this and the different views held by European and Australian doctors.

I am surprised that the doctor failed you, so here is some good news. Yes there is a difference of opinion between UK and Australian doctors as regards a blanket ban on anyone with any sort of asthma diving. Over here we realise that some forms of

"A mild asthmatic allergic reaction to cat's saliva and dust mite faeces, he signed me off as being permanently unfit to dive."

asthma contraindicate diving but others do not.

You have what is called allergic asthma; cats and mites being your triggers to wheezing. It would be a pretty weird dive if you came across either of these underwater, so modern medical thinking is that you are at a low risk of getting an asthma attack whilst diving and you should be fine. The sorts of asthma that stop you from diving are where the triggers are exercise, cold or emotion. You still need to go through a full medical with a doctor who will check your lung function before passing you as fit.

Now, in Australia it seems that this is not accepted, and anyone who has the asthma label cannot ever dive. This is probably because it has become one of those group opinions that just become entrenched into the psyches of a body of doctors, and they have never been lobbied by a large group of asthmatics to review their rules.

I suggest that anyone who is going to learn to dive and has asthma gets checked over in the UK first of all because you don't want to take the risk of being disqualified nonsensically out there and the Barrier Reef is pretty boring if stared at through a glass bottom boat.

I am a very fit 30 year-old man (I cycle 12 miles a day) and have been diving exclusively in the UK since last August. I am also a worrier and recently managed to get myself in a stew about my blood pressure for no good reason, so I went to my GP to get it checked. Of course it was fine but when I mentioned that I was going to go for a diving medical he did a spirometry test on me just out of interest, using a simple spirometer with a sliding scale. You can imagine my surprise when I couldn't manage more than 575 litres/min peak expiratory flow rate. My GP said it should be 640 litres/min for a man of my age but did not seem greatly concerned and asked if the results of the medical could be copied to him for my notes.

The thing is I am now worrying if I am asthmatic. I have never had any problems with breathing and can still breathe well on strenuous exercise. I have had a slight wheeze on strenuous exercise in cold air but I certainly wasn't gasping for breath.

Another worry is that if I'd not panicked about my blood pressure I would never have known anything about my breathing and would have carried on diving on self-certification indefinitely. Am I just being a bit of an old woman?

Yes you are. So put away your knitting, get that hanky out of your sleeve and calm down. From the top, with the blood pressure then, as that was your first worry. Basically there is no problem with BP: If it's normal then you dive, if it's abnormal we treat with diver friendly anti-hypertensives such as losartan and… you dive.

You didn't have spirometry from your doctor; you had a peak flow. Two very different things. Spirometry measures lung volume and how much you can exhale as a percentage of that volume in a certain time. Peak flow (PF) measures the fastest you can exhale. Your score may have been a bit low for age and height; however the problem with PF is that it is very technique dependent. If you can cycle 12 miles a day, then the chances are that you do not have asthma that's exercise triggered. So, get proper spirometry to set your mind at ease and take a big deep breath and relaaaaax.

"…put away your knitting, get that hanky out of your sleeve and calm down."

BAROTRAUMA

What is a pulmonary barotrauma? Is it life threatening? Does it mean you can have a heart attack under the water?

Burst lung. Yes. No.

Pulmonary barotrauma happens when the air in the lungs expands on ascent faster than a diver can exhale it. This is why we are all taught to exhale on an emergency ascent on our PADI Open Water Course. It's not difficult to imagine what can happen to the lungs if the air inside them expands at a rapid pace. The very tissue and structure will be torn apart. Air bubbles will get into your arterial circulation, go through your heart and off to raise hell in all other parts of your body. Without normal functioning lungs there's no oxygen supply to the rest of the body, and this is what can kill you.

How you tell a diver has this problem when they are back on the boat depends on the extent of the lung burst. A very mild case may not be noticed at all, but as it gets more severe, problems associated with the actual lung damage will become apparent, such as shortness of breath, blue lips and a cough, all the way through to a case where the diver is coughing up blood-stained frothy sputum and rapidly becoming shocked.

It's not just a panicked diver on a rapid ascent that can get this problem though. It's one of the reasons that asthmatics are so strictly controlled as divers. If someone were to get a constriction in the bronchi or lung tubes through which the inhaled and exhaled air flows, then all that air inhaled under pressure at depth can't get out properly on ascent. The resulting problem is pulmonary barotrauma.

Dealing with it is very simple for the dive crew onshore or the boat: quickly put the diver on their back, give 100% oxygen and call a chopper in ASAP. We doctors will do the rest but the key is recognising the problem quickly and not being afraid of calling the Emergency Services as fast as possible.

> "Without normal functioning lungs there's no oxygen supply to the rest of the body, and this is what can kill you."

As for a heart attack underwater, it won't cause this but an indirect effect may be to decrease the amount of oxygenated blood getting to the cardiac muscle so it dies, which is, by definition, a 'heart attack'. By this time, however, the diver is so well and truly screwed that it's only of interest to the poor old doc doing the autopsy.

So all you asthmatics: get passed as fit by a diving doc, and for the rest of us, remember the words of the Prodigy: exhale.

I sometimes have trouble clearing my ears when I start to descend in the water, but I get a clear warning in the form of pain when this happens. Would I get a similar pain signal in my chest if I were to ascend and not breathe out?

I must say I've never been asked that before. I assume you want to know what it would feel like if you weren't exhaling quick enough in relation to your speed of ascent.

Well, my first thoughts are that you must always exhale and never breath-hold whilst ascending. Pulmonary barotrauma, or lung damage, is always the result. So long as your throat is open and epiglottis in the right position, the expanding air will always come out and you needn't worry.

As for how it would feel, well, it would be like when you sneeze but stop it just before or similarly letting a full party balloon deflate through your lips when you have just taken a full breath. I don't suggest you try this though, Nugget, just exhale normally.

I have been diving for a couple of years now and I am qualified to Rescue Diver level. I have asthma, but this is mild, well controlled, and only ever presents a problem if I suffer a chest infection. I had one recently which has lingered a bit and did end up upsetting my asthma so that I had to use prednisolone tablets.

I was feeling a lot better and virtually back to normal and decided to dive this weekend. I did a wreck dive at an inland quarry to a depth of 18m. The descent was fine and conducted slowly. On reaching the max depth and beginning to circle the wreck I began to feel that my breathing was a little laboured and uncomfortable. This did not feel like an asthma attack as my breathing wasn't fast or panicked, just heavy and uncomfortable. I immediately signalled the problem to

"I must say I've never been asked that before. I assume you want to know what it would feel like if you weren't exhaling quick enough in relation to your speed of ascent."

my buddy and we ascended slowly to 5m, completed a three minute safety stop, and then went to the surface. The total dive time was 18 minutes.

Since then I have felt an uncomfortable heaviness in my chest and have been quite weak and tired all the time. I have used my reliever inhaler which helps the breathing but does not remove the heaviness. It doesn't feel like regular asthma. It seems to be getting better with rest but I want to be sure I haven't done any lasting damage.

Yup, you need to see a diving doc ASAP. And one that works near a dive chamber too. There is a theoretical risk that you could have DCI. Let's say the infection had not cleared fully, or there was some sort of gunk plugging your bronchioles, then expanding air could pop an alveoli and release bubbles into the system. This could give you the funny chest feeling, and other symptoms to boot.

So you need lung assessment, and you need it fast.

PNEUMOTHORAX

Many years ago, I had on two separate occasions a spontaneous pneumothorax. If memory serves correctly it was on the same side. The doctors told me that this is a common occurrence amongst young, tall and thin men. I am now older and heavier (and still only 5'10"). As it has been seven years since I was last affected by this, can I assume that it is safe to start Scuba diving?

A pneumothorax is when you burst the outer lining of your lung. What then happens is that the air you breathe in, instead of being exhaled normally, can escape out of the newly blown hole into the chest cavity. Your chest cavity is all enclosed, so the more air that escapes, the more this air can then crush down on the lung, eventually collapsing it. So, imagine a situation where air under pressure is inhaled when you dive, a pneumothorax occurs, and then as you ascend this air expands. You would be breathless in seconds and in some cases the venous blood flow back to your heart can be cut off too. Nothing in to the heart, nothing out and then death.

The stats on pneumothorax are that it can occur, often during exercise, for seemingly no reason (the actual causes are little blebs or bullae: weak pouches on the lung surface that are more likely to rupture) in young tall fit people (usually men) and can reoccur soon after the first event. If it happens, the victim usually feels a sudden shortness of breath and chest pain on the side of the problem. Fortunately, if a period of four to five years goes by without a recurrence then it is unlikely to come again. Smokers have a dramatically increased chance of recurrence.

The key factors as a diving doctor are: what are the risks of a repeat episode, and will that happen when you are diving? We assess this by both waiting a number of years after the first event and also having a special scan of the lungs to see whether there are any abnormalities (blebs) that will cause another pneumothorax. This is called a CT scan. If it is at least five years post initial pneumothorax and your CT is normal as well as lung function studies then you should be fine to dive. You can have an operation to stick the lining of the lungs to the chest wall, thereby eliminating the blebs, but usually they will disappear on their own over time, hence the CT scan.

This throws up an interesting issue though, that I have come across many times with divers in your situation. Because diving is a recreational activity, the good old NHS will not do your CT for free as it is deemed non-essential to your continued wellbeing. This means that you have to fork up for a private CT which comes in at about £300 to £400 before you can dive. I personally think that this is a mad situation as you have been honest about your problem and you now have to foot the bill through no fault of your own. If you had been a smoker and suffered lung problems then all CT scans would be free. Write to your MP on that one.

My lungs collapsed in a car crash 16 years ago and I was on a life support machine for 10 days. Unfortunately the crash happened out in Saudi and so I was not allowed to take any of the medical records out of the country. I'm now 30 and fighting fit. Can I learn to dive?

The chances are good for you. The reason for this is because although you had bilateral pneumothoraces (punctured lungs in effect), it is more allowable to have had these if they were caused by a traumatic event, than if they were spontaneous and occurred as you were ambling down the street. In such a serious accident as this, often the ribs will break, puncture the lining of the lungs (the pleura), and cause air to enter around the lung on each breath, which then crushes the lungs slowly. Life threatening stuff, and in need of a great big tube in through the chest to decompress the lungs, but once resolved, as your lungs were in good nick before, they should be fine after. You will need this checked with a test called spirometry as well as a CT scan to assess resolution of lung pathology. Contact your local dive doctor for this.

Bit odd, though, them not letting you take your medical records with you. They would be useful, so call the British Embassy out there, drag the ambassador away from his Ferrero Rocher and tell him to go get 'em.

"...you now have to foot the bill through no fault of your own. If you had been a smoker and suffered lung problems then all CT scans would be free. Write to your MP on that one."

As part of an investigation into abnormal levels of iron in my liver, my consultant wishes to perform a liver biopsy. This involves a 1 in 1,000 risk of a punctured lung. I am a very active diver and would therefore not like to risk this. Would an 'accidentally' punctured lung heal?

Medical risk is an interesting concept. What does "1 in 1,000" mean to you? If I told you that the chance of needing emergency treatment in the next year after being injured by a bed mattress or pillow is 1 in 2,000, would that make you more or less likely to take this 1 in 1,000 risk?

Oodles of stuff has been written about 'risk perception' – how an individual understands and judges risk (and how that influences behaviour). People are much more willing to accept voluntary risks (such as driving a car, where the lifetime risk of dying in a crash is 1 in 100) than risks where they have no control. The risk of lung cancer from a pack a day habit is about 1 in 125 over a lifetime; for skin cancer from sun exposure it's a staggering 1 in 3 (although most are non-fatal). 1 in 1,000 is about the same probability as a 4-4 draw in a football match. A 5-5 score would be 1 in 10,000 and winning the Lottery about 1 in 3,000,000 so get down to William Hill rather than buying scratchcards. According to the HSE, the average annual risk of death from Scuba diving is 1 in 200,000 dives. Pretty safe, really.

Ultimately then, each individual has their own perception of risk, which is shaped by their personality, previous experiences and probably hundreds of other factors yet to be determined. On this aspect, it's therefore difficult to give black and white answers.

The bottom line with punctured lungs is that we are talking here about a so-called 'traumatic' pneumothorax, where the cause of the lung injury is known (in this case an errant biopsy needle). So there is no reason to suspect that the underlying lung tissue is more susceptible to barotrauma or another puncture. Most of these types of injuries heal up and all that is required is some confirmation that the repair is complete, usually a CT scan and some lung function tests.

Word of advice for now: take care in the bath. There's a 1 in 685,000 chance you'll drown in it within the next few years.

> "According to the HSE, the average annual risk of death from Scuba diving is 1 in 200,000 dives. Pretty safe, really."

SMOKING

I've been diving for 30-odd years and was a smoker until five years ago (I'm now 48). Unfortunately I think I left giving up a bit too late: I was diagnosed with chronic obstructive pulmonary disease (COPD) six months ago. The docs say it's mild but because I smoked for 20 years (an average of 40 a day) it's likely to get worse. I do wake up coughing and have to clear some fairly putrid-looking oysters (sorry) in the morning, but otherwise I'm pretty fit (still run and cycle to work). Can I still dive?

Your typical COPD case is picked up in those aged 45 or older, with a smoking history of at least 20 pack-years. (Pack-years is a quick way of estimating long term smoking exposure; one pack year is equivalent to smoking 20 cigarettes a day for one year, so in your case you have a 40 pack-year history.) Early symptoms such as frequent throat clearing, breathlessness on mild exertion and an irritating cough are often blamed on aging or lack of fitness. Progression to chest tightness and wheezing may take years, but other behavioural signs may appear first; avoiding the stairs in favour of the lift, taking longer to mow the lawn etc.

Lung infections become more common and severe as time wears on. Your major achievement has been to stop smoking, which is the most important treatment. There's nothing you can to do to reverse the damage, but at least it won't accelerate now. Medications can help widen the airways and treat infection, and no doubt these have been discussed with you. I'm afraid your diving days are numbered though; poor lung function will reduce exercise tolerance and put you at risk of barotrauma. Borderline cases with very mild symptoms and satisfactory lung function tests might get away with it, but it's difficult to be certain of safety and personally I wouldn't risk it. Time to hang up those fins.

Like many divers who enjoy a holiday in the Red Sea, I have partaken in the local custom of smoking on the hubbly bubbly

pipe otherwise known as shisha, or hookah. Can you clarify whether or not smoking these things can or will damage a person's health?

There can't be many visitors to Egyptian shores (or the Edgware Road) that haven't been tempted by, or at least curious about, these splendidly ornate-stemmed water pipes. They do elevate smoking from a squalid habit to what some deem a fine art. The expatriate British lawyer William Hickey, renowned for his thoroughly debauched existence, wrote this about hookahs in 1775, after arriving in India: "The most highly-dressed and splendid hookah was prepared for me. I tried it, but did not like it. As after several trials I still found it disagreeable, I with much gravity requested to know whether it was indispensably necessary that I should become a smoker, which was answered with equal gravity, 'Undoubtedly it is, for you might as well be out of the world as out of the fashion. Here everybody uses a hookah, and it is impossible to get on without' [... I] have frequently heard men declare they would much rather be deprived of their nightly sex than their hookah."

As to the wisdom of a pipe after a day's diving, the crux of the matter is whether they use tobacco or not. Shisha comes in various lurid and herbaceous guises, but unfortunately most of them are around a third tobacco, with the rest made up of spices and fruit pulps. Thus you are effectively smoking flavoured cigarettes. Many studies have shown that the health risks are similar to cigarette smoking, indeed potentially worse: the average shisha session (try saying that quickly) of 40 or more minutes can deliver considerably more smoke than a pack of cigarettes, and the cooling effect of the water combined with the intoxicating fruity aromas may lull those who indulge into a false sense of security. The water filter does not rid the smoke of any impurities or nicotine (most of the toxic chemicals and nicotine are not water soluble). The pipe sharing aspect does also expose the smoker to gum infections or cancers.

For the hardened hookah hedonist there is hope, however; tobacco-free flavoured herbal blends are available, which are theoretically less harmful, and various attachments can be added to the basic device to filter out the nasties. A number of Smoking Research Institutes (which I envisage are rooms full of white-coated scientists furiously dragging on nefarious nicotine delivery devices) are looking at the long term effects of hookah smoking, but at present the jury is out.

> "There can't be many visitors to Egyptian shores that haven't been tempted by, or at least curious about, these splendidly ornate-stemmed water pipes."

I regularly dive to about 40m and would like to learn technical diving that will include depths of 40m+, Nitrox and Trimix, and wreck and cave diving. I take bupropion and read it can increase seizure risk. Will the Lamictal I take for mood-cycling counteract this?

I'm a bit concerned about this. Bupropion is a drug that was originally developed in the States as an anti-depressant, but is often used in Europe as an aid to giving up the fags (the name Zyban may be more familiar to some readers). When it was first introduced in 1985, there was a high incidence of people fitting on the maximum standard dose of 600mg. It was withdrawn a year later, and remarketed in 1989 at a lower dose. Anything to claw back all that R&D money. Anyway, to my mind this is still a problem, as we all know a seizure underwater is likely to be fatal. Bupropion commonly also causes dry mouth, nausea, tremor and tinnitus: not great for the aspiring technical diver.

The other drug you are taking, Lamictal (or lamotrigine), unfortunately has similarly problematic side effects, with the added bonuses of dizziness, blurred vision and headache. It's an anti-convulsant with particularly good mood stabilising properties, smoothing out the manic peaks and depressive troughs of bipolar disorder sufferers. Authoritative data on the interactions of these two drugs and diving is not available (which is not unusual), but several animal studies have shown that the blood brain barrier becomes more permeable with pressure changes, effectively increasing the dose of drugs that act on the brain. My worry, therefore, is that you have here a potent cocktail of nitrogen, significant depth, and two drugs being delivered to your brain in unpredictable doses. If I were you I'd steer clear of all things technical until you come off these medicines.

> "My worry, therefore, is that you have here a potent cocktail of nitrogen, significant depth, and two drugs being delivered to your brain in unpredictable doses."

As part of a health drive this year I've decided to quit my 20-a-day habit. Having been a smoker for 30 years I didn't think I'd make it by going cold turkey so I've been using nicotine patches for the last 12 weeks, and (bar one relapse on my birthday) I've not had a cigarette since starting. I'm going on a liveaboard in a couple of weeks and wondered if it's safe to dive with nicotine patches.

I think you can be safely reassured. The nicotine in a patch is not in gaseous form, so pressure won't have any effect on it. Soaking the patch in saltwater could conceivably modify the rate at which the drug is released or absorbed by the skin, but I doubt whether this effect would be significant, and after 12 weeks you're probably nearing the lower dose ranges as well. So congratulations on quitting, the money you've saved has probably already covered half the cost of your holiday.

Being honest, I'm one of those annoying on-off social smokers who's always scabbing cigarettes off people at parties and never buys their own. Normally I go out on Thursdays and don't smoke Friday so it clears my system before I dive on the weekend. This year though, I've been getting bunged up on Saturdays and Sundays and had loads of equalising problems and sinus squeeze. But last week we went out Friday, I smoked a pack and was fine diving: it's almost like it cleared everything out. What's all that about?

Being honest myself, it's always difficult to give concrete explanations for quirky individual symptoms like this. I suspect though that after a day of withdrawal (your usual Friday off the fags), your lungs are beginning their recovery and consequently your respiratory tract produces more mucus, causing congestion in your ears, nose and sinuses. By smoking that pack last Friday you beat your poor cilia back down into submission, so rendering the system 'clear'. Sadly this delaying tactic will only postpone inevitable (and bigger) problems. Social smokers run pretty much the same risks as full timers: they tend to take more drags, and inhale deeper and for longer, so their overall exposure is similar. The same goes for smokers of 'light' cigarettes: research suggests they still get as much heart disease and lung cancer. Giving up totally is really the best option.

OTHER

A few weeks ago I had an unsuccessful op to repair a **Patent Foramen Ovale (PFO)** following 'undeserved' decompression sickness. I had a further bubble study done, and while they are confident I don't have a PFO, there was still bubble migration between the right and left chambers, at an interval of seven to nine cardiac cycles. The doctor suggested it might be pulmonary, and said I should have an angiogram and/or a **CAT scan**, but I am no closer to knowing what the solution is than before.

What does "it could be pulmonary" actually mean? Can I dive?

"I am no closer to knowing what the solution is than before. What does 'it could be pulmonary' actually mean? Can I dive?"

What your doctor is referring to here is a pulmonary arteriovenous malformation (AVM) as it is most likely, in the absence of an obvious PFO, to result in bubbles showing up on an echo test after more than five cardiac cycles. A pulmonary AVM is basically an abnormal communication between the pulmonary artery and pulmonary vein, which allows blood (and bubbles) to bypass exhalation by the lungs and re-enter the blood stream on the arterial side. They can be diagnosed by CT scan or pulmonary angiography. Most are congenital (ie present since birth). They can be treated, either surgically or with embolisation, but this depends very much on the exact type and individual circumstances of each case. Whether diving is possible afterwards again is difficult to say – the cardiologist would have to be sure that there is no residual right to left shunting. So, there's no definite answer here until you've been fully investigated I'm afraid.

Can you confirm what range or percentages a normal result from a lung function test falls into. I've started doing a lot of yoga including breathing exercises and my most recent medical showed I was exhaling 115% of my predicted capacity. My yoga instructor has just done her open water training and her result read 170%. Does a higher than average lung function have any advantages or disadvantages when diving?

Big lungs are generally better for diving (less gas consumption, in theory) and you tend to find that people who dive regularly (such as commercial divers) get progressive increases in their FVC (forced vital capacity, which approximates to your total lung capacity). Most divers tend towards an increase in FVC with age but the general conclusion that divers tend to have larger vital capacities than non-divers was not confirmed by a study of 126 saturation divers by Thorsem et al (1989). They suggest that the increase is transient and that later there is a greater decline. Any change of vital capacity probably has little effect upon the diver's general health.

There have been some studies that suggest divers develop a degree of air flow obstruction due to airway narrowing over the long term, however more recent studies have not confirmed this, and actually in a group of military divers there was no evidence of obstruction compared to non-divers. In divers who smoke however, there was a much more marked decline in lung function so there's an obvious message there.

Some swimmers and divers I know use resistive training devices such as the PowerBreathe to improve their lung function and there is good evidence that this helps asthmatics: it can strengthen the inspiratory muscles and produces similar changes to yoga breathing exercises. So adopt that wind relieving pose, stop smoking and watch your lung capacity and bottom times soar.

"So adopt that wind relieving pose, stop smoking and watch your lung capacity and bottom times soar."

I am a fit and healthy 25 year-old who plays a lot of sport. I developed what I believe now to be coldwater induced pulmonary oedema at the end of my 50th dive in the UK. I had a chest injury at the time and felt that that it was due to this.

After a year's break and consulting a cardiologist, I returned to diving. I had all manner of medical tests: ECG, PFO, exercise test, CT scan and all showed that I was in good condition.

I kept on diving in my wetsuit. I am cold on my dives but I tend to grin and bear it. Recently I was doing some deeper and longer dives and on my 70th dive, it happened again, at above 3m. I recognised it immediately, dekitted, got in the boat and put myself on oxygen. Like last time, it cleared in 15 minutes. I went back to see my cardiologist and he suggested that I refrain from diving, but from what I have read there seems to be a lack of medical consensus on the subject.

I feel that the cold was a critical factor and that if I was using a drysuit this may well not have happened. I don't think you will find many people who have done as much diving as myself in a wetsuit in these waters.

I would like to return to diving but I would definitely be more conservative as regards temperature. Any advice is welcome.

The main mechanism behind this is as follows: on land, quite a lot of blood sits in peripheral veins, but when the body is immersed in water, the peripheral veins shut down, and the blood in them physically shifts to the deeper vessels, moving centrally. If the water is cold, the effect is more pronounced. This increases the amount of blood reaching the heart with each pump, as well as increasing the resistance against which the heart is pumping (as the peripheral vessels are shut down). Sort of like a pump trying to squeeze water through furred up pipes. There is also a theory that the chest constriction caused by a tight wetsuit might contribute. The net effect of all this is to cause fluid to leak out into the lungs.

Bizarrely, the patchy pattern of lung changes seen in pulmonary oedema in divers is very similar to patients who have overdosed on cocaine. But that's not important right now. What is important, is that the changes resolve very quickly with appropriate treatment. The body somehow cleverly shunts blood away from the fluid-filled (non-functioning) alveoli, towards the ones that are still working, so that the lungs can still do their job while the damaged alveoli heal.

Although it often resolves with no long term complications, to have had it twice at your age does suggest some predisposition to it. Interestingly this is similar to high altitude pulmonary oedema (HAPE), in which there is a definite genetic component (and similar treatments). Your investigations sound pretty thorough so I would assume they have found no cardiac or pulmonary cause for it.

Certainly this is a grey area in terms of recommendations for future diving. Obvious measures such as dry suit diving and steering clear of cold water would be mandatory. Other than that, however, one of the issues is that the onset of pulmonary oedema is often acute and unpredictable. Personally I would be reluctant to consider diving again other than in very safe and non-challenging conditions.

Doc, I'm getting fed up with my dive club making jokes about how bad my gas consumption is. I admit I'm not the slimmest

card in the pack but I've been trying to exercise more; going to the gym and swimming twice a week. My girlfriend does yoga and thinks I should try it as she reckons it makes your lungs bigger. I always thought it was a bit weird but I'll give it a go if it makes me less of an air pig. Is this true or would I be wasting my time?

Yoga has come a long way from being a vaguely disconcerting habit of quirky hippies in the herbaceous fug of the 70's. It's now so uber-trendy that you can't bend over backwards for Om ornaments and Buddha bling. Myriad variations on its central theme (the 'bringing together of parts in order to create a union' – no sniggering at the back there) have resulted in splinter forms springing up everywhere. There are now specific Scuba-orientated yoga trips the world over, from the Bahamas to the Red Sea. So how can gaining inner peace benefit the humble diver?

Let's start with the physical aspects. The common Western perception of yoga is that it's all about impossible contortions and ludicrous postures. Modern society has made us stiff (apparently) and this is why we find the poses so tough. For a diver though, the essential elements of yoga can significantly reduce the likelihood of injury. Specific exercises can improve core stability, working on the lower back to protect it from the trauma of twinsets and weightbelts. Targeting the legs and hips can improve finning (both technique and stamina) and make that long slippery trip in full kit from the car park to the water's edge a joy. Or at least less of an ordeal. Stretches before and after diving will keep the muscles going for longer, especially on those long liveaboards, and, by improving flexibility, can help the burgeoning wreck or cave diver in and out of awkward tight spaces. More generally, the breathing exercises that are fundamental to yoga are also ideal for improving lung capacity and encouraging effective steady breathing during hard exertion. Ultimately this will extend bottom times and reduce feelings of panic underwater, which we all want, don't we?

And what of the more, ah, spiritual aspects to the ancient Yogic arts? Well, the original goal of yoga was to intertwine the body and the mind so that the two could become one. I'm not saying we're going to find the answer to Life, the Universe and Everything underwater (it's 42, in case you'd forgotten), but there are parallels between this aspiration and many divers' urge to find the solitude and peace they miss on dry land. Visualisation techniques in yoga are often practised by freedivers, and can help prepare any diver

> "Yoga has come a long way from being a vaguely disconcerting habit of quirky hippies in the herbaceous fug of the 70's."

for challenging or particularly strenuous dives.

So before belittling the posh toffs of yogaland too much, it's worth giving the practice a chance to make us better divers. Particular poses I'd suggest include the Sun Salutation at Stoney, or the wind relieving one at Wraysbury…

I had surgery on a tumour which had invaded the diaphragm and wall of the inferior vena cava. Both were patched with Dacron. I am now fully fit and have no health problems. Does this count as blood vessel surgery on the medical questionnaire, and can I go ahead with the PADI certificate?

It does and you do need a medical. I am not sure what sort of tumour it was but it does sound nasty. However, if you have been lucky and it's all out now then there's hope.

Dacron is used to patch up vessel walls after surgery. It is not compressible at depth and so should not be an issue. But the patched up hole in the diaphragm needs further exploring. If it moves fine and does not restrict breathing, then all is OK. To assess this you will need spirometry. Get this done at your local dive doctor.

GASTROINTESTINAL AND GENITO-URINARY PROBLEMS

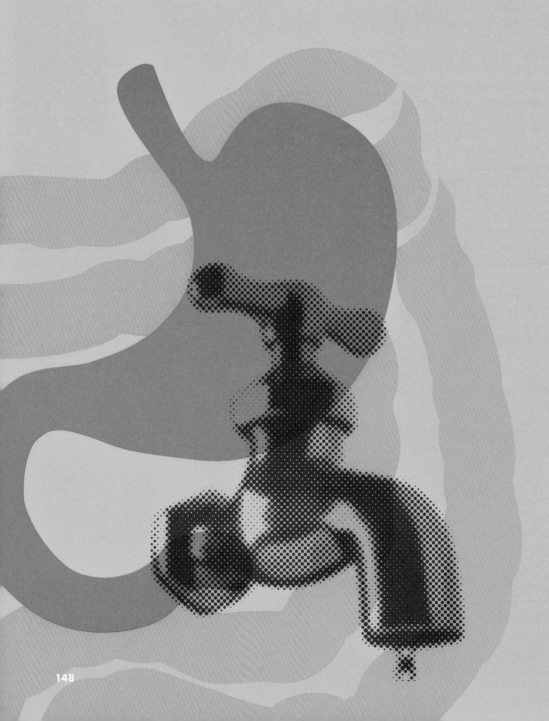

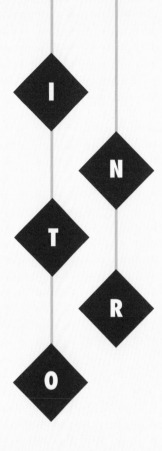

I've amalgamated GU and GI here for an unbelievably puerile reason, and it's not because their acronyms both have 'G's in them. If you can't work it out, I commend you on your esoteric and highbrow nature.

It is, of course, completely medically inaccurate of me to combine them like this. The GU system really is a miracle of modern technology and I raise a toast to whoever invented it. All that sorting and separating. Unfortunately, I have been on various diving trips with people who insist on utilising it a bit too close to the end of the dive, rather than as a quick way to warm up at the beginning (except in a drysuit, you at the back), forcing everyone to talk loudly about anything other than wee in order to pretend there's nothing wrong, as they rapidly change tanks on the dive deck afterwards.

The GI system, on the other hand, isn't even considered properly internal as anything that goes in and isn't absorbed takes a straight road all the way from the mouth through to what is technically known as the bumhole. If it wasn't for various rings of muscle and a few tight corners, when you yawned on a bright day, the sun really would shine out of... Look, what I'm trying to say is that we're food tubes, essentially. Like worms but with arms and legs and MP3 players.

I'm sure there's lots of amusing things one could find to say about diarrhoea and so forth, but I haven't filled my pants with poo since Valentine's Day 2002 (in Bangkok), so I can't think of anything off hand. Anyway, this is a mature work, so I really wish you'd take your mind out of the gutter for just long enough to read on and learn something.

Honestly...

Tip: If you're going to have explosive accidents in these areas, it's usually best to do so whilst out of water and in the comfort of a water closet.

DIARRHOEA

A query about a rather mundane medical condition I'm afraid. I am off to the Red Sea for a diving holiday and would appreciate your advice on the most effective way of dealing with an upset stomach. Some divers tell me an anti-diarrhoeal (eg Imodium) is the best way to deal with this, although I believe these can cause constipation. Others say to just drink lots of fluid. Which is best and, if some kind of medicine is advisable, what would you recommend?

There's nothing mundane about diarrhoea, and as a bowels obsessed traveller myself, here are a few tips on avoidance and treatment.

The first thing to consider is that diarrhoea in a normal tourist is a drag but not really life threatening. It may be an embarrassment on a long bus journey but on the whole, most get over it without much ado. However, in the diver it really can be a problem, as if you combine the fluid loss from it with a hot environment, a bend can become a real possibility. Why? Well, with less circulating blood volume there's less ability to remove the nitrogen from your tissues, so with divers I always advise that you take precautions to avoid it.

Wash and peel all your fruit. Do not take ice in drinks as it can sometimes contain a surprise amoeba. Try to stick to a diet that you are used to and nothing too exotic for a pampered Western intestinal system.

Now, if you do happen to get diarrhoea, I suggest that you hit it hard with an antibiotic called ciprofloxacin. It has been shown that a simple one off dose of 1g can stop 80% of diarrhoea in its tracks. Either take this with you or try to get it where you can.

You will need to replace the fluid you have lost, and this is best done with oral rehydration salts such as Electrolade or Dioralyte. Go for the citrus flavour as it's the nicest. Using Imodium or Lomotil is OK

"In the diver [diarrhoea] really can be a problem, as if you combine the fluid loss from it with a hot environment, a bend can become a real possibility."

too as it will slow down the bowels and reduce fluid loss. However, be aware that if nothing works, you are going more than five times a day, and you see blood or become really dehydrated, then you need to see a doctor. This is because an amoebic dysentery or salmonella should be treated only after a medical opinion.

So when should a diver with diarrhoea stay out of the water? Well when they are borrowing their best mate's drysuit, or even when cage diving, especially if there is no cage. Apart from that I suggest that if there is any vomiting and dehydration as well, then stay in your hotel room. And as before, if there is blood in your stool then you should be at the doctor's rather than on a boat.

Is it safe to dive on metronidazole 400mg tablets BP? I am currently taking three a day.

Metronidazole is fine to dive with. It's an antibiotic used for treating protozoal and anaerobic infections. The latter is where the bugs can breed without oxygen; the kind of stuff that causes gangrene. It's unlikely you'd be up for diving with that, so I assume it's for something else – diarrhoea caused by amoeba maybe? If this is the case, then you can dive but make sure you are not suffering dehydration at the time or a bend will ensue.

Interestingly, it's one of the few meds you really cannot drink alcohol with. It blocks the enzyme in the alcohol breakdown process making you feel off your head on a little tipple. I know; one day I shall tell you about my story of being on metronidazole, drinking a pint of cider, and meeting Lionel Blair in Weymouth. Let's say I was lucky to get off with a caution.

I've recently returned from a week of diving in Malta, during which I picked up a particularly nasty stomach upset: Campylobacter according to my doctor, whom I visited upon my return.

I'm off to El Gouna in the Red Sea this coming Friday for another week of diving (tough life) and frankly I want to go prepared for anything. I was thinking of taking ciprofloxacin with me, but is this antibiotic on prescription only?

The answer to that is yes. Ciprofloxacin is a prescription only antibiotic, and in fact all antibiotics are scrip only. This does present a problem if you are like most people and leave it until the last moment before trying to get some before you fly away. Your GP is unlikely to let you have an emergency appointment to get it and if yours is like most doctors now it's a two week wait.

Ciprofloxacin has been in the news as it's the most effective drug to use against anthrax and the company that makes it, Bayer, have had their arms twisted to reduce the price so it may well soon find its way as an affordable antidote to diarrhoea in most divers' bags.

The infection you suffered in Malta is a particularly nasty bowel bug and presents with loose bowels tinged with blood. It is important to treat this early and effectively so ciprofloxacin is the right thing to use. A one off 750mg dose will knock it on the head with general diarrhoea but for your particular type, a 500mg twice a day regime for at least five days is required.

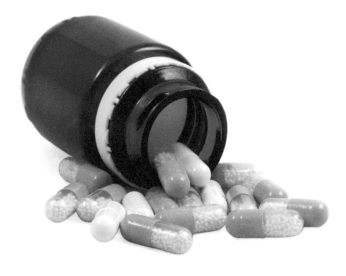

GASTRO-OESOPHAGEAL AND STOMACH

Since starting diving I have noticed that every time I finish a dive I get heart burn and have to have Zantac 75 on hand to get rid of it before my next dive. I am wondering if this is just a minor problem or whether it is something that could possibly affect my diving future.

Heartburn, or reflux oesophagitis, is one of the things highlighted on the medical declaration form. The danger here is that if it's uncontrolled, good old gastric acid can spill up into your oesophagus on a dive, into your throat and either come out as a vomit through your reg, or more lethally, be re-inhaled. This will cause a spasm in your breathing tubes, laryngospasm, it's known as. If you get this underwater, your next sight will not be a little wrasse but the Grim Reaper himself.

The reason you may get this diving is because of your body position and your gear. A horizontal dive position with a tight BCD and weight belt can squeeze your abdomen forcing up the acid. So if that is the issue, then consider an integrated weight belt or a larger BCD.

However, as you are getting it so regularly I suggest you see your GP and consider a course of Omeprazole to really knock the problem on the head. This is an antacid that is better at long term prevention of gastric acid problems. If this does not help then it's a gastroscopy for you. That's a 50cm flexible tube they shove down your oesophagus to have a look at what lies within. Not a lot of fun but better than having a chunder at 30m.

While diving recently, I began to cough and retch small amounts of blood at 25m. This unfortunately led to me aspirating some of the blood, making breathing difficult. I ascended slowly and got to the surface safely, but felt very weak and required assistance exiting. Due to a slightly over enthusiastic response, I wound up spending a few days in hospital until my oxygen saturation had picked up a bit. It has been established that I

"If you get this underwater, your next sight will not be a little wrasse but the Grim Reaper himself."

have got a small recurrence of varices but the specialists don't intend to treat them as they regard them as fairly small. Now, if I am to continue as a DM or progress further I will require a HSE medical. What are my chances of passing?

This is pretty serious stuff. Varices, or oesophageal varices as they are known in long hand, are blood filled swellings in the oesophagus caused by a problem with the vasculature in that area. The issue here is that they can bleed at any point, sometimes disastrously. In your case they have done that and you inhaled the blood at depth. Lucky to be alive, and I guess this is a testament to your 'sang froid' underwater.

Now imagine if you were DMing and it happened again. You would be putting not only your life, but those of your other divers at risk. So it's no diving for you I am afraid.

What the hospital considers small and not worth operating on though needs another look. If diving is your life and you want to continue, then you need to find out why you have varices and if they could fix them with a guarantee you will not bleed again. If they can do this, then you may well be able to dive and DM in the future.

Is my SAGB (Swedish Adjustable Gastric Band) likely to be affected by diving, especially as I work towards deeper dives? Since having it, I've lost 47kg. None of my dive club pals knew me then and it is something I'm reluctant to bring up with the instructor: vanity as well as the fact the procedure is not that common in the UK (I went to Lyon for it) so they probably won't know anything about it anyway.

Thanks for explaining the acronym as, to tell the truth, I have never heard of it before. Likewise anything Swedish and adjustable could easily be assumed to affect the bedroom rather than the stomach, but I think I'm right in assuming it's a band that is put around the stomach to squeeze it smaller so you need less food to feel full. It involves putting an inflatable device around the top part of the organ via keyhole surgery. This 'band' creates a small pouch above it, which therefore fills quickly and produces a 'full' sensation, while also slowing down the passage of food through the rest of the stomach. In theory this means the wearer feels full more easily, eats less, and loses weight. The tightness of the band can be varied by injecting or withdrawing saline from it, until a happy medium is found. Very clever stuff.

So what about diving with it?

"Likewise anything Swedish and adjustable could easily be assumed to affect the bedroom rather than the stomach..."

As it is not air filled that's fine, as long as there's no gas trapping in the stomach. The only real issue is if it causes any reflux of gastric contents back up the oesophagus. If it does (because it's too tight or you are trying to get too much food in you for your new stomach width), then that is a real problem. Acid regurgitation with a reg in your mouth can be fatal. On dry land you can retch merrily away to spit the acid out, or even rush to the pharmacy to get the Gaviscon. However down with the fish there is a chance that you can inhale the acid; go into a paroxysm of coughing; reg comes out; you drown.

Only you know if you get any reflux. If you do, don't dive until the band is off. If you really don't then I hope you enjoy your trip to Egypt. There is also a particular side effect associated with gastric bands charmingly referred to as 'PBing' (Productive Burping), which can result in regurgitation of food from the upper pouch. Fortunately, your regs are designed to let 'productive burps' through (I've had a few when diving with a hangover) and luckily, with some of the local delicacies I've seen out there, you don't need an operation to put you off eating.

I went on a Red Sea liveaboard a month ago and the first couple of days were fine, great in fact, but from day three, after each dive I started to notice slight bubbling/gurgling sounds in my chest. These got worse over the week, and I started getting burning pains as well. By the end I had to bail out of the last two dives as my chest was so sore. I felt sick too, and half the time couldn't sleep as lying down made it worse. I'm only 40 years-old so I'm praying this doesn't mean the end of diving for me.

Don't panic, this is actually quite a common complaint and thankfully it's unlikely to terminate your diving career prematurely. These are the typical symptoms of gastro-oesophageal reflux disease (GORD), which are often exacerbated by diving. Think of your stomach as a bottle filled with acid, and your oesophagus (food pipe) the long neck of the bottle. Normally a handy little sphincter stops acid entering the oesophagus, but in some situations (for example lying down, or being horizontal in the water) the acid refluxes through it, up the long neck of the bottle, and causes your typical heartburn and nausea. Pretty unpleasant during a dive.

The risk factors for GORD are numerous: certain foods (fatty or spicy stuff, chocolate, caffeine, citrus fruits), certain drugs (nicotine, alcohol, anti-inflammatories), obesity, advancing age and tight

"On dry land you can retch merrily away to spit the acid out, … However down with the fish there is a chance that you can inhale the acid; go into a paroxysm of coughing; reg comes out; you drown."

clothing are those most prevalent in the diving community. If any of these apply then address them. Luckily, there are also plenty of medicines to help. Some coat the lining of the oesophagus, others stop the acid secretion from the stomach, and sometimes a course of 'triple therapy' will eradicate pesky bacteria that can contribute to the symptoms. So before your next dive ask your GP to give your gullet the once-over.

When I return to the boat after a dive, I sick [sic], but this is only when I try to get on board. I am OK if my head is below the water but this is very embarrassing. Is there anything I can do about this?

I have given this a lot of thought, consulted some of the wisest sages that have learnt the arts of Hippocrates, and all we can come up with is a guess.

If all is OK on the dive; up from your safety stop with your head bobbing above the water, but then you paint the deck as you pull yourself up, the only thing it could be is an increase in intra-abdominal pressure brought on by the exertion of hauling yourself up whilst still in full kit.

On your next boat dive here are my tips: don't eat for at least two hours before you dive, so your stomach is empty; remove your weight belt before getting onto the boat; and remove your BC and tank and let the boatmeister haul them up for you.

This should work, but if not then I suggest you either get the same guy to gently lift you onto the vessel, or tape a sick bag onto your face so you have your hands free to hold a mop and bucket of water if it blows.

"…I suggest you either get the same guy to gently lift you onto the vessel, or tape a sick bag onto your face so you have your hands free to hold a mop and bucket of water if it blows."

HERNIA

I have a congenital inguinal hernia on the left side and want to know if I can dive.

A hernia is caused by a loop of your bowel pushing through a weakness in the muscle wall of your abdomen. Yours is the most common one to get, and what has happened is that the track left by your testicle as it descends from your abdomen to your scrotum has been left open. In most people this will close so that the bowel can't get through this 'inguinal canal'. The problems associated with this are that if you increase the pressure in your abdomen like when trying to use the toilet when you are constipated, sneezing, or when you lift heavy objects, it can pop the bowel out and down towards your scrotum.

All hernias are dangerous, in that every one poses the threat of incarceration (where the bulge becomes trapped), strangulation (entrapment with loss of blood supply), obstruction (blockage of the intestinal flow) and the possibility of death if the obstructed gut perforates.

That a hernia should be repaired goes without saying. It is a simple procedure, often done as a day case, where a strong mesh is laid over the weak area of muscle to hold the contents in. An unrepaired hernia should be considered a contraindication for diving until it is satisfactorily repaired. The diving danger has to do mainly with the effects of pressure on gas inside a loop of intestine. Without repair, a previously asymptomatic hernia can be pushed out through the ring of the hernia and become trapped. If this occurs with the straining and lifting of heavy tanks and gear, and the person then dives to depth, the air in the trapped bowel expands due to the effects of Boyle's law on ascent. This leads to strangulation-obstruction and a requirement for emergency surgery. Getting to a good surgical facility may not be so easily done in some of the places that we go to dive.

> "A hernia is caused by a loop of your bowel pushing through a weakness in the muscle wall of your abdomen."

Returning to diving after hernia surgery should only be after the wound has completely healed, normally at least six weeks following the op. Although recurrences are uncommon you have to bear in mind the factors that caused the problem – carrying of heavy dive gear is a major consideration after hernia surgery.

I have been diagnosed with a 4cm hiatus hernia and require laparoscopic (keyhole) surgery. I would like to know if I will be able to continue diving after the op. I have researched this matter in depth and there seems to be conflicting opinion. I approached my local diving medical referee, and he was of the opinion I could dive whilst controlling the hernia with PPI's (acid suppressants) but stated I would not be passed fit to dive post repair due to an elevated risk of gastric rupture.

The thing is, I know of several divers who are diving post surgery for the same complaint. I also know of people diving with the condition and controlling it with PPIs. If I do have the repair will I be able to continue diving?

Rather than being an obvious groin bulge, a hiatus hernia is a bulge of the upper part of the stomach through the diaphragm, into the chest cavity. The confusion (and thus controversy) arises from the different types of hiatus hernia, and the unpredictability of complications following the surgery.

Two main types of hernia are distinguishable, since they have different implications for fitness to dive. By far the most common is the sliding hiatal hernia (95%), where the upper portion of the stomach slides upward into the space occupied by the oesophagus (food pipe). This hernia can cause gastroesophageal reflux (giving you that acid burning in the chest), but it often has no symptoms. The second type (5%), a paraoesophageal or rolling hernia, is a protrusion of the stomach through a separate opening of the diaphragm.

If you have significant gastroesophageal reflux then it should be treated before diving (usually with PPIs), as there is an increased risk of acid reflux and aspiration (inhaling stomach contents) with the horizontal or head-down body position adopted during a dive, but otherwise a sliding hiatal hernia does not by itself contraindicate diving. However, part of the stomach can become trapped within a paraesophageal hiatal hernia, and could rupture during ascent, so this kind of hernia is considered a contraindication to diving.

"Rather than being an obvious groin bulge, a hiatus hernia is a bulge of the upper part of the stomach through the diaphragm, into the chest cavity."

Do you know which type of hernia you have, and the name of the procedure you are going to have? The most common one is called fundoplication, where the surgeon wraps (or 'plicates', a lovely word) the upper part of the stomach (the fundus) around the oesophagus, thus stopping it from moving. A few who have had surgical repair of their hiatal hernia can suffer from gas-bloat syndrome, which is associated with gaseous distension of the stomach. This is believed to occur due to an inability to expel swallowed air by belching. During an ascent, this distension can lead to gastric rupture. The symptom usually resolves within a few weeks. If the distension persists, however, diving is not advised.

It would be worth discussing this with the surgeon before deciding one way or the other, as it's difficult to predict who will suffer from this gaseous distension.

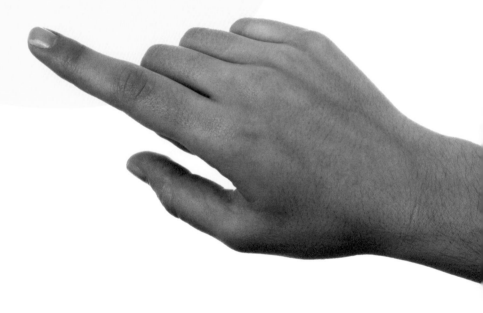

INTESTINAL

I recently had a Hartman's resection to remove 50cm of damaged colon (due to colitis or diverticulitis) following a fistula between bowel and bladder. This has left me with a stoma bag (hopefully for only four to six months), after which a reversal will be carried out. I wonder if you could let me know whether you see any problems with Scuba diving with a stoma bag and after a major operation.

I don't see any real issues with the bag. This sits across the piece of bowel that has been extended to come out of your abdominal wall. They do this to give the lower bowel a rest before the rejoin. The bag has a super sticky ring that goes around the fleshy stoma and obviously collects the intestinal mulch coming out. So as long as putting on and removing a wetsuit won't tear it off, and it doesn't come loose inside a dry suit leaving you with one hell of a cleanup job, then that should be fine. Stay away from windy foods, you know the sort, as theoretically if wind is produced at depth in the bag, it will expand on ascent. And I don't want to be flippant but a stool filled plastic bag bursting on the deck of a liveaboard would have the same consequences as that scene in Trainspotting.

Give it at least eight weeks post op before diving again.

"...I don't want to be flippant but a stool filled plastic bag bursting on the deck of a liveaboard would have the same consequences as that scene in Trainspotting."

I have recently been diagnosed with gallstones and will need to have my gallbladder removed in the near future. How long should I leave it after having it removed before I go back to diving?

Also, can I continue to dive before it is removed?

I wonder how many people are wandering about with gallstones without knowing it. About one in three women and one in six men form gallstones at some stage in their life. Most people don't know they have them because they generally sit in the gallbladder doing nothing, except perhaps growing bigger. In this situation they can be safely left well alone. In three out of 10 people however, they cause symptoms which may be colicky type abdominal pain or occasionally jaundice. In a few people the gallbladder gets infected and this causes severe pain, often with fevers and vomiting, usually resulting in hospital treatment and an early gallbladder removal.

There is no harm in diving if the stones don't cause you symptoms, but if you get colicky pains underwater there is a high chance of dropping your reg or panicking with potentially dire consequences. Diving after the surgery depends on how long the wound takes to heal. Generally, I would suggest a minimum of six weeks for this.

I have in the past had some bleeding on defacation due to internal piles. These episodes did not last for more than two or three days. I have seen a consultant about managing this, and he recommended no intervention other than topical cream for the moment if/when there is a recurrence. Am I OK to dive?

Apart from inventing psychiatry, the greatest contribution Sigmund Freud made to medicine was that his name rhymed with haemorrhoid. Don't worry about your Siggys, they'll be fine. If your arse-surgeon has given them the all clear, then all should be fine underwater. Piles have three degrees of seriousness: internal; internal, come out but you can pop them back in; or external. The latter would be an issue diving, as it would attract the bottom feeders, if your wetsuit came off in one of those sitcom sorts of ways. But judging by your doc's advice you are in the first two degrees, so no worries there.

"Apart from inventing psychiatry, the greatest contribution Sigmund Freud made to medicine was that his name rhymed with haemorrhoid. Don't worry about your Siggys, they'll be fine."

I was diagnosed with irritable bowel syndrome (IBS) recently. I've done a few open water dives and I find that I get really 'gassy' during them. Afterwards, my stomach feels bloated and I have to pass a lot of wind. Is this normal?

Apparently a certain four letter 'f-word' is one of the oldest in the English language. Chaucer describes one of his characters "letting fly a fart as loud as a thunder-clap" into the face of a rival in one of his Canterbury Tales, nearly blinding him. Nice. Unfortunately, production of some intestinal gas is an unavoidable part of digestion. A human can generate anything up to two litres of wind a day, although your average is nearer 600ml. Its major component is nitrogen but sadly, farting a lot does not reduce your DCI risk.

The problem of course is that all this gas has to obey Boyle's Law when diving, so it will expand and contract and generally cause maximum discomfort unless it is expelled, from either end of the gut. Some IBS sufferers do generate a lot of wind, and diving will therefore exacerbate the discomfort, but as long as there is 'light at the end of the tunnel', as it were, then the gas will escape and relief will ensue. The best advice I can give is simply to avoid anything 'flatogenic' on a dive trip. The obvious culprits include beans, cabbages, onions, mushrooms etc., but also fizzy drinks and milk. With any luck you can then spare your cabin buddy a fragrant night on your first liveaboard.

I am 37 years of age and have been diving for about six years; three of them as an instructor but I have not dived since being diagnosed with Crohn's disease two years ago. In hindsight I can see I had this disease for a number of years, but dived without any apparent adverse effects.

I intend to go back to teaching sometime this year but can't find out very much from my GP with regard to diving with Crohn's.

There is no absolute contraindication to diving if you have Crohn's disease. However there are a few issues you should be aware of.

Firstly, anaemia can be a result of your condition. This will be a problem if you dive as your oxygen carrying capacity will be lowered making things more difficult if you have a hard counter current, surface dragging a tired buddy kind of dive. So if you are tired in yourself, short of breath, and friends comment on how pale you look, get a blood test before you go.

Secondly, one of the treatments for Crohn's is high dose steroid tablets that keep the inflammation at bay. Steroids have also been linked to cataract formation. These are opacities in the lenses of your eyes, most commonly found in the elderly. This is a rare side effect of steroid treatment, however another equally rare cause of cataract formation can be breathing higher concentrations of oxygen. The concentrations in some higher O2 gas mixes shouldn't really cause this but if you are on steroids, it's worth seeing an optician quickly if you feel your vision deteriorating.

Any of the treatments for Crohn's that suppress your immune system can lead to a bigger risk of picking up infections from dirty water.

There are also problems with arthritis, and this in the knees and hips will affect your finning abilities.

"There is no absolute contraindication to diving if you have Crohn's disease. However there are a few issues you should be aware of..."

Lastly, Crohn's disease can cause air trapping in your bowels. This is called intestinal obstruction and can be a danger with diving as the air can expand on ascent with obvious consequent problems. This, though, is a very intense pain and I doubt whether you would be in any condition even to contemplate a dive as it usually signifies a worsening of your condition which would need a visit to the hospital.

So, as long as you are aware of these factors, you shouldn't have much trouble getting signed off by a dive doc.

I recently had a laparoscopy examination under general anaesthetic (GA) for investigative purposes only. During this, my abdominal region was pumped with carbon dioxide, as is normal in these procedures. I was told that it would take a few days for the CO2 to work its way out of my body. The specialist did not seem concerned that I would be flying to Barbados five days after the operation for a diving holiday. However, I have since heard that it can take up to three weeks for all traces to leave my body. I would like some advice as to whether I should dive or not.

Insufflation, that's what they call it. A lovely word indeed. When there's trouble in the tum, and the surgeons need to take a look, they have to blow up the abdomen with this gas. That's so that when the pointy steel visual thing goes in through the umbilicus, they all get a clear view. Your doctor is right, the CO2 does clear fairly quickly, being absorbed by the tissues, so flying is fine. You should not expand like that baddie in the Bond movie who explodes comically over the alligator pool. But I do have a reservation with diving so soon. Five days after an op that involves a GA with the abdominal wall pierced is too soon. Normally you'd be looking at two to three weeks.

I suggest taking it easy, and if you must dive, keep it shallow: 10m max, and only a couple at the most. No heavy lifting either, and that includes your kit. With easy exits too. Come to think of it, just chill and drink rum.

My husband is a very keen diver but was diagnosed with cancer of the pancreas and bile duct. He had a Whipple's Procedure (removing half stomach, half pancreas, bile duct and duodenum), made a very quick recovery and was released from hospital after only 15 days. He has just finished his six month

course of chemotherapy and has been given the all clear. We are planning a holiday soon and he is wondering if he can dive.

This is an incredible recovery. Stats show 80% of folk with this diagnosis cark it, so well done him.

Diving depends on two factors: which chemo he had/what effect that left on him; and how strong he now feels. Man enough to lug those tanks and weak buddies, if the diving doc feels that there has been no collateral damage from the chemo, and he passes any fitness tests, then he could well be back in the water soon. Call this a wake up message to get out and enjoy life to the full. In the words of the pianist from Spinal Tap: "Have a good time, all the time."

DIETARY

I'm writing to ask if I would be allowed to Scuba dive with an asthma condition. I have an average peak flow metering of 450 and take terbutaline sulphate 500 microgram Turbohaler and Pulmicort Turbohaler 200.

I also have an eating disorder which means I keep on binge eating and have found that my breathing has become a lot shorter than before. Would this affect me at all?

The asthma here is the least of your problems. A well controlled asthmatic, with no exercise inducement of the problem, is OK to dive, as long as they pass the medical that involves lung testing.

It's your eating disorder that worries me. These normally fall into three categories: anorexia, where you don't eat; bulimia where you eat too much; and bulimia nervosa, where you eat and throw up.

Yours obviously falls into the latter two categories. The problem with over-eating and vomiting is that there is a risk of inhaling some of the acid in the vomit. This can cause spasm in the lung tubes, and shortness of breath. It could be what is happening to you. And made worse by pre-existing asthma, where these tubes are prone to spasm anyway.

So, where does that leave you? I think you really need to address the eating disorder. It is often caused by subliminal issues, often from childhood, and often centred around 'control'. If you are on the edge and bingeing, you may well have psych problems underwater and be a risk to yourself and others.

Go to a psychologist and get control of the problem. When this is sorted, getting the asthma passed should be a breeze.

I'm going to Thailand for three weeks, where I plan to do a seven day detox fast (no solid food, just fruit juices twice a

"The asthma here is the least of your problems. A well controlled asthmatic, with no exercise inducement of the problem, is OK to dive, as long as they pass the medical that involves lung testing."

day) at a spa in Koh Samui. I am a 35 year-old healthy female, 170cm tall, weighing 60kg. Can I dive whilst I'm fasting?

My theory is that you can tell how good a nation's food is by the amount of restaurants in London. No Chilean, some Brazilian, but a hell of a lot of Thai. Good luck starving yourself in the culinary capital of the world. But I have to say, if you dive and starve, you're gonna risk a fine blend of DCS and cramps. Fruit juice twice a day is not enough fluids in a hot climate. If you dive dehydrated, then there is an issue that you won't be able to off-gas your nitrogen as easily. Likewise, not enough carbs then a difficult energetic dive, and you could cramp up.

So, as you have a three week trip there, detox merrily away, but do not dive. There's plenty of time in the other two weeks to do that when you are eating and drinking healthily. Spend your time in that week helping the C-list celebs examine the results of their colonic irrigation. Aaah, isn't that the duck pâté from the Groucho?

I am a 26 year-old female with anorexia nervosa and have just got an ECG test back that said my heart rate was slower than normal (in the 50s). Does this put me at an increased risk for diving? I've been a diver since I was 14.

Anorexia nervosa is not a new illness. 'Fasting girls', a Victorian term for non-eating pre-adolescents, have been around since the Middle Ages, and were often claimed to have miraculous or magical powers, usually by exploitative museums. Sadly, whenever these claims were tested, the girls in question starved. Today, the condition is a formal psychiatric diagnosis, an eating disorder that causes low body weight, body image distortion and an obsessive fear of gaining weight. In general terms, the problems that this would cause for diving are several. Reduced strength and exercise tolerance are common, meaning kit-carrying and hard finning may produce early fatigue. Psychological issues might jeopardise safety, with panic and phobic behaviours a prominent feature. Any medication taken for the disorder might have repercussions also.

As far as your specific heart rate query goes, a slow pulse can be a sign of a very fit heart. If the ECG is otherwise normal then the rate itself would not put you at any increased risk of diving problems. Nevertheless, I would suggest you are cleared by a diving doc for the reasons outlined. The fact that you have been diving for 12 years should be in your favour though.

"Today, the condition is a formal psychiatric diagnosis, an eating disorder that causes low body weight, body image distortion and an obsessive fear of gaining weight. In general terms, the problems that this would cause for diving are several."

GENITO-URINARY

I am very prone to getting bladder infections, which I treat with various over-the-counter remedies. I'm due to go on a long live-aboard to the Red Sea soon and a friend has told me that I ought to take some antibiotics with me, just in case. Which ones should I take and is there anything I can do to prevent it from happening?

Your friend is right. You suffer from what we call cystitis, which is where bacteria that normally inhabit your lower gastrointestinal tract can find their way to your bladder and multiply causing you the symptoms of pain on urination, increased frequency of urination and often an odd odour to your urine. The reason that women get it far more frequently than men is due to the length of their urethra. This is the tube that takes the urine from the bladder to the outside world and is considerably longer in men than in women.

Back home, if the problem doesn't get better with the over the counter remedies you can quickly see your doctor who can prescribe you the antibiotics needed. But of course on safari you may be a long way from medical help and if left untreated the real problems can set in. Leading into the bladder from the kidneys is another tube called the ureter, and in some cases the bacteria can ascend this tube and cause a full on kidney infection. This would lead to a severe fever, vomiting and pain in your lower back at the side of the infection. This can sometimes lead to dehydration, delirium and hospitalisation.

What I suggest is that you take your usual remedies with you, and if you get symptoms of cystitis then you should try these for a day. If there is no improvement after this, then you need to really increase your fluid consumption to about five litres a day, especially as you will be in a hot climate and will be dehydrating at a faster rate than at home. You should also start the antibiotics immediately. There are several you can take and currently I would suggest either trimethoprim 200mg twice a day for three days or cephalexin

250mg twice a day for the same time. The strongest and widest spectrum antibiotic is called ciprofloxacin and is taken at a dose of 100mg twice daily for three days as well. If you are going for a long time I recommend you get hold of two courses of one of the first two and one course of the ciprofloxacin for your medical bag.

To prevent it occurring in the first place, always drink plenty of fluids, especially cranberry juice (the theory is that this makes it more difficult for bacteria to adhere to the bladder wall), make sure you wipe your bottom from front to back after going to the toilet and try to pass urine as soon as you can after intercourse as this can also aid the passage of bacteria up to the bladder.

On a final note, if you are suffering cystitis that often then you should make sure that your doctor has screened you for diabetes as this can make you prone to these recurrent infections.

Just recently I have been diagnosed with BPH (Benign Prostatic Hyperplasia). At the age of 44, would the prescription of one capsule of tamsulosin hydrochloride 367 micrograms affect me diving in any way?

You can happily continue to dive with an enlarged prostate. There are, as usual, one or two caveats. The profound diuresis (increased urine production) that immersion in water induces can become more problematic with existing BPH, so take care to empty your bladder before and after each dive (and preferably not during, unless you're wearing someone else's wetsuit). Tamsulosin, or 'Flomax' (its deliciously literal trade name), can cause significant nasal congestion, so you'd be wise to make sure you can equalise properly in the shallows before leaping into the depths. It can also drop your blood pressure, which shouldn't be an issue unless your BP is low already, in which case it may cause you to feel faint or short of breath. Again, a few cautious shallow dives should highlight any impending problems or susceptibility to this.

"Take care to empty your bladder before and after each dive (and preferably not during, unless you're wearing someone else's wetsuit)."

I have to urinate in my wet suit on each dive, sometimes twice and on the odd occasion three times. I try to hold it back but it becomes so painful and uncomfortable that it ruins the dive if I don't go. I go to the toilet just before the dive but it makes no difference.

I drink lots of water as most of my diving is in tropical climates and I know diving dehydrates the body. I have not kept any

data about whether I urinate when I dive below certain depths or over certain lengths of time. There have been times when I need to go after ten minutes in the water and there are other times, very few and far between, when I don't go at all during the dive.

I am very passionate about diving and don't want to stop because of this embarrassing problem. I have been told that the pressure on your kidneys makes you want to urinate more and we have all seen divers rushing to get their gear off to get to the toilet at the end of a dive.

Got me here. I can't say I've come across this a lot. Sure, some people need to pee maybe once underwater, but three times is overdoing it a bit. And if it's happening every time you dive then I can see how you would have problems with a smelly wetsuit.

Hydration is important when diving, less fluid in you means less blood to take away the nitrogen. So I always recommend drinking enough to make your pee pale straw yellow before you dive. If it's clear urine then I think you are over-hydrating. Likewise tea, Coke and coffee will make you want to urinate more often, so avoid those drinks before a dive. Just stick to water.

It would be an idea to get a quick check for both diabetes mellitus and insipidus, as their early symptoms are urinary frequency. See your GP for this. However, my hunchy bits here say that it's probably just one of those things, and you're going to have to live with it. I think a Velcro flap is a good idea so you can go underwater without soiling the suit. Just don't wave your old boy around too much. Little pink fish are at the bottom of the food chain.

About two months ago, I underwent an operation to correct hydrocoele and to remove varicocoele around my testis. Are there any dangers associated with my operation and diving? Currently I do suffer from some pain in the area.

I bet you are all dying to know what these are! And if you are a ballsy bloke you're gonna wince. So look away.

A hydrocoele is a collection of fluid around your tessy. It causes said organ to lie in a giant pool of straw coloured sticky stuff, rather like a prune floating in a sac of golden syrup. Normally you stick a needle into this big old bag and suck out the liquid. Just make sure

> "...tea, coke and coffee will make you want to urinate more often, so avoid those drinks before a dive. Just stick to water."

the doc doesn't miss and put it into your nad.

A varicocoele is a varicose vein around your tessies. You know you have one if the ladies complain of feeling worms around your nuts when your first date gets to the hotter phase. There's only one thing to do here. Op and snip the little vessels out. You've got to do this as they can raise the temperature of your plum and cause your sperm to die in a hot sweat, rendering you infertile.

Can you dive? Very much so. Give it four weeks post op as they may still be painful, and we all know what a dry suit squeeze can do for the pitch of a diver's voice. But once healed, dive on, and never tell anyone what you had.

I have been suffering with renal colic and last week the specialists finally found a stone just below my left kidney. During an operation to remove it, they found they didn't have a scope with a long enough reach and put a 'double J Stent' in instead. As far as I'm aware, it links my kidney to my bladder to allow the kidney to drain.

I'm getting married in three weeks time, and my best man has organised a diving stag party in Weymouth next weekend. As the dives should be quite shallow, will I be able to participate or should I sit them out? I have been given Voltarol 50mg tablets to control the discomfort at the moment, but I only have them for another two days.

"I can see 10 bleary eyed divers, still pissed from the night before, as hydrated as a Bedouin's mouth, merrily vomming into their regs at the first sign of a swell."

Phew, you're a brave man. A diving stagfest. We'll prepare the chamber immediately. I can see 10 bleary eyed divers, still pissed from the night before, as hydrated as a Bedouin's mouth, merrily vomming into their regs at the first sign of a swell.

The kidney stone and stent will be the least of your problems; just make sure you drink plenty of water to keep everything flushed through. If the stone is still there, then there is a risk that it can move a bit more, causing a lot more pain. I am surprised you were not offered 'lithotripsy'. That's where they can ultrasonically vibrate your stone to pieces, rather like an opera soprano and a wine glass. If they haven't referred you for that, I suppose you could add it to your wedding list.

If you are still on the Voltarol at the time, then once again that is allowable with diving. So, good luck, brave groom, and one last tip. Don't bother bringing your weight belt. You're going to be handcuffed to a Mondeo anyway.

I have just been diagnosed with prostate cancer and radical surgery is advised within four to six weeks. Can I dive in the meantime? I am asymptomatic. Also, will I be able to dive after the op?

Poor you. I hope it all works out. If you are asymptomatic, no metastases to the bone or local invasion to important vessels, and you feel well enough then diving is no problem. Once it's been removed and you have been given the all clear, give it a few weeks and diving should be fine then too.

Point to note here: thank medical science for progress. In the old days one of the cures for prostate cancer was orchidectomy. That's castration to you and me. Ouch.

CENTRAL NERVOUS SYSTEM

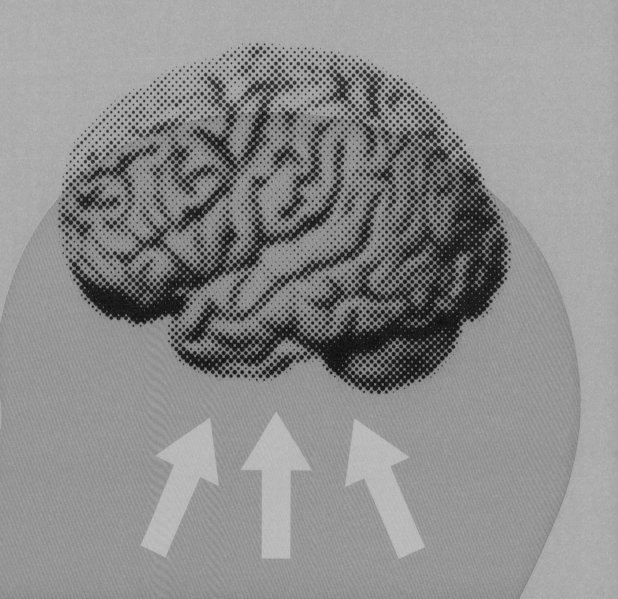

INTRO

Back when I was administrating pensions and contemplating suicide every day, I was docked a day's wage for taking a day off and claiming I had a headache, rather than a migraine. The thing is, I'd heard about how debilitating migraines are and I didn't want to tempt fate. In much the same way, a month later I took two weeks off on the grounds that I didn't want to come in, rather than risking poetic justice by claiming to be depressed or dead or something. I got sacked for that, which actually cheered me up no end.

So, you'll notice from this chapter that a central nervous system is useful for being able to move and feel things. Unfortunately, sometimes it mutinies on you and makes you fall over or puts you through agony just for its own amusement. When you're 16, it makes you shake so uncontrollably that you can't sign a nightclub membership card in front of the person who's just given it to you after you've shown them a fake ID. Then all your friends use their central nervous systems to laugh at you.

Tip: If you don't have one, you can't dive.

I can reliably inform you that having a functioning brain and set of nerves is excellent for playing Nintendo and confusing with alcohol, but useless for administrating pensions (which is what we have robots for; that and coming from the future to terminate people) and not always much help in coming up with reasons for skiving off work.

Mind you, René Descartes spent a lot of time worrying whether we were plugged into The Matrix or, in the language of his day, whether everything we perceive with the central nervous system is nothing other than our senses being deceived by a malevolent demon.

It's not possible to prove the idea wrong, so you might as well just take the demon diving instead.

MIGRAINES

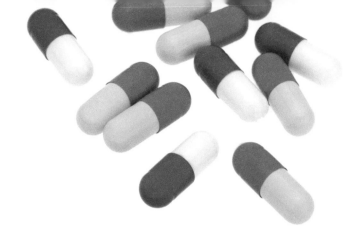

I am 49 years of age; male, non-smoker and teetotal. I have had a recent diving medical exam and was passed fit to dive. I swim train four times a week and go to the gym three times a week. My BP (at the last reading) is 125/76; pulse 56 at rest; weight 85kg; height 5'10".

I am a certified NAUI diver up to level Advanced Diver and have completed Assistant Instructor, but that certification has lapsed. I want to re-enter Scuba diving and have joined the local **BSAC** club with a view to starting again at the beginning so that I can be sure a) I am fit and capable, and b) that I am not missing out on any developments over the intervening years of non-diving.

Seven years ago, I had two or three minor migraine attacks over a two week period. Cause unknown, but probably work/stress related. These attacks were minor in that there was no headache or spatial disorientation. The most severe symptom was pinwheel vision which cleared if I sat still with eyes shut for ten minutes or so. Since then, I have had no recurrence at all. Prior to that, I had one migraine attack as described above while in the Army in 1970.

Would you consider me precluded from Scuba diving because of migraine?

> "Seven years ago, I had two or three minor migraine attacks over a two week period. Cause unknown, but probably work or stress related."

No booz, no tabs. Exercise seven times a week. A blood pressure a Kenyan 1,500m athlete would be proud of. But you've had a couple of migraines in the past, so are you fit to dive?

Well I think it's a huge YES for you. You are probably the fittest bloke who ever took to the water, but sadly a victim of inflexible medical declaration forms. There is a point to not diving with migraines. If you have recurrent attacks and are at risk of having one on a dive then it may well be better that you don't go underwater. A throbbing headache, visual auras and paralysis are some of the consequences of this problem when it is severe. And getting this will risk a diver's life if they are down in the deep. But yours are mild and haven't been back for many years. So I think you can declare yourself as fit to dive and well done on the health standards you set yourself. You put most of us other divers to shame.

A final point though for anyone with severe migraines. There is still a chance you can dive but you will need to discuss with an experienced diving doctor all the factors that trigger them. Also, what treatment you are taking and what problems you actually get. Anything that can occur underwater and risk you and your buddy sadly may well end in a ban until an effective treatment can guarantee they won't occur on a dive. Some people who get migraines get an aura (their migraine is preceded or accompanied by a variety of sensory warning signs or symptoms, such as flashes of light, blind spots or tingling in the hands or face). This can mean they have a PFO, which could raise their risk of DCI, so anyone in this category needs checking out by a dive doc before they dive.

About four years ago I completed a normal profile dive and within an hour I experienced visual disturbances, with flashing lights and opaque sections of vision. At the time I was put on oxygen and after about 30 minutes my sight was fine. I suffered no other symptoms. After a couple of days I resumed diving with no problems.

However (and four years later), on a plane journey yesterday I was sitting at the front of the aircraft right next to the main door. On ascent, I experienced very similar visual disturbances; this time very specific, with arcs and triangles of red and yellow. Clearly this worried me, but it stopped about 25 minutes into the flight. My colleague said it was the first flight where he had experienced a very marked change in pressure. Although the episode passed I would like to know if the two incidents (although years apart, and I have flown many times since) are related, and if you have any advice to give me.

They could well be related, but there are a few possible causes for these episodes. In the first case this could have been a symptom of DCI as it responded so well to oxygen. In the second, although cases of overt cabin depressurisation are unusual, a similar DCI could happen...

"About four years ago I completed a normal profile dive and within an hour I experienced visual disturbances, with flashing lights and opaque sections of vision."

But there are a variety of other possible explanations. Migraine with visual symptoms is not uncommon and doesn't always give you a headache. Your arcs, triangles and flashing lights do fit the criteria for migraine with aura, and migraine is often under- or misdiagnosed. Your GP might be able to help if you are getting more episodes. Occasionally, floaters and flashing lights can signify an imminent retinal tear or detachment, so a visit to the optician should be top of your list as if caught early these conditions can be treated. There are a few weird and wonderful neurological problems that can present with visual hallucinations but most are rare. Importantly though, if it occurs again after a dive, then get some oxygen and call your nearest chamber.

FITS

I am a student just starting my second year in a Marine Biology/ Zoology course in North Wales. Although diving is not an essential part of my course it would be very helpful to learn, and I could then join in various excursions and activities with the sub-aqua club.

The problem is that a while back, I was diagnosed with having epilepsy. The fits have been occurring since I was five but there was a long break of about 12 years in between. I am now on lamotrigine, 150mg/day. The fits are described as 'petit-mal', so are not violent and only last about one minute.

Am I allowed to dive? My last fit was recent but due to an operation on my knee.

I'm surprised that diving is not essential to being a Marine Biologist. It's rather like a doctor never seeing a patient in their normal environment. Hang on, that's the District Nurse's job isn't it? Maybe you have a point. I must also say that I envy you your course. If I hadn't managed to get into Med School then Marine Biology at Bangor was my calling and sometimes when faced with a case of anal itching first thing in the morning, I dream and regret not being able to study dolphins in the Bahamas and calling it a job.

And now for the bad news, I'm afraid. Diving is a non starter for you. Epilepsy, whether petit mal, grand mal or any other of the varieties that can occur is absolutely forbidden for anyone who wants to dive and there are no exceptions. The reason is obvious: a fit underwater will be fatal and not just endanger your life but also your buddy's as well.

Petit mal is an odd sort of epilepsy as it is characterised by so called 'absence seizures'. These appear unannounced and the sufferer will suddenly go blank, stop moving and not be responsive to any stimuli for a short while. You say yours are only for a minute, but

"A fit underwater will be fatal and not just endanger your life but also your buddy's as well."

a minute is long enough for the regulator to drift out of your mouth and for you to lose your buoyancy and your buddy. Missing diver would be the result.

On top of this is the fact that anti-epileptic medication can bring on narcosis at a very shallow depth too, and is banned for a diver. I suppose it's possible that the use of Nitrox might lessen this, but there is a bigger issue to consider: no one knows how the drug's metabolism is affected by depth and pressure. Metabolism of medication is normally a consequence of either kidney or liver function, or blood flow to these organs. These organs will break the drug down and excrete it at a normal rate giving a drug what we call a 'half life'. This is different for different drugs; hence you take some drugs twice daily and some four times. Now, when you go diving, blood flow is affected to different organs, and the metabolism of certain drugs can be increased. If this were to happen with antiepileptic medication, the consequences would be disastrous as the medication may wear off underwater with a fit ensuing. Now, this has not been researched because of ethical issues but also because there is little point: no one would be allowed to dive on these tablets, since taking them is an admission that there is still a risk of fitting.

There may be hope there on the horizon, but nothing that can get you underwater before you finish your course of meds. If you stay fit free and off medication for five years it is deemed that you are at a low enough risk of another fit that you can then learn to dive. As to when you come off the medication, this is a decision only your neurologist can make for you. So it's no-go for now but maybe in the future when you have finally paid off your student loans you'll be in a position to get back into debt by taking up diving.

I have had no medical problems while diving, however one evening on a recent holiday I fainted and had what looked like convulsions. As I had not been in the water for two days, I don't think it was caused by diving. I had CT scans at the hospital in Egypt and epilepsy was ruled out. The diagnosis was convulsions brought on by hyperventilation, although low potassium levels may have also contributed to the initial faint.

Am I still fit to dive?

We need to look into this more closely with you. Firstly, as epilepsy is a massive diagnosis to give a diver, it's an automatic ban on

"You say yours are only for a minute, but a minute is long enough for the regulator to drift out of your mouth and for you to lose your buoyancy and your buddy. Missing diver would be the result."

diving. Yes, the CT was normal, but CT scans can't always rule out epilepsy. An EEG (electroencephalogram) would be useful too, along with your previous history of fits or faints.

Secondly, untrained eyes looking at a 'convulsion', can get it wrong. A tonic-clonic epileptic fit is a specific thing. An occasional twitch in a fainter can look bad, but not be epilepsy. We need to explore this.

WHY is diving with carbamazepine barred? WHAT sort of problems can it cause under pressure eg increased narcoses, susceptibility to DCI etc.? Is there any epilepsy medication that is less likely to cause problems? I want to make an informed decision.

Serious stuff this. The original question was the old epilepsy and diving one. The usual response from me of "five years fit free and off all medication before you go" brought this response. So why is this rule in place?

To tell the truth I find it a bit rigid as well. Yes, there is a risk of getting narcosis at shallow depths, but, so what? We all get narked and continue to dive merrily without risk to life and limb. There are thoughts about increased turnover of antiepileptic medication under pressure of depth. This may lower the bioavailability of your meds and hence bring on a fit. But no one really knows for sure, hence the rules.

Personally I would like to see a trial of some of the newer meds with Nitrox to see if it's really as bad as they predict. But once again, the researchability of this is difficult. Ever made a goat epileptic, stuck it full of lamotrigine and tried to tie a mask to its face in a chamber? No, nor have I. So you see the difficulties. When it comes to epilepsy I often have to say, if you want to get buzzing and wet, try rafting down the Nile. If the crocs don't get you, the hippos will.

"When it comes to epilepsy I often have to say, if you want to get buzzing and wet, try rafting down the Nile. If the crocs don't get you, the hippos will."

Would a single seizure two years ago preclude, in itself, a HSE medical for Scuba diving? It was a one-off seizure. An MRI scan showed nothing unusual, no medication was prescribed and I was told by the neurologist that it was not epilepsy.

Then what was it? The HSE medical does need us docs to be very accurate about past medical history. A seizure is a serious thing, and yes, the rules for sport divers are that you have to be fit free and off all meds for five whole, long years before diving again. The HSE are tighter. Any history of epilepsy will bar you from being a commercial diver. Now, as it is not epilepsy in your case, there may be some flexibility, but we do need to know what they thought it was.

So this means a chat with the neurological team, and a clear cut diagnosis. Stress, hypertension, coming off illicit drugs. That sort of thing. Then we can go from there.

NERVES

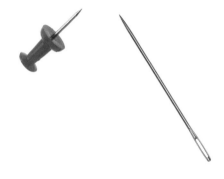

I just spent the weekend attending the PADI Open Water Referral Course, but unfortunately did not complete the full set of confined dives.

While underwater, I experienced a strange pins and needles sensation in my finger tips, on the outer sides of my hands, and on my lower arms. I sometimes have a swollen feeling in my fingers when I am out running and mentioned this to my instructor. He felt it would be a good idea to mail you for advice before continuing with my confined dives, and eventually the open water ones. While the pins and needles feeling subsided a short while after I left the pool, and though this may not be anything to worry about, I just wanted to double check to be sure.

You should be fine. For starters, this has nothing to do with nitrogen, bends or whatever. DCS does not come on under water and go when you get to the surface. With tingling, pins and needles, or paraesthesia as we docs call it to seem intelligent, it might have more to do with the nerves in your arm. A BCD can cut up into your armpits, crunching a nerve and cause these symptoms. Over breathing due to anxiety can also cause these symptoms. So can a borrowed wetsuit tight around certain body parts.

I don't know what's going on with your hands when you jog. Perhaps God's punishment for being so fit. A herring with a pinkish tint methinks.

So, don't worry, get back in the water, get a loose BCD, custom wettie and if it does continue, go see a neurologist.

I have been on long-term sick leave with post viral fatigue and trigeminal neuralgia. With the fatigue syndrome, I sometimes feel perfectly OK but some days I feel totally drained; sleeping for periods varying between four and forty hours. There is no way of predicting when the good or bad days are going to come, but they are each unmistakable.

With the neuralgia, I have a permanent numbness on the right side of my skull. I also experience various aches and pains in the right side of my face, jaw, neck and shoulder, which mainly occur in the morning. I occasionally take Diclofenac to ease the pain.

As a 54 year-old safety-conscious diver, I would appreciate your opinion whether there is any reason why I should not carry on with my beloved hobby.

Your diagnosis of post viral fatigue syndrome is not a bar to diving in itself but there are a few issues surrounding the problem that you should be aware of. When you get your phases of extreme tiredness, you can see the problems that would ensue if you were to dive. You may well be in a situation where your buddy needs your physical assistance, so if you were too weak to help this could be disastrous. You say you cannot predict when the bad days are going to be, so if the fatigue sets in on one of these days you'll have to cancel any planned diving.

Other issues are brought up with your problem of trigeminal neuralgia. This is a condition where the trigeminal nerve, which supplies the sensation to large parts of the face, can cause extreme pain to the area where it causes sensation. The fact that you have numbness there makes me suspect a different diagnosis and it would be a good idea to see a neurologist to confirm that it is what you think it is.

You also have a range of other symptoms in your shoulder and jaw, and what I always suggest is that you see a diving doctor in your area to get a good map of the numbness and where exactly the aches are. The reason for this is that if you ever had a problem on a dive that could cause a bend, such as an uncontrolled ascent, then your pre-existing problems could easily be construed as the signs of decompression sickness. But if you were to be able to tell the examining doctor what you had before, then this wouldn't be mistaken for an episode of neurological DCS.

The other point is that many dive centres all over the world will make you fill in the Health Declaration Form before they let you dive with them. You are obviously going to have to tick the Yes box to a few of the questions, and it is always easier to have a Fit to Dive Certificate with you then as they are well within their rights to ask you to see a local doctor, who may be hard to track down, to pass you as fit if you don't have this certification.

Finally, one of the treatments that is often offered to people with trigeminal neuralgia is a drug called carbamazepine, but this medication cannot be taken if you want to stay diving as it can cause narcosis at far shallower depths than usual (even deco stop depth), so stay with a simpler pain killer.

I have a friend due to travel to Cyprus soon and she has every intention of learning to dive whilst there. About six weeks ago she contracted Bell's Palsy. There has to date been no real improvement although she is fine in herself. Should she continue with her plans or shelve them until there is either a full or significant improvement in the condition?

The implications I can think of are the fact that her left eye will not close at the moment and she is obviously now a bit 'saggy' around her mouth.

Imagine waking up one morning, tottering downstairs for that half asleep bowl of cereal, and the milk won't stay in – it keeps pouring out of your mouth. Something similar happened to George Clooney when he was a boy, and an astute physician diagnosed him with Bell's Palsy. It was during his first year in high school too: not a good time to have half of your face paralysed, although it doesn't seem to have done his career much harm.

Named after Charles Bell, the Scot who first described it, this is a peculiar disease of a single nerve (the facial nerve) which controls the muscles of facial expression. Only one side of the face is affected, so sufferers develop a sort of Billy Idol sneer when they smile, and cannot wrinkle one side of their forehead when they frown. It's most often impossible to find a cause, although some cases occur after shingles and it is more common during pregnancy. Interestingly, there are some cases that have been caused by diving; air expanding in the middle ear on ascent can exert pressure on the facial nerve (which passes close by), causing a reversible Bell's Palsy, much like the temporary pins and needles you get when you bang your inaptly named 'funny bone'. There is no reliable treatment, but most cases resolve on their own in two to three weeks, and almost all within a few months.

"Imagine waking up one morning, tottering downstairs for that half asleep bowl of cereal, and the milk won't stay in – it keeps pouring out of your mouth."

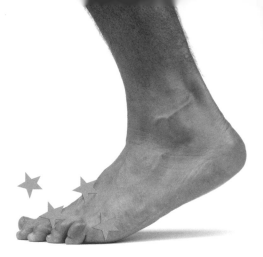

As far as your friend's diving goes, the implications are several: the ones you mention are significant, in that an eye that does not shut properly is susceptible to injury or infection if her mask comes off. Trying to hold a regulator in a saggy mouth is a bit haphazard also, and might expose her to an increased risk of salt water inhalation or free flows. The chances of diving depend on the severity of the symptoms, so she would be best off being assessed by a dive doc. I suggest it would be better to wait until all the symptoms have cleared up before learning to dive.

I was diagnosed some time ago with Peripheral Neuropathy (PN) which was mild then but has increased in severity over the years. Luckily, I only have problems with my toes/feet, eg numbness, pins and needles, burning sensations, occasional cramps; all the usual PN stuff. I am on no medication for this but take Lansoprazole (15mg) for Barrett's Oesophagus. Otherwise I am reasonably fit for my age (63) and engage in 30 minutes of fairly testing cross-country machine training five times a week.

Do you perceive any problems related to recreational diving with PN?

Not really with the peripheral neuropathy. This illness, where nerves in the periphery stop doing what they are supposed to do, can be a real pain, as I am sure you know. But the deal with diving is that as long as you have sufficient strength there to fin, haul out a buddy, and get back on the boat, then it should be OK. It is worth seeing a dive doc to get passed as fit, as well as getting a neurological mapping of your deficit. Numbness and pins and needles are classic bends symptoms, so you need to have a good idea of what's going on baseline, as it could save five or six hours in a chamber if you had a problematic ascent and an overzealous doctor.

The Barrett's though is an issue. This is caused by hyperacidity in the oesophagus, and needs the antacids to prevent pain and burning. As long as it does not affect your diving, causing reflux or pain when you are horizontal, then cool. If you are a gastric belchy sort of diver then there could be a risk of an acid vomit, so get that all checked out when the doc is stroking your tootsies with cotton wool before jabbing a pin into the big toe.

At the beginning of December last year I fell through a glass window and severed the main artery and median nerve in

"Luckily, I only have problems with my toes/feet, eg numbness, pins and needles, burning sensations, occasional cramps…"

"…get that all checked out when the doc is stroking your tootsies with cotton wool before jabbing a pin into the big toe."

my left upper arm. The scars have healed and my strength is coming back, however my hand is still numb and I am only able to move the base joints in my thumb and index finger due to the severed nerve. I have been told that the nerve will have to fully grow back before all the symptoms disappear. My self-declaration is due at the beginning of May. Will I need to have a medical?

In these sorts of cases, it's not so much the injury but the level of recovery, and how it specifically relates to diving and your responsibilities as a good buddy.

My first thought concerns your trigger finger and your inflator hose. It is also the hand you may need to grab your buddy's occy if you have an out of air situation. Likewise, if you are having to lift a diver up from the deep and keep their reg in their mouth, you are going to need both hands functioning. From this logic, I would say wait until the power has increased in these digits. Work on the physiotherapy to get full power and function too.

When it is strong enough to do all the above, you may have a bit of sensation loss still. Get this mapped by a dive doctor, as you don't want it to be mistaken for a cardinal sign of a bend if ever you have a rapid ascent.

OTHER

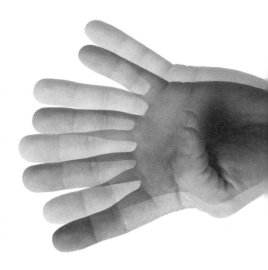

I have a problem with feeling somewhat disorientated and dizzy (as though the boat is still moving) after spending three to four days on a dive boat. Usually this clears up with Stemetil, but I'm not sure if it's that which is curing it or whether it's just settling by itself.

I am due to go to Sharm for Christmas and whilst this feeling does not interfere with my diving at all, and I have a totally clean bill of health, I am loath for it to spoil our leisure time there. My doctor has prescribed more Stemetil for this trip. Could I take it as a preventative measure, or is this just something I will have to get used to?

Poor you! I've only had this once or twice and it's really irritating after coming off a boat. People look at you swaying and whisper about alcohol and problems. Stemetil, or prochlorperazine is OK to take for this though. Unlike other medications which can be used for dizziness like the antihistamines, it is less likely to cause drowsiness. A 5mg tablet is the standard strength, and it can be taken two to three times a day. However, as you don't seem to get the problem on the boat itself, it may be wiser not to take it for the beginning of the liveaboard. Then, as shore approaches towards the end, start taking it the day before you disembark. It should kick in to stop you feeling so swayey when you get your feet on the ground.

"It's really irritating after coming off a boat. People look at you swaying and whisper about alcohol and problems."

I am planning on doing my Open Water Course, but am a little concerned because I've suffered from hydrocephalus since birth and was 10 weeks premature. This means that I am shunted to enable the fluid to drain from my brain.

At first I had two shunts, but now I only have one. In 1996, my shunt was revised twice due to age of the mechanics and (touch wood) I do not have any troubles at present, although I have yearly out-patient visits to my consultant. Otherwise, I live a normal life, bar participating in rugby, kick boxing and pub brawls. If you would be able to shed any light on the safety of Scuba diving with my condition I would appreciate it.

That's what I like to hear. Good old British pastimes. They can take away the fox hunting, but they can't stop us fighting in pubs. Get tooled up with your PADI card. I assume your shunt goes into your abdomen. The high pressure cerebrospinal fluid has to be taken away from your brain as it can't go the normal route out. The tube takes it safely into your tummy cavity, and as there's no air involved, all is not compressible at depth. So all's OK, just get a fit to dive cert first.

About four years ago, I had a brain scan after my ophthalmologist noticed I had nystagmus on a routine eye test (nystagmus is a repetitive involuntary oscillation of the eyes, like watching a lengthy Federer-Nadal tennis rally without moving your head). The scan showed up Arnold Chiari malformation, Type I. I have no other symptoms and was told by a neurologist that I could carry on diving, however I am concerned about the pressures on the body and would greatly appreciate your opinion as I would not like to make the situation worse.

To tell you the truth, I have never come across this in a diver before and having extensively searched the diving literature, it seems no one else has either. As always, an anatomy lesson for starters. In those human beings lucky enough to possess one, the brain sits happily in the skull, linked to the spinal cord which traverses the whole length of the vertebral column (backbone). The aperture in the skull through which the spinal cord passes is called the foramen magnum (Latin for 'ice cream' 'big hole'). At this junction there is a chunk of brain called the cerebellum, which deals with co-ordination of various senses and motor control. It's this portion we're testing when we do all those 'standing on one leg with your eyes shut' manoeuvres in dive medicals. Arnold and Chiari were both German pathologists who independently noted cases where a part of the cerebellum had protruded ('herniated') through the foramen magnum, sometimes with other abnormalities such as spina bifida. This herniation can block the flow of blood and the cerebrospinal fluid that bathes and protects the spinal cord, resulting in a variety of symptoms; dizziness, odd eye movements (such as your nystagmus), muscle weakness, numbness, headache, and problems with co-ordination and balance. Basically, a checklist of DCI symptoms. There are several types of Arnold Chiari malformation, with Type I luckily being the most benign.

"It's this portion we're testing when we do all those 'standing on one leg with your eyes shut' manoeuvres in dive medicals."

Here are some musings regarding diving. Firstly, there is the perennial problem of diagnostic confusion, as the symptoms of the malformation can be so similar to those of DCI. Secondly, and more seriously, if you were to suffer a case of cerebral decompression illness then it is possible that some herniation of the lower parts of the brain could occur through the malformation, which could be fatal. How likely this is is anyone's guess, but it's the severity of this consequence that leads me to the conclusion that it is probably too risky for you to dive safely. I would have no problem with you snorkelling, but without any other evidence it's the only safe recommendation I can make.

I would like to go diving in the coming August as part of my summer holiday. Unfortunately, I was diagnosed with a low grade glioma (brain tumour) last year having had a seizure whilst asleep. I have since had the tumour removed and have not had any more seizures.

I sent a mail to the diving club at the resort I will be staying in and they said I need to get confirmation from a diving doctor before I can dive. What do you think?

Firstly a random tangent on glue-sniffing (all will become clear). The pronouncements of the oracle at Delphi, which had profound influence on much of ancient Greek life, were not so much prophetic visions as the ramblings of minds made euphoric by glue. This bombshell was suggested by geologists recently when they discovered that the original site of the Delphic temple sits above two fault lines, through which high levels of methane, ethane and ethylene suffused. Whether this led to the coining of 'glia' as the Greek word for 'glue' I don't know. Glia these days refers to support cells in the brain and spinal cord, the 'glue of the nervous system', which provide nutrition and insulation for nerves, and remove dead ones after a big night out. A glioma is a tumour of these cells, which can be very slow-growing, or quite aggressive. Symptoms of a glioma depend on where the tumour is: in the brain they cause headaches, seizures and vomiting; in the optic nerves, visual loss; in the spinal cord, pain, weakness, or numbness in the extremities. Treatment is often a combination of surgery, radio and chemotherapy.

So to the question: fit to dive? The brain is enclosed in a decent hard case, so pressure will not normally affect the structures inside. Surgical approaches to tumour removal can have diving implications though. Boring through the skull will render that area more susceptible to external pressure and possibly infection. The

"The pronouncements of the oracle at Delphi, which had profound influence on much of ancient Greek life, were not so much prophetic visions as the ramblings of minds made euphoric by glue."

eye-watering nasal approach to some pituitary gliomas can impair sinus function and increase future barotrauma risk. Sometimes the treatments can result in loss of neurological function, so you would need to be assessed in person for this. If your single seizure was due to the glioma which has now been dealt with, then you are at no further risk of another. Provided you are not taking anticonvulsants and all else is well, I suspect you'll be found fit to dive.

I have never dived before, but would very much like to during my upcoming trip to the Maldives. Unfortunately, I developed vertigo a few years ago after being on a small boat in Barbados; I was never sick only slightly nauseous, however the feeling of swaying stayed with me for a few days after the trip. By the time I reached the UK, I was experiencing such severe spinning and dizziness that I was unable to drive. It persisted for nearly six weeks before I returned to normal.

Last time I went to the Maldives it happened again, thankfully it was very mild and lasted no more than three days. It probably helped that I refrained from snorkelling and generally tried to rest. However, later that year, I again returned to the UK from Egypt with severe vertigo that lasted around five to six weeks in total. I was signed off work for two of those weeks because I wasn't even able to sit at my computer.

I'm a 27 year-old female who leads a normal active life. Since the first episode I have cut out unnecessary salts and high fatty foods from my diet and I barely drink alcohol and never fizzy drinks or coffee and tea. I'm currently training for the Edinburgh marathon this year, so in general my fitness is good.

The doctor examined my ears thoroughly the first and second time I had the vertigo, and could find no perforated ear drum or obvious reason for the symptoms. He gave me some eye exercises to follow. After the third occasion he prescribed me four different types of medication, but there was little or no improvement and as with the first episode it seemed to eventually dissipate by itself.

Can you help?

Phewee, let me get this right. You've never dived, but you have been on a boat on two occasions. You don't say whether you did in Egypt, so it could be three. And each time you get vertigo lasting from three days to six weeks. And I assume it never happens after, say, car journeys or a Waltzer, which you must have done. And the drugs don't work, thank you The Verve, with normal ears too. And you wanna go diving. Something where boats come in handy on rough, wavy seas.

Sometimes you get a medical feeling that as many tests you do, as many opinions as you get, there will never be an answer. So let me suggest this: go for the open water course and see how the pool work affects any vertigo. If there's none then go for the next stage. Shore dive, calm sea entry for your four cert dives, eg Jordan. If all's OK, then either stick to this for diving or try slowly going onto boat diving in ultra-flat seas. At any point if you get vertigo in these easy conditions, then sadly forget it. Choose a safe leisure pursuit that won't involve brain operations or wavy seas.

I guess that rules out 'Dynamite Surfing'. Anyone for Ninja Cribbage?

"Sometimes you get a medical feeling that as many tests you do, as many opinions as you get, there will never be an answer."

TRAUMA, SURGERY, ORTHOPAEDIC AND DENTAL PROBLEMS

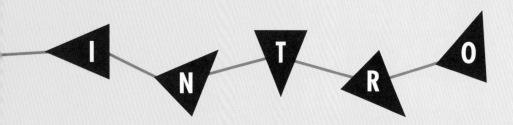

INTRO

One of the best things about bodies is that when you gouge, separate, or smash bits of them, or expose parts that should otherwise remain concealed (not like that, you at the back), they have this incredible ability to repair themselves. Providing you survive the initial incident. It is truly amazing and is a shoo-in, year after year, for a top ten place in the best things that bodies can do.

You can't grow limbs back though, generally speaking. Not if you're a mammal. Dr Curt Connors tried doing it with reptilian DNA but now he keeps turning into a lizard, which means he keeps getting kicked-in by Spiderman. Another clear warning to us all, as if any were needed, of the dangers of science.

As a species, we probably live a bit too long nowadays (although it's probably preferable to the alternative: I'll be honest with you, I don't know, I've yet to try it), which means that bits of us get worn down. Inexplicably, there's no consumer-friendly store of replacement parts to be found, not even on the whirlynet (except in urban myths about organ thieves), which is an unintelligent design flaw if ever I heard one. To be fair though, by day six it was technically the weekend and so God was probably fairly keen to get finished up and go and watch the football. I do hope it was a good match because this chapter also deals with dental issues and wisdom teeth are rubbish.

Fear not though, because the news just in is that many of these worn out knees and so forth can be replaced by bits of metal and plastic and whatnot. Probably best not to try replacing them yourself, though, if you want to be able to dive again afterwards.

Tip: Whilst being sawn in half is excellent fun, it is a procedure that should only be performed by a qualified magician, and doctors recommend that Scuba diving should only be undertaken by those whose bodies forms one contiguous unit.

JOINTS

I need to book my first HSE medical but have badly damaged knee joints caused by cartilage removal over 20 years ago. My colleagues tell me that part of the medical involves climbing steps and I am very concerned that I won't be able to do this (sometimes, if I'm feeling unstable, I have to lean on banisters to support myself whilst going upstairs). Is it possible for me to exercise some way other than putting a strain on my knees?

Ooh, I can think of plenty of different exercises to get the heart rate up, that won't mess up your knees any further. As long as the heart rate gets to the max predicted and comes down to normal when it should, then I don't really care if you do headstands, ride a bike, or press-ups like a Latino lover who has been told he has a week to live.

A word of caution though: if your knees do stop you from finning properly, or dragging a bent diver out of the water, then think carefully about DMing, as you are the support man for the trainees around you.

I would be grateful for any information you could give me about the effects and recommendations of diving on the drug naproxen. I take two 250mg tablets daily and have done so for a couple of years. I very rarely take any other medication with them other than beer.

OK, hands up anyone who wouldn't value a doctor who can get away with prescribing beer as a medication. Mothers used to be offered a choice of a bottle of Guinness or Mackesons every day that they were in the maternity wards in the late 1950's, and in return "Guinness is good for you" was their advertising slogan for years. Sadly it's not being funded by the NHS anymore. Naproxen, on the other hand, is. It's a variant on the anti-inflammatory theme, particularly good for mild pains, stiffness in the joints and for menstrual cramps or painful periods. It's probably not a good idea

"I take two 250mg tablets daily and have done so for a couple of years. I very rarely take any other medication with them other than beer."

to take the two together: beer and anti-inflammatories are a perfect recipe for creating stomach ulcers, or at least some good-going gut erosions. The good news is that if you have no side effects, then naproxen (and all other anti-inflammatories) are safe to dive with. The bad is that beer isn't; apart from the obligatory post-dive cold ones, obviously.

I fractured my wrist four months ago, My consultant has said it is fine for me to dive once I feel that my wrist is strong enough (which it is now) although I do have a steel plate in my wrist which is compressing the median nerve & causing light numbness in three of my fingers. Can I start diving?

You sure can.

As you say you have full power and ability in the hand. So you can use it to dump, fiddle with a loose weight belt, and do that fine finger co-ordination needed to pull the last of the snot from your nose after a dive.

Make a note of the sensation loss in the hand, and if ever you end up having a rapid ascent then tell the dive doc you had it anyway as it is a classic bend symptom. You don't want five or six unnecessary hours in a pot due to an overenthusiastic diagnosis.

I had a pneumothorax as the result of a fractured rib two years ago, which I am now fully recovered from. At the same time, I also had a seizure due to head trauma, which occurred whilst unconscious. I have had none since, take no medication and have been declared medically fit to drive. Finally, I sustained some fractures in my pelvis and upper left arm. Both have healed and I have no problems. Can I dive?

There are three issues here to deal with. As your punctured lung or pneumothorax was as a result of injury, rather than being spontaneous, it is more likely that you will be fit enough to dive. You still need to have your chest examined by a qualified diving physician, and our regulations also call for a CT scan of your chest to make sure that all is well now before we can recommend you dive again.

Your seizure is less of a problem. In normal cases of head injury the length of any amnesia or presence of a seizure will decide the lay off from diving time. You have been fine for the last two years with

"As you say you have full power and ability in the hand. So you can use it to dump, fiddle with a loose weight belt, and do that fine finger co-ordination needed to pull the last of the snot from your nose after a dive."

no problems, so I think that this should be OK.

Finally, the fractures you sustained are of relevance only if they stop you from kitting up on a RIB, or mean that you would not be able to look after your buddy if they had a problem. The other thing to have checked by your diving doc is if there are any residual problems left by the injury which could be mistaken for a bend. By this I mean areas of numbness or joint pain in your pelvis or upper left arm. It's best to have these documented now, so you are not incorrectly diagnosed as bent in the future.

I am an experienced diver who had a double arthroscopy operation last year. I am considering booking in to do a 50m dry dive in the chamber. Will this be OK?

You'll be fine. An arthroscopy is fairly weedy in the scale of ops you can have in our fine hospitals and is more investigative rather than operative. A little nick, and then a steel rod into your knee, so the orthopaedic surgeon can have a gander at your cruciates and menisci. It causes little damage, so a dry pot dive is fine.

It is worth noting here that damage and scarring to areas of your body won't necessarily invoke a bend at depth. True, they may off-gas slower, but they on-gas more slowly too.

I have Kienbock's Disease and was concerned about increased chances of DCS when diving. Also, in the past I dislocated a knee, which chipped bone from underneath it, and chipped a piece of bone off an ankle, which healed but the chipped bit has healed away from where it should be. Both these have been fine since, but I just wanted to check I'm OK to dive.

Another issue, another eponym... Kienbock was an Austrian radiologist who first described the breakdown of the lunate, a moon-shaped bone in the wrist. The precise cause is unknown, but it's rare and most likely a complication of trauma. The initial injury can be innocuous (even a mild sprain can lead to so-called 'avascular necrosis', where the bone dies as its blood supply is interrupted). Pain, stiffness and swelling are the most common symptoms, which eventually start interfering with manual dexterity. At this point surgeons generally intervene, although quite how is controversial (surgeons in my experience don't agree on much).

There is some anecdotal evidence that DCI occurs more often in previously damaged or scarred tissue, but there is no scientific data to back this up that I am aware of. So as long as the Kienbock's does not impair you functionally at all (in terms of the use of your hand), I'd say you could dive safely with it. Similarly, this would be the case with the ankle chip and the knee: if you've had no problems in the recent past, then finning should not cause a further dislocation.

I recently suffered a grade three shoulder separation which was operated on.

They drilled holes in my collar bone and used something like tape to wrap it around my scapula to hold it in place. They had to harvest ligaments. Will my shoulder be able to stand the water pressures of Scuba diving?

When you dive, pressure only affects and compresses air spaces. Middle ears, sinuses, those sort of things. Because shoulders are made of bone, muscle and tendons, the pressure effects will be fine.

My only concern is with what function you are left with after the op. You must be able to move your arm easily, especially if it is your left. Wrist dumps on a drysuit and inflator hoses on a BCD all need good free left arm movement. If the surgery has limited this then you may need to review your gear. Only you know this, and only physiotherapy can help.

"My only concern is with what function you are left with after the op. You must be able to move your arm easily, especially if it is your left."

For about two weeks I have had a swelling on the elbow, diagnosed as 'olecranon bursitis' and have been prescribed 600mg Ibuprofen to help reduce the inflammation.

Can I dive?

It's a functional thing. If your elbow is able to bend to do all those divey things, like putting on the kit, launching the SMB, and reaching for the 'up or down button' on your BCD, then go for it. However, if there is pain or gross limitation of movement, forget it.

The elbow joint, where the radius and ulna articulate with the bottom of the humerus, is all held together by a fibrous sac called a bursa. Inflammation here will fill up the sac with fluid and cause this olecranon bursitis. Normally it looks like your elbow has grown an apple in it. That's the fluid. I hope your doc has stuck a needle in and drained some of it out, as that speeds the healing process, but for now stick with the ibuprofen, and wear a tight elastic support stocking-like thing on it to prevent any more fluid build up.

I have just been diagnosed with a ganglion on my wrist (a small lump the size of a one penny piece). It appears that I may have to wait some time for an operation. Is this going to affect my diving at all?

You have absolutely no problem here. A ganglion is a small cystic swelling that occurs in relation to a joint or the sheath that surrounds a tendon. They always seem to occur around the back of the hand or the wrist. They are filled with a jelly like substance called synovial fluid that is similar to the liquid that lubricates our joints. The theory is that they arise from a tear in the tissue that surrounds a joint, which is supported by the fact that they can arise after trauma to an area.

Ganglions are mostly painless but can cause aching in a joint, so I would suggest that you make a good mental note of this and are aware of where the ache is before you dive, so you don't end up on a six hour recompression in a chamber afterwards as the joint pain has been mistaken for a bend. There will be no detrimental pressure effects to it underwater, so don't worry on that count.

A ganglion can be treated by syringing out the fluid, but this is only temporary as they always seem to recur. The best thing is to have the fluid and the wall of the ganglion excised surgically. Sadly, this is low priority in our Health Service and you can often wait for over a year, but once it is done it should never come back.

After all operations you should wait until the wound has healed properly before diving again, but this will be quick after yours as it's done through a very small incision with only a stitch or two which come out after a week. Leave it two weeks to be safe and I hope you can get the op done this side of the next World Cup.

I have recently had both knees totally replaced and will build up the muscles again by walking, exercising and swimming. At what stage will it be safe for me to recommence diving? Will I be more prone to a bend in the knees?

I am 58 years old and overweight, but with no other medical problems.

"Ganglions are mostly painless but can cause aching in a joint, so I would suggest that you make a good mental note of this and are aware of where the ache is before you dive..."

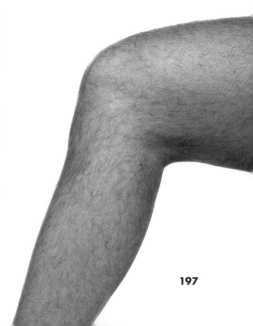

It's a pretty major operation you have had there, but one from which you should make a good recovery and be able to dive again soon. I would say that you need to talk to your orthopaedic surgeon about exactly when you should go back into the water, but as a rough guideline people usually regain full function after eight to ten weeks post operation. I think you should wait this long but you also need to really work on your thigh muscles to get them as fit and strong as possible for proper finning, and I think you should stay well away from strong counter-current dives. It would also be a good idea to get the best set of fins you can, as these will really help you if your knees are weaker than before. Also, try to lose as much weight as you can. Your new knees can only take a certain amount of wear and tear and so the less weight you have going through them, the longer they will last. Besides that, if you are too overweight you shouldn't be diving.

As for whether you are more prone to a bend in the knees: well, as they are now made of metal, you wouldn't really be able to tell. However, in the area surrounding the replacement, as the operation may have slightly affected any tiny capillaries then there is a theoretical risk that it may be harder for any nitrogen to be transported away, so always dive well within the tables. I don't think you need to restrict your depth of diving to any particular level but you should only dive as deep as you are qualified to.

Another very important point to note is that one of the side effects of this operation is damage to the common peroneal nerve. A lack of sensation above the instep of your foot would indicate this, and it should be noted if you do experience it as it could be misinterpreted as a symptom of DCS in the event of a suspected bend. Paying attention to such details could save you five or six hours of recompression.

Finally, I would add that on long flights you may have a greater chance of getting a clot in your legs, ie a DVT (deep venous thrombosis), so always stay well hydrated and make sure you take a walk down the aisles every hour or so.

"As for whether you are more prone to a bend in the knees: well, as they are now made of metal, you wouldn't really be able to tell."

RHEUMATISM AND ARTHRITIS

I was diagnosed with Polymyalgia Rheumatica five years ago, and have been taking steroids for most of that time. At the moment I am trying to reduce the dose to 3/4mg (of prednisolone) on alternate days with a view to getting off them completely once and for all.

Since I have been on steroids, my doctor has urged me to take HRT to reduce any chance of osteoporosis (which my father has). I had a scan last year and my bone density is OK. I am also taking thyroxine (75mg daily), which I would also like to wean myself off from.

Am I safe to dive? Last time I went diving I had several small nose bleeds on surfacing. Is this indicative of a problem?

Bad luck with the triple drug whammy, it must be a bore taking that lot each day, but as I say to my patients who are in a similar situation, you eat two or three times a day so just think of the tablets in the same sort of way.

Polymyalgia Rheumatica is a condition where the sufferer gets arthritic pains around the more central joints of the body, usually the shoulder and hips. If you are fit and with your treatment don't find that there is a limitation of function, then the case in favour of you diving is increased. If this were a bad case with poor movement of your hips, finning would be impossible, and I would think that if you couldn't move your shoulders, donning a BCD and helping a distressed buddy would also be unfeasible.

One issue with long term steroid medication is that it can cause fluid retention. This would be a problem if it were to gather in your lungs and prevent you from breathing properly when you were exercising hard on a tough dive. You need to get your lungs checked and even an exercise test to make sure this doesn't happen. In fact, I am a bit surprised that you weren't referred to a diving doc before you did

"...you eat two or three times a day so just think of the tablets in the same sort of way."

the course as you must have ticked 'yes' to several questions on the health form.

Thyroxine isn't a problem with diving. It is a medication you will be on for life so thoughts of coming off it are premature. This is also the case with HRT; if you have a family history of osteoporosis then there is a high chance you may contract it also. Taking a daily HRT tablet should seem a tiny burden compared to losing six inches from your height and lying in a hospital bed with a hip fracture, which are the sad consequences of osteoporosis later in life.

As for the nose bleeds, this is a common problem in new divers who are equalising incorrectly, due to too much too late. What happens is that in the first few metres the diver is more intent on checking gauges than sorting out the middle ear so they have to blow quite hard as the Eustachian tube collapses and becomes hard to open at depth. This can result in burst nasal capillaries. So remember, feet first, little and often, and take it slowly down.

I'm 45 years old and as a younger man I was extremely active. I was a physical training instructor in the Paras and since leaving have kept up with plenty of running (minus the Bergen and rifle).

Four years ago I was diagnosed with osteoarthritis of my left hip, which the consultant was convinced was down to overuse. Recently, the joint has deteriorated. As an instructor I kneel on pool surfaces etc. and I really notice the discomfort and limp noticeably for a while afterwards.

After a recent consultation with a specialist I have decided to opt for MoM (Metal on Metal) resurfacing, but don't want to go for an op that will end my dive career prematurely. Any advice on this would be greatly appreciated.

This is the classic 'wear and tear' arthritis that prematurely grinds down the hips and knees of athletes, particularly runners. The hip is a ball and socket joint, and as it wears out, the area becomes stiff and gives constant pain that eventually limits even walking. The approaches to dealing with this are twofold: you can either replace the whole joint, which involves hammering, fairly brutally, a metal stem into the thigh bone; or you can carve away the worn areas of the existing joint and reline them with metal equivalents. The latter has several advantages: less bone removal, a more stable joint and a greater range of movement. One website offering resurfacing goes

"…you can either replace the whole joint, which involves hammering, fairly brutally, a metal stem into the thigh bone; or you can carve away the worn areas of the existing joint and reline them with metal equivalents."

by the wonderfully apt name of www.zimmer.co.uk; thankfully not a frame in sight though. After 20 years of practice the orthopaedic surgeons are exceedingly good at doing this procedure.

Diving-wise you need not worry: it won't rust. Because the prostheses are solid with no gas-filled spaces, they will not be affected by pressure or depth. Obviously you will need to wait until the wound is healed and you are back to full weight-bearing activities before diving, as climbing a boat ladder with a twin set and wet dive gear puts a huge amount of strain on the back and hip joints. There are unsubstantiated theories about scar tissue from surgery taking up nitrogen preferentially (ie making you more prone to DCI), but as yet these have no hard data to back them up. So hold tight for a little longer and you will soon be giant-striding like a youngster again.

My osteopath has just diagnosed me with PMR. To date there is no medicine prescribed. How will this affect me diving, assuming I cease to remain quite so immobile and as stiff as a bloody plank?

Another acronym for you: PMR stands for Polymyalgia Rheumatica. Ever noticed how we docs attach a long name to diseases for which we don't know the cause? Here is a classic example. PMR is a debilitating illness which causes stiffness and aching in the muscles of the neck, shoulders, hips and thighs. Sometimes this is so severe that the poor victim becomes bed-bound, literally unable to lift a finger. It also causes fatigue and a general lethargic listlessness. It can come on suddenly after a viral illness but its exact cause is unknown. Most cases occur in the over-50s and a blood test called ESR (an acronym which would take too long to explain) is used to monitor the condition. Although it cannot be prevented, PMR can be treated with steroids and anti-inflammatories which produce a rapid improvement.

Now, as far as diving goes, the issues are simply practical ones: would the stiffness stop you from getting suited and booted for a dive; and would the lethargy impede your ability to fin and exercise underwater? Such questions need an individual assessment, and the answers may vary with time. The medications are perfectly compatible with diving, at least initially, so as long as you had no side-effects these would not be an issue.

Looking a long way ahead, some PMR sufferers have to be on steroids for so long that their bone-thinning and fluid-retaining side effects can become a problem, and a set of lung function tests is required. At this stage though, a bit of physio and some brisk, weight-bearing exercise will often work wonders for the skeletal flexibility so your days of stiffness will hopefully soon be over.

I am 25 years-old and seem to be developing arthritis in my hands, feet and knees. No official diagnosis yet, but my sister (who is a doctor in Canada) from hearing my symptoms over the phone is of the opinion that it's the start of rheumatoid arthritis (RA), although still fairly mild. My doctor here doesn't seem to think that there's anything wrong, since my blood test for RA was negative. Is it safe for me to dive?

It seems you need to get a good, firm diagnosis first. It is possible to have what is called a sero-negative arthritis where some arthritic conditions have a normal spectrum of blood tests. Also, rheumatoid arthritis itself can be negative on the blood tests yet you could still have the disease.

However, whatever the diagnosis, the only problem with diving is related to whether you are limited in your capacity to fin or help your buddy in an emergency. If your problem means that you cannot walk very far or find that the joint stiffness is so bad that gearing up or holding your buddy in a head up position above water is affected, then I would hold back from diving until you are sorted out by a rheumatologist.

"…whatever the diagnosis, the only problem with diving is related to whether you are limited in your capacity to fin or help your buddy in an emergency."

I'm disabled and my buddy (a nurse) and I have been diving since 2003. I have polyarthritis and take 7.5mg meloxicam and 40mg amitriptyline to control it. I have co-codamol for extra pain relief but rarely take it as I use hand reflexology instead and a bit of Tai Chi for fitness. I was a chronic insomniac all my life before the amitriptyline, and it's possible I have fibromyalgia as well, which is why it was first prescribed. My condition was later diagnosed as polyarthralgia when I was off work with a flare-up, so take your pick of diagnosis. But can I dive on these meds?

Good news for you. The meloxicam, as a straight forward non-steroidal anti-inflammatory will be fine. I can't see an issue there unless it is causing rip-roaring stomach burn. The amitriptyline should be fine as well. It's used as an anti-depressive at a higher dose of 75-150mg, but at a lower dose it is great against nerve pain or can help with insomnia. It does have side effects though:

dry mouth and racing heart to name a couple that can impinge on diving. So the best thing to do is to see a dive doc and get checked over for the latter.

On another note, your diagnosis seems to be one of those 'don't quite know what it is so let's give it an esoteric name' sorts of things. Whether you have polyarthritis, fibromyalgia or whatever, make sure you are strong enough to dive and save your buddy.

HEAD AND SPINE

A while ago I was playing football and received a blow to my head. I was knocked unconscious for about 10 seconds. I felt OK at first, started to get tunnel vision and tinny hearing for about five minutes, and then felt OK again until I was being driven to A&E, at which point I had trouble speaking properly and was unable to remember things like my date of birth. I got to the hospital and was given a CT scan, which was normal.

I was kept in overnight for observation and given pain killers for a pretty mean headache. I was discharged the next day and felt fine. I had headaches for about three days afterwards, but since then am back to normal and can take part in exercise without any discomfort. I have been swimming and can get to the bottom of a four metre pool without any trouble.

Do you have any advice?

Advice? OK, big round balls are wrong, take up rugby instead. In the UK, over a million people visit hospital each year with a head injury. The vast majority of these will be trivial bumps and have no serious consequences, but things like unconsciousness and disturbances of brain function can be signs of more severe trauma. The question therefore is how to pick out the nasty few from the more benign many.

"Advice? OK, big round balls are wrong, take up rugby instead."

As far as diving goes, the two main potential difficulties are post-traumatic epilepsy and altered cognition. The chance of a seizure is directly related to the severity of the injury. Impaling one's cranium on iron railings is far more likely to cause a fit than being hit by a squash ball (although it did quite hurt when it happened to me last week). The risk of fitting drops sharply with time after a mild head injury with only brief unconsciousness, but is more difficult to forecast with penetrating trauma. Anyone who needs anticonvulsants will not be able to dive as the drugs are sedative and can cause unpredictable susceptibility to narcosis. Altered cognition (such as

memory problems) can be immediate or delayed but, if ongoing, would be detrimental to diving performance.

The UK Sport Diving Medical Committee has some helpful advice on this. They suggest using the length of post-traumatic amnesia (PTA) as a guide to the severity of the injury, and delaying return to diving accordingly. So for a PTA of less than an hour, you should have three weeks off; for between one and 24 hours, two months off, and if the amnesia exceeds 24 hours, at least three months off is advised. As your CT scan was fine, and assuming your memory problems and cognitive function are now back to normal, then you could start diving a minimum of three weeks from the accident.

I had a central herniated disc S1/L5 and 18 months ago I underwent a circumferential fusion S1/L5. A subsequent SPECT scan indicated that the fusion had taken successfully.

Do you think I can continue to dive?

The only real problem you face having had a fusion of these two vertebrae in your lower back is to do with tanks and weights. Because your scan shows the two bones have successfully joined you shouldn't get any problems with your disc herniating out, which would have caused problems with diving if left untreated.

However, after any op in that area you may get the odd niggling pain and weakness there, so you need to be sure you can carry your tanks well enough, especially on long walks to a shore entry. I think it would also be wise to use an integrated BCD as a traditional weight belt would hang down right over where you had the fusion and may exacerbate any remaining problems.

I had a bicycle crash last week in which I sustained multiple fractures of the cheekbones and lost a few teeth. All seems to be healing well, but I'm wondering how this could affect ear clearing and the risk of embolism in the face on ascent. I didn't have an operation; just broken teeth removed, but can't get work done on them until face bones are healed, which could be one to two months. I have a diving trip booked in a few weeks time and worried I might be faced with a mandatory three month lay-off.

There is the potential here for gas to have entered the facial tissues, or for abnormal conduits to have been made between the usual

> "...for a PTA of less than an hour, you should have three weeks off; for between one and 24 hours, two months off, and if the amnesia exceeds 24 hours, at least three months off is advised."

> "I had a bicycle crash last week in which I sustained multiple fractures of the cheekbones and lost a few teeth."

gas-containing spaces in the head (sinuses, ears). Gas in the tissues is referred to as 'subcutaneous emphysema'. The classic diving-related manifestation is when the lung tears on a rapid or breath-holding ascent, with consequent leaking of the air into the tissues. I can remember the first patient I saw with this: the crackling sensation when I felt his neck was just like popping bubble wrap. Although the commonest symptoms are breathlessness and chest pain, sometimes the only one is a high-pitched or unusually nasal voice, as the free gas reaches the larynx and distorts the vocal cords. Happily the gas is reabsorbed fairly quickly so the treatment is simply supportive; oxygen and bed rest will usually do the trick, but obviously the cause of the escaped gas needs to be corrected (often more difficult).

In your case, the question is whether there is any gas trapping. Hopefully, the X-rays and imaging you had would have revealed any abnormalities, but it's difficult to exclude small pockets of gas in the tooth sockets with such tests. But, following the same principles, gas will normally dissipate within days, and if the repair work is going to be delayed then it shouldn't be an issue. I'd suggest you get a check up with a diving doc nearer the time to make sure, but I don't see any need for a compulsory three month layoff. Take care when you next mount your two-wheeled steed.

I had spinal surgery to correct a scoliosis and have made a 100% recovery.

Could you tell me if I would be OK to dive?

A scoliosis is a curvature of the spine in a left/right direction, or lateral to be a tad medical. This is in fact quite common but needs correction or you will get a lot of knock on effects later in life. The good news is that the actual nervous tissue of the spinal cord is usually not affected, just the bones of the vertebrae, so can be seen dive-medically like any other bony operation. When you come along for a dive medical, we will make sure that if there are any neurological abnormalities, they are noted at this stage so that if you ever have a suspected bend, any loss of sensation or power related to your condition would be known in advance and not mistaken for DCS.

I have never known a mild, pre or post op scoliotic patient fail a Fit to Dive (or HSE) medical for that reason alone, so I think you should be fine provided you are strong enough to lift a tank onto your back and your buddy out of the water.

"A scoliosis is a curvature of the spine in a left/right direction, or lateral to be a tad medical. This is in fact quite common but needs correction…"

Seven weeks ago, I had an undisplaced fracture of my left zygomatic complex (cheekbone). There were no other symptoms other than a tender area on the face and a slight pressure pain upon sneezing. After two weeks, the pressure pain disappeared and in three weeks time I want to go diving. Can I?

All seems fine now. You will be 10 weeks post fracture, and so pretty much there on the healing front. All I can suggest is that your mask can sit fairly tight across your cheek bone at times, so make sure you have a nice loose fit. Don't let it squeeze, ie pull even tighter across your face as you descend. Breathe out tiny amounts through your nose as you go down.

I have just been told I might have ankylosing spondylitis. I am fit and go to the gym regularly, but can I carry on diving?

Yes, you should carry on diving. Ankylosing spondylitis is an arthritic condition characterised by young onset and lower back pain due to inflammation of the joint within the pelvis called the sacroiliac joint. The only problem that may occur at this early stage is difficulty in gearing up in cramped conditions, due to any pain and restriction of movement. Later, this disease can cause rigidity of the spine so you would find it hard to bend down with your legs straight. If this happened you should make preparations with your kit; such as getting a weight-integrated BCD, so you don't have to bend over to get the buckle tight, and also make sure that any dive boat has an easy means of reboarding after a dive, so you don't have to flop into it like a seal.

I'm currently undergoing treatment for a compressed disc at C6, in the mid-neck, which is causing pain in my hands. After having physio and traction it is no better and I have been referred to a surgeon who discussed surgery with me. I have the choice of fusing the bone or inserting a new disc. Which of these would cause the least problems while diving?

Disc, bone. Bone, disc. Hmmm.

I go for bone here. The issue with the disc is that by slipping, it causes the nerves to compress, hence the pain and tingling. A new disc could do this again, I guess. A bone fusion, strengthens the whole area. Nodding might be odd, but all the symptoms should stop. That's my call. But it does also depend on the surgeon's ability and experience. Ask them what they are better at doing. You are allowed to do that, and if they say they've never fused a C6, run a mile and find someone who has.

HANDS AND FEET

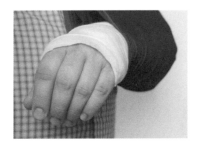

My boyfriend recently broke his hand, which had pins put in yesterday and is now in a cast. We are going on a diving holiday on Thursday and his surgeon has signed a letter saying he is fit to dive as long as he keeps the cast dry. He bought some waterproof covers which on arrival don't appear to have a proper seal. Do you have any suggestions on ways to keep the cast dry?

No doubt he was defending your honour in a mightily chivalrous manner, and thus deserves a good holiday. Apologies, then, but I feel I have to make your boyfriend aware that there are a few reasons why diving with a fracture is not a good idea. Obviously, there can be loss of dexterity in the broken part, making that bumpy ride out to the dive site a little trickier. It might affect your ability to rescue yourself or your buddy, and be more susceptible to infection by marine nasties. Reinjury to the area is possible, as it's weak during repair, and sometimes the surrounding muscles lose some strength as they waste away a bit with disuse. The other theoretical problem is that the disrupted bone may preferentially take up inert gas, increasing the risk of DCI. So in general I would suggest not diving until the injury is healed and full function is back; a ballpark figure is around four to six weeks.

However, if it really is the unpostponable holiday of a lifetime, then go for a waterproof cast construction if you can. GoreTex liners can be used instead of the traditional cotton wool and elasticated stocking getup, allowing evaporation but maintaining enough water repellency to permit swimming, baths etc. A fiberglass tape is then wound around the liner to give the equivalent strength of the more usual plaster-of-paris deal. You'll be glad to hear they come in a wide variety of offensively garish colours too.

I will soon be having surgery on the misaligned fifth metatarsals of each foot. This involves cutting, re-shaping and pinning them. Apparently I'll be walking around OK in two weeks, and back

"No doubt he was defending your honour in a mightily chivalrous manner, and thus deserves a good holiday."

to running in four to six weeks. Would you suggest any time limit after the op before diving?

You can see why orthopaedic surgeons are thought of as carpenters by some in the medical world.

Well, after this bit of re-modelling your only real concern is finning. There will be swelling, there will be pain, but at six weeks, if your surgeon feels you can run, then you should be able to fin. Before you do, make sure that your fins still fit properly as you will have different shaped feet. They will probably be narrower. So check before you dive and wear a thicker neoprene boot or sock if you don't want to splash out on a new set of flippers, as they are called by tabloid travel writers.

DENTAL PROBLEMS

I'm taking 400mg of Nurofen four times a day for toothache. Will I be OK to dive?

As someone who suffers frequent and various tooth disasters I have to sympathise whole-heartedly with you here. That constant nagging, gob ache makes me reach for the painkillers they usually use on horses. The issues here though are two-fold: is your dental problem going to stop you diving; and how strong can you go before the side effects of the meds make you too woozy to dive?

With the former, the only real problem would be if you had a cavity with a narrow entry. Air can get in here on the way down and the reg can block it from leaving the tooth on the way up. Expanding air in a closed tooth space feels worse than an amputation without anaesthetic. So check with your dentist that you don't have any holes.

On the subject of painkillers, Nurofen is fine. It won't knock you out, but then again it might not be strong enough for the pain. There are many analgesics that are tougher but some of the strong codeine based ones can space you out. Best you try something like Nurofen Plus, it's got a low dose codeine at 15mg, and enough ibuprofen to hit the inflammation in your mouth. One before a dive should be fine, but you can also take two after diving to do the trick. Also consider oil of cloves. It's brilliant when rubbed directly on the problem tooth and I never leave home without it.

If I have had a root canal work or fillings in the past, what are the considerations for diving?

Ouch. You think seeing the dentist can be a bad experience: just wait until you have a tooth blow out on an ascent.

Like most things that cause you pain underwater, it's all about air spaces. We all know that the middle ear and sinuses will traumatise

"That constant nagging gob ache makes me reach for the painkillers they usually use on horses."

and squeeze if they are not properly equalised or cannot release air upon ascent. Well, there is a third potential air space not a lot of divers know about and it's right there biting onto your mouthpiece.

Normal teeth are a solid mass of dentine, enamel, nerve fibres and pulp, and so don't compress on descent or ascent. But when these healthy teeth become diseased and begin to get a hole or two in the middle of them, things can go wrong. These holes are either due to being forgetful with the toothpaste for a few years, or when you have succumbed to your wallet and been to a bad dentist. What can happen is that the pressurised air breathed at depth can make its way into a tooth cavity underwater. If, eg the filling dislodges during a dive or you bite down on a different part of the mouthpiece and the air gets trapped in the tooth, it will expand on ascent, press on any nerve in that tooth and cause the sort of pain that can only be described as being hit by Tyson in a debate about a fender bending. The same goes for badly fitted crowns as well. If you get a tooth squeeze there's not a whole lot you can do except take the pain, figure out how you are going to take revenge on the dentist later that week and reach for the whisky on surfacing. Sometimes, moving your mouthpiece to a different bite may work or sucking on the tooth may remove any detritus that blocks the now air filled hole.

Now, root canal work is different and I speak from experience. This is a long, literally boring and expensive procedure and should deaden the nerve in the tooth. If there were a potentially fillable air space then you wouldn't feel anything as the nerve has been killed. Bad dentistry could still lead to a space, which could blow a tooth, but it would have to be really bad dentistry and on surfacing, forget the painkillers and just call a lawyer.

I'm due to go to Malta, but my 13 year-old daughter has been told by her orthodontist that she will be having braces fitted a couple of weeks beforehand. Will this prevent her taking her Open Water course and diving?

Braces come in all shapes and sizes, but generally aren't a problem for divers. The (obvious) principle is that your daughter should be able to hold the reg in her mouth and form an adequate seal around the mouthpiece. There are tabs on the mouthpiece of the regulator, just like a snorkel, and there are occasional reports of these snagging on braces.

You can get mouldable mouthpieces which would solve this if it

"...it will expand on ascent, press on any nerve in that tooth and cause the sort of pain that can only be described as being hit by Tyson..."

becomes a problem. If she can open her mouth to eat then breathing through it should be fine. There are some elaborate orthodontic constructions that reduce the bite diameter, but I doubt whether these would allow you to get the mouthpiece in at all.

I'm due to go diving three weeks after having a wisdom tooth taken out.

I have been having trouble equalising due to the tooth interfering with my ear, so thought by having it out I might be able to pop my ears more easily, but is this date too close to diving and should I postpone the extraction?

I'm not really convinced that a wisdom tooth, inflammation around it and all, will really affect your ability to equalise. Certainly pain from the tooth can be referred to the ear, but a tooth so far back in the mouth is nowhere near any of the relevant tubes. However, if it's causing enough aggro for you to want to remove it, then it's best you go ahead.

Three weeks should be OK from the op to a dive, however I have seen tooth extractions go merrily awry. Post op infection, constant bleeding, etc. so I think the safe thing to do is not book the trip until a week before. If you are fine two weeks after the op then you will be fine to dive, but any inflammation and infection will prevent you from biting on your mouthpiece; a dangerous problem even in the mildest current.

I've had to undergo the removal of a front tooth which has been the bane of my life since the age of 14, when my brother first kicked me in the mouth and broke it. I now have to wear a palette with a false tooth for six months before they can bridge the gap.

Although it's quite a good fit, I can still move the palette up and down away from the roof of my mouth. Will it cause me any problems by creating air pockets when I descend?

"When my brother first kicked me in the mouth"? Sounds like a tough upbringing in your household. My sympathies.

I think you should remove the palette before you dive. The reason is not air pockets, which won't happen by the way, but mainly obstruction. The palettes slide in and out, I believe, and there

"'When my brother first kicked me in the mouth?' Sounds like a tough upbringing in your household."

could be a situation where it gets caught up or even prevents quick accurate placement of your buddy's occy if you had an out of air situation. It would be mad to be struggling to first place your teeth in line before biting on a reg in an emergency. When the bridge is in, all will be back to normal again, so don't worry about your smile when you get back on the dive boat. That's not the first thing blokes look at anyway.

I have a swelling in my jaw on the left hand side, under a molar that was root filled about six years ago. I went to the dentist yesterday, had an X-ray, and the results proved to be uncertain. The dentist is trying to get me an appointment at the hospital for a second opinion. She thinks I have two problem areas, one of which is between the molars and the bigger area is underneath the root filled molar, which might be cysts, although she was uncertain and a bit surprised. She has put me on amoxicillin 250mg three times a day, as well as metronidazole 200mg three times a day.

Could this be related to diving? Maybe I have my mouthpiece positioned incorrectly or I'm biting down too hard. My jaw does feel tired at the end of a full day's aquatic activity.

This is unlikely to be diving related. The antibiotics you are taking are the standard dental ones, so I assume they are fleshy infected cysts, rather than the bony hollow ones that sometimes occur. When you grip a mouthpiece, you are using the molars and pre-molars, where your problem is. The amount of time in reality that you have a mouthpiece in is small compared to other things you do with your mouth, like chewing. However, when you bite the rubber, so to speak, during a dive, it could worsen a pre-existing problem.

There is something you could try where no bite is involved. It's called the Manta mouthpiece and it has wings that pop out toward the cheeks, pulling the reg up against the mouth so you don't need to bite. While you are waiting, finish the antibiotics and it all may end up with further root canal work. Good luck, I know how much fun that can be.

I am having a new orthodontic treatment called Invisalign. If you haven't heard of it, it basically does the job of braces by using very thin plastic aligners that look kind of like gum shields only a lot more fitted.

My query is whether I am allowed to dive with these in my mouth. They do not cause me excessive pain or discomfort. My only worry is that if some air got caught in-between my teeth and the aligners it might cause a problem.

At last someone has invented something to stop the shame and embarrassment of our nation's children. And adults, for that matter. I can't see a problem here at all. If it lies outside your teeth, away from the nerves, then even if air got in, it should be able to get out as well whilst you ascend. The only potential disaster is if air gets in and under at depth, and then you block it in by biting on your reg mouthpiece too closely. Air would expand on ascent and, I suppose, could cause pain. But if you got this, then ease off the bite on your reg and all should be fine.

From the other side of the coin, do ask your dentist fitting it if there would be issues having a rubber mouthpiece close to it for two hours a day. If there is a risk of dislodging it or breaking it, then maybe get it fitted after your dive hols as from my experience there's nothing cheap in the world of teeth, and you don't want to see a couple of grand settling on a sandy bed in the blue.

FEMALE PROBLEMS

INTRO

There is a certain class of person that will say: "How come there's a chapter on 'Female Problems', but nothing for blokes?". Well, one answer is that I can only think of two questions in the entire book that would really have fit into such a category, but the correct response is actually to knee them sharply in the nuts.

I expect most people would agree that the biggest female problem is a hundred thousand years of unfair stereotyping by men as being some sort of emotionally unstable, baby-making machine and the inequality reflected in the social order as a direct consequence. That and periods. But it used to be a lot worse.

As a random example, I read HG Wells' seminal 1897 sci-fi classic The War of the Worlds recently and stumbled across the following line: "His endless muttering monologue... drove me... almost to the verge of craziness. He was as lacking in restraint as a silly woman."

Having said that, men don't get off much easier. At the beginning of the great exodus from London, the narrator's brother has this to contend with: "His landlady came to the door, loosely wrapped in dressing gown and shawl; her husband followed, ejaculating." Typical bloke really, but when Martians actually do attack the Earth (and they will), I feel that whilst it will be fairly exciting, I might react differently.

Clever eh, using War of the Worlds as an analogy for the differences between the sexes? Not really; I only noticed it when I was halfway through that last paragraph. I don't think HG Wells had that in mind either, even though the Martians do all die from man-flu. Still, there are differences between the two species (women and men, not humans and Martians), and although we can't explain why there aren't as many of them diving (women, not Martians), some of the gender-specific issues are dealt with in the next chapter. And although anyone looking for info on tentacles and tripods will have to look elsewhere, it's not all just tits 'n' bits. It mostly is, though.

Tip: If a representative of the company you've been diving with claims that being female is the problem, or makes any reference straight from 1962 about "women d[r]ivers", kick them in the nuts then go diving. If symptoms persist, call a diving doctor who will hold them down for you whilst you aim.

PREGNANCY

What are the risks to the mother and the foetus (if any) of Scuba diving while pregnant? To the extent that there are risks, can they be mitigated by not exceeding a certain depth or by not diving at all during a certain part of the pregnancy?

Here's why you cannot dive if pregnant, or even trying to get pregnant: one of the issues with diving is that for all the tables and dive computer algorithms we have, there is always a chance, however remote, that you could get a bend. I have seen many divers who have stuck rigidly to the limits of no decompression diving, and still gotten bent. This is because there are many variable factors to take into account. Now, we all take the risk and dive without problems as this decision concerns ourselves only, but the question with pregnancy is what could happen to the unborn child if a problem occurred.

There are some case reports in which pregnant mothers with carbon monoxide poisoning were treated with hyperbaric oxygen in a chamber without adverse effects on the foetus. Conversely, many animal (and some human) studies have noted an increase in the incidence of foetal abnormalities and spontaneous abortions in those who dived whilst pregnant.

Very early in pregnancy, up to two weeks or so, there is no effective blood circulation between the placenta and foetus, so problems are unlikely. Once such a circulation develops, there might be.

Nitrogen bubbles are easily absorbed by neuronal or nerve tissue. If a pregnant diver got a hit but it stayed undiagnosed (as it often does), then the foetus could easily have neurological DCS and you wouldn't be aware of it. This could cause problems later in the unborn child as the nervous system developed in pregnancy. Now I know that a lot of this is speculation as there is not a lot of research on the matter because it wouldn't get past the ethics committee.

> "Now, we all take the risk and dive without problems as this decision concerns ourselves only, but the question with pregnancy is what could happen to the unborn child if a problem occurred."

Of course, there are also a lot of women who have dived whilst not realising they were pregnant and without any problems, but the key issue is that if you dived, had a bend, and there was a deformity in your child when born, you wouldn't know if it was due to the nitrogen or some other cause. If it was the nitrogen and it could have been avoided by not diving, it would clearly cause severe levels of guilt in the mother.

So, I always say to just leave it for nine months, as this is not that hard when the downside could be disastrous.

We are due to go on a diving holiday booked prior to finding out that I was pregnant. I have since had an incomplete miscarriage and am due to have an Evacuation of Retained Products of Conception (ERPC). I have been told that I will not be able to swim for four to six weeks after the procedure due to the potential for infection, but would it be OK to dive in a drysuit?

Sorry to hear that, not a pleasant experience for anyone to have to go through. Infection is one of the risks after this procedure so wetsuit diving would indeed be out for the sort of time period you mention, but I don't see any reason you shouldn't dive in a dry suit: the infection risk is negated, and it would probably be a good idea to have a holiday after the trauma of an ERPC.

There are similar advisory delays for diving after a normal delivery or a Caesarean. Basically once the uterus has shrunk to its normal size, vaginal discharge is negligible, any wound has healed sufficiently and the woman is sufficiently recovered, then diving can resume.

Two months ago I gave birth to a beautiful baby girl by Caesarean section. How long before I can dive again?

I think you have waited long enough before diving. Your new addition has of course exited you and entered the world via a route through your abdomen rather than the usual more painful way. So the issue here is: can you lift your tanks and weights post op without breaking the scar? I think eight weeks is enough. If you have had any delay in healing the wound then maybe wait a little longer, but the call is up to you.

The really hard thing of course is deciding who gets to hold the bairn on a perfect dive day when the baby sitter's failed to turn up.

But knowing hungry youngsters they will probably need a feed just as the boat is about to leave, so be prepared to hand your partner a bottle full of expressed breast milk and tell him that you'll get some good shots of the mantas for him.

VAGINA, UTERINE, OVARIAL AND MENSTRUAL

My doctor has just put me on a tablet called Cyclokapron for period pains and heavy bleeding, which I have to take once a month. As an instructor, is it OK to dive whilst taking this medication or should I just put up with the pains?

This is one of the in-vogue treatments for your problem. Cyclokapron is also known as tranexamic acid and it is useful in period pains as it is an 'antifibrinolytic'. This means that it prevents the substance that breaks down blood clots, which basically means that you bleed less each period.

Now there's little evidence to suggest that this medication will cause any problems for you when you dive, and it may well even help you to dive more healthily. By this I mean that there is a link between getting the bends and having your period at the time (although the evidence is still being slowly researched as to exactly why this is the case). There may well be a function of the blood loss involved and if this tablet can decrease that during a period, then it may mean it is a tiny bit safer than not taking it.

I am considering having the contraceptive intrauterine device (IUD) fitted. Are there any risks that the coil could be crushed, pushed out or even damaged while diving due to the pressure on the body at depth? What about the contraceptive implant, does the pressure when diving interfere with the amount of hormones released?

It's extremely unlikely that you'll encounter any problems with the IUD whilst diving. Most are small, solid structures that are snugly situated in the womb, protected from any harmful effects of external water pressure. Sometimes they do lead to increases in amount and length of menstrual flow, which might prove less than ideal on a liveaboard with one tiny toilet and 20 hairy male divers. But newer types such as the intrauterine system (IUS) tend to diminish flow so it's probably wise to discuss the various options with your GP

> "…there's little evidence to suggest that this medication will cause any problems for you when you dive, and it may well even help you to dive more healthily."

before plumping for one. There's no available evidence on whether pressure affects the release of hormones from the contraceptive implant, but there's no theoretical reason why it should.

I have noticed that whenever I dive below 18m I experience a vaginal bleed. My menstrual cycle is regular and I take the Oral Contraceptive Pill (OCP). As you can imagine this is not only inconvenient but can also be embarrassing. Is this normal?

You say that you take the OCP and I find that in some women, one pill may not be as effective as another and so cause mid cycle spotting. This may not always happen topside, but could occur at depth, so perhaps a pill with a different progesterone may be worth a try. But before you assume it is that, you should have a gynae check up to make sure you don't have any cervical erosions. These are small ulcers on your cervix that can cause your problem and they should be the first thing to exclude as there is a link to early cervical cancer. You need a chlamydia screen too as there is a link with bleeding mid cycle as well, and this is a disease that can cause infertility later on if it's not caught early.

So, get a gynae check up first, if that's OK then try a different pill, and if it still occurs then you will have to try diving with a sanitary towel in a dry suit.

I recently had a vaginal hysterectomy. I'm 37 and generally fit and well. I'm returning back to work later this month and have started driving a bit again. My check-up after the op is not until three weeks from now. How long until I can try diving?

There are two ways of doing a hysterectomy: vaginally; or abdominally where they go through a bikini line incision on your lower abdomen.

The advantage of the first method is that it does not involve cutting through your abdominal muscles, so your overall recovery time is quicker as you can lift, strain and heave sooner. This naturally will benefit the diver as they rig up on a busy RIB.

I normally suggest that six weeks is a reasonable time to wait post-op before diving again, but if it's the first time for you and you are doing the Open Water Course at a pool in Chiswick, then a couple of weeks should be fine for the simple pool work and theory. Leave it another three to four weeks though before doing your four open water dives.

"The advantage of this method is that you can lift, strain and heave sooner."

37 is quite young for this sort of op and it may be worth considering the implications of the condition that warrants this on diving. If it's for uncontrolled heavy periods, then that's fine, however if it's for any sort of tumour then we may need a rethink.

What is the effect on women putting a tampon in during Scuba diving?

I imagine trying to do this in water, wearing a drysuit and gloves would be beyond the skills of all but the most dexterous women. The absorbent blighter would undoubtedly wriggle free, swell to gargantuan proportions and be rather difficult to insert. But if deployed wisely on dry land it's a different story.

Tampons (or "Satan's little cotton fingers" as they have been referred to by a particularly hysterical American Baptist church) can be used whilst diving and there is no evidence that they cause any harm. Menstruation itself may be an issue in terms of decompression illness, as there is some evidence that diving in the first week of the cycle (ie whilst menstruating) is associated with an increased risk of DCI. There are theoretical reasons why this might occur to do with hormonal and vasomotor changes, so it would seem sensible to avoid diving at this time if possible. Concerns about attracting sharks though are unfounded (you'll be glad to hear) with no evidence of increased numbers of attacks.

Incidentally, if you happen to be passing through the outskirts of Washington DC, you might want to visit the faintly disturbing 'Museum of Menstruation', run (apparently) by a 50-something bachelor in the basement of his home. Sounds a bit 'Silence of the Lambs' to me...

Is it OK to dive with large ovarian cysts?

"Referee, I hope your mother has an ovarian cyst the size of a grapefruit". One of the better insults I have heard at Stamford Bridge in the last few years. So, Mrs Collina, listen up. It is fine, as long as they are not prone to something called torsion. That's where they twist on their own axis and cause a lot of tummy pain. If this happened underwater it could be an issue.

I assume the gynaes would have removed them by now if this was the case, so dive on, as these fluid filled lovelies won't compress or burst with pressure.

"Tampons (or 'Satan's little cotton fingers' as they have been referred to by a particularly hysterical American Baptist church) can be used whilst diving and there is no evidence that they cause any harm."

To delay my period on my diving holiday to the Red Sea, I am going to take norethisterone twice a day, and I just wanted to check this would not increase the risk of DCS.

Ladies wonder drug, that. Fed up with periods? Worried about sharks? Can't buy 'you know what' up the jungle? Never fear, norethisterone is here. It's basically a hormonal analogue that makes your pituitary/ovary/uterus axis think: "Hmm, not time for my period yet, let's delay for a while".

So this is a widely used drug by those on honeymoon, models on photo-shoots and yes, divers. The rules are simple. You take the drug each day, start a few days before you expect your period, and as long as you take it the period will not come until a day or so after you stop. The maximum time you can take it for is to block two periods, so that's two months, but most ladies will just do a couple of weeks whilst away.

Side effects: a little fluid retention (no bad thing with diving) and maybe a feeling of uterine fullness. All should be well as there's no DCS risk. And don't worry about the shark gag, they prefer surfers and cameramen. It's the bull seals that like the laydeez.

"Fed up with periods? Worried about sharks? Can't buy 'you know what' up the jungle? Never fear, norethisterone is here."

I have just had a laparoscopy with diathermy to endometriosis and a Mirena IUS fitted. It was my fourth laparoscopy and it eliminated all the endometriosis which remained from the previous ones. I insisted on a three mile walk the day after the op thinking it would build up muscles slowly and enable progression to running, swimming and diving. Unfortunately, the walk, persistent cough (which is at last on its way out) and my four year old jumping on my stomach the next morning have not helped. I am still bleeding internally but that could be the Mirena. Externally there is hardly a trace, the lower cut just looks like a scratch and the one in my belly button is not much more, just a little bruised. Please could you let me know when I can dive?

I think if they have dived into you four times to frazzle the little bits of uterine tissue lying outside the womb that cause endometriosis, and your little scamp of a child has been using you as a trampoline, then it's best to leave it for six weeks. I know this may be ultra-conservative, but it's no mean thing having this sort of op.

What has happened here is the womb lining somehow gets out of the uterus and into the fallopian tubes, the abdominal cavity, and even into the uterine muscle too. Then, each time you have a period, the hormones make this tissue expand as well, and get bloody, causing monthly, agonizing pain. Thank the Lord for Y chromosomes. Though it's gone for you now, four entries through the abdomen wall with the scope can make healing less quick, so leave it six weeks to be sure.

The bleeding is due to the coil. Mirena is a progesterone covered coil, and this hormone can cause abnormal bleeding for a few weeks after it has been fitted.

MENOPAUSE

I am approaching 50 and for several months have been getting menopausal symptoms. Before I go to my local GP, please can you advise me if any of the HRT preparations are 'banned drugs' as far as diving is concerned. I would rather put up with the menopausal symptoms than have to stop diving.

And what a fantastic advertisement for diving that is. The joys of the deep exchanged for five years of the misery of anger, night sweats, facial flushing and a dry you-know-where, although your husband might not be so pleased when you take a chainsaw to his neck for leaving the loo seat up.

HRT is fine to dive with. Just make darn sure you are given the right one. Take the tablets not the patches. The latter tend to float off your arm underwater and who knows what can happen to them then. I would hate to see how an oceanic whitetip behaves when crammed full of oestrogen.

I have recently turned 55, am a female in good health who regularly works out but going through the menopause. I am not taking HRT or any other medication except glucosamine. I get the usual hot flushes and have aching limbs, particularly shoulder/neck (result of an old whiplash injury) and lower back. Sometimes the aching is really quite severe.

I was in the Bahamas recently and went Scuba diving on two occasions; two morning dives on each day. I was buddied with the divemaster for the first dive, which was to 45ft with a bottom time of 30 minutes, followed by a half hour surface interval. The second was another 30 minute dive but this time to 40ft. Five days later, I did a wall dive where I only wanted to go to 50ft, but the visibility was so good that before I knew it I was at 55 plus. I came back up to 50ft immediately and after a 30 minute bottom time, came up slowly and made a safety stop, followed by a 15 minute surface interval. On the second dive we hit a

"…your husband might not be so pleased when you take a chainsaw to his neck for leaving the loo seat up."

maximum of 25ft with a 45 minute bottom time.

We flew back to the UK two days later. I cannot say for sure that my aches and pains are any worse since coming back and have put it down to age and time of life, but given the little bit of bobbing up and down on the wall dive I would be grateful to know if you think I could have a problem.

I think you're OK here.

The profiles are fairly shallow. The surface intervals long enough, especially with the four day break between the two sets. Yes, you did have a bit of a yo-yo, but not enough to fizz you up inside.

If the pains you have now are in a completely new area and of a type you have never had before then it may be worth a consult with a chamber. Even so, in all likelihood menopausal aches can flit around, and you had them before, so I am 99.9% sure you do not have DCS but something that would respond better to a HRT patch than five or six hours on a Table 62 recompression.

BREAST

Hi, I have recently given birth to a baby girl and am breastfeeding. I had been hoping to return to the water as soon as possible but I have concerns about the effect the pressure changes may have on my milk supply. Is there any advice you can give me regarding when I can return to diving and the effects it will have for continuing to breastfeed, or if it is likely to cause mastitis?

Congratulations on bringing another potential diver into the world. This is a question that has been looked into in some detail. Milk supply does not seem to be affected by pressure, although it may cause a bit of leakage (probably unnoticeable in the water). Engorged breasts can be a bit tricky to squeeze into a tight-fitting wetsuit, so you may have to prepare for some discomfort. One way round this is to use a breast pump to empty the blighters before you dive or, better still, give the little nipper a quick feed just before going in.

There have been concerns voiced about possible transmission of inert gas bubbles to the baby, but these are unfounded: nitrogen bubbles have not been seen in breast milk, and even if microbubbles did form, they would only end up in baby's gut which is full of gas anyway (as you have probably discovered by now). Mastitis (infection of the breast tissue) from marine organisms is possible, particularly if the nipples are cracked or sore, and so I wouldn't dive until the nipples are healed over. There is one other potential issue: breastfeeding and prolonged immersion can both precipitate dehydration, so it's vitally important to keep the fluid intake up, both to avoid DCI and any reduction in the volume of breast milk produced.

"One way round this is to use a breast pump to empty the blighters before you dive..."

I had a mastectomy two years ago. Unfortunately, I got an infection shortly after the surgery and the wound opened up into an abscess about the size of a 50 pence piece which went down to the bone. It took quite a while to heal as I'd had radiotherapy on the area a few months previously. Tissue built

up from the bottom of the wound and it eventually healed up in about three months.

Having finished chemo six months later, I went back to diving last weekend. We did two dives; the first had a max depth of 21m, and the second was to 15m. When I showered later that evening I noticed a lot of bruising and blood blisters around the edge of the scar tissue. It certainly wasn't there that morning. The scar is around the same place as my chest valve would be on my dry suit. As this area is completely numb I could have bruised the new scar tissue whilst using the chest valve without realising it. I just wanted to check that it couldn't be an indication of air trapped in the wound or some other weird diving-related problem.

In surgical circles they call this delayed repair 'healing by secondary intention', a fantastic cop-out term that implies it's all a bit of an afterthought. Basically it means the surgeons are powerless to do anything about it so it's left to heal by itself. Six months down the line, I doubt there would be any air trapped in the wound, as the healing has been slow enough to allow any gas to diffuse out. As you say, the more plausible explanation is that the bruising and blistering came from a suit squeeze and/or direct pressure from the valve on the area around the scar. After a mastectomy numbness is not uncommon in and around the wound, so although numbness can be a sign of DCI I think it's more likely to be due to the knife in this case.

So rest easy, allow things to clear up before you next dive, and if it happens again it might be time for a new dry suit.

I would like some advice on breast enlargement (versus diving). I have a condition which means that one of my breasts is about half the size of the other, and have been offered an enlargement of the smaller breast.

Could you tell me if there have been studies on the effect of the pressure etc. of diving with implants? As my plan is to become a dive guide abroad within the next few years, this would drastically change my plans if there were any implications.

No worries here for you. Remember it is only air that gets compressed underwater, so unless the surgeon is going to use an inflated lilo for your op, you will be fine.

"...unless the surgeon is going to use an inflated lilo for your op, you will be fine."

Breast enlargement utilises either silicone or other fluid filled sacs for the desired effect. These are not compressible at all at depth. There has been some research I have read, but it mainly concerns slow leakage from the sacs due to pressure from a tight wet suit or over inflated BCD. Ask your doctor for the most sturdy of implants, as if you are going to guide there could be a lot of wear and tear in the chest area.

If the implants are silicone-based they may affect buoyancy as they're heavier than water (saline ones are obviously neutrally buoyant). Clearly you shouldn't dive around the time of the procedure, but once all has healed up you'll be fine.

Three months ago I did one dive to a depth of 33m. We had a surface interval for one hour before travelling back over the hills. While travelling I had a slight pain in my right breast so I undid my bra and removed it, but then the pain started in both breasts. It was really unbearable. Later that day I noticed unusual marks around them. Today is Monday and they're still tender. Was this a skin bend?

Steady on there, sister, I'm feeling rather faint: no more breast-baring on the way home please! There are sporadic reports of breast pain as an unusual symptom of decompression illness in the literature. The interesting thing about your story is that the symptoms seemed to appear soon after the diving, and worsened as you crossed the hills on your way back, with only a small increase in altitude. If there were any provocative factors on the dive, such as dehydration, missed safety stops or rapid ascents, then you would have to consider DCI as a strong possibility. It is also worth noting that bends such as these have a high correlation with PFO (Patent Foramen Ovale, one of the so-called 'hole in the heart' conditions that can predispose to DCI), so that would need to be checked out too. Some female divers do experience breast tenderness as a regular post-dive phenomenon however; something for which there is no reliable explanation that I know of. Theories abound of various hormone imbalances causing the pains, in much the same way as with pre-menstrual breast tenderness, but there is no adequately explained reason this should happen with exposure to pressure or compressed gases.

I had a malignant tumour in my right breast which was removed last year. At the beginning of this year I underwent radiotherapy and was additionally prescribed tamoxifen. I am worried that

"Steady on there, sister, I'm feeling rather faint: no more breast-baring on the way home please!"

my lung tissue may have been damaged by the radiation although I feel healthy now and have started exercising again. I would like to do a few dives in the English waters every now and then (neither deep nor especially long) and spend a relaxed holiday in Egypt in autumn. Can I?

This is always a tricky one as there is no definitive 'yes' or 'no' answer. The reason for this is that radiotherapy (and chemotherapy) is highly targeted to the tumour in question, so one patient's treatment is invariably different to the next; the best recipe changes depending on the tumour type, how advanced it is, whether it has spread etc. Generally speaking, both chemo and radiotherapy can induce scarring of the lung tissue and render a diver more susceptible to pulmonary barotrauma, embolism and pneumothorax. So you would need to have some investigations to assess these risks, usually involving a CT scan of your lungs together with lung function tests, before diving again.

That said, the odd shallow UK dive and some relaxed drifting about in Egypt should be well within achievable realms, and would probably be just the ticket after what sounds like a pretty traumatic year.

I have been taking 100mg of danazol maybe twice a week, for hormonal breast pain which is no longer intense but more of an inconvenience. Now, I'm about to start taking Lariam, due to a six month posting to Kenya.

Can I take both at the same time and can I dive?

Good news all round for you.

Yes there is no problem in taking danazol with Lariam. The two drugs work completely independently of each other and so there is no synergistic effect that will cause you to explode or break out into weird rashes.

There is also no problem with diving and danazol, and you may find it even helps protect you from a bend. The reason being that there is a link between a hit and having a period, and danazol will also cause the cessation of menstrual bleeding. The deal with Lariam is different as it has too many side effects that could either cause a panic underwater or be mistaken for a bend. However,

> "Generally speaking, both chemo and radiotherapy can induce scarring of the lung tissue... So you would need to have some investigations to assess these risks..."

those who have taken Lariam and have absolutely no problem with it, will be OK to dive.

Malarone is the alternative but it is a daily tablet and for six months the cost can really add up. So unless you have just won the lottery, stay as you are.

DISEASES
AND VIRUSES

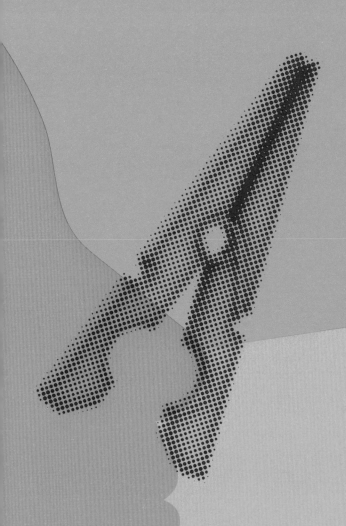

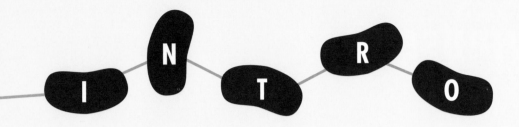

It's quite fashionable these days to describe the human race as a virus, as it seems to be reproducing almost without limit, consuming all resources in its path, and evolving (culturally) to overcome perhaps every obstacle it has thus far faced.

Don't worry, though, it's not your fault: it's your DNA, which is a worse virus still. Ever since that little acid learnt to copy itself, that's pretty much all it's ever done, evolving (literally) to overcome perhaps every obstacle it has thus far faced. Your entire body is nothing more than your DNA's wish to replicate into future generations and thrive. And drink beer. And Scuba dive. And go shopping, play Nintendo and watch the football.

Possibly the greatest obstacle the human virus (and our genome) has faced is disease and, well, proper viruses; a battle which we have fought with medical culture. I'd say we're about 3-1 up, which means we can worry about more important issues: not whether some bug is going to kill us but whether we can dive with it. The Shaman is on the front line of that war, and I reckon he's about 3-1 up as well, as you'll see in this chapter.

Still, though, am I the only one thinking that the common cold is the most annoying virus there is? OK, having just had a flick through some of the real illnesses in this section again, I suppose there's every chance I am. But still, you can do absolutely anything with a cold except what?

Dive. And why would you want to do anything else?

Tip: Don't inject yourself with any diseases or viruses just because we say they're easily curable.

CHEST

After having a cold and cough for approximately a month, I developed a pain to the right side of my ribcage. My GP says I cracked one of my ribs and it may take four to six weeks to heal itself. This was about five weeks ago. The pain has generally gone, but I get discomfort on sneezing, etc. and after vigorous exercise. Is there a recommended time I should refrain from diving?

I think that you have waited long enough to get back in the water. If you suffer a rib fracture for whatever reason then it will be pretty much healed in six weeks. The thing to watch out for is the pain and the way it may limit your ability to inhale.

If you find on inspiration that when the chest expands it catches and makes you cough, then this is a problem underwater. On top of this is the effect of an inflated BCD pushing onto the painful area. My tip is to put on your BCD at home, orally inflate it and try to breathe in as deeply as you can. If there is no pain and you can inhale fully then you should be fine to dive.

A point though from what your doc told you. There are other reasons for late presentation localised chest pain if you start with a simple cough. Rib fracture is rare, but there could be a chance that you have a pneumonia or pleurisy. This is where the outer lining of the lungs get infected and can cause a similar sort of pain. I think that if you are still getting pain now a chest X-ray would be useful as you shouldn't dive with the latter two.

"If you find on inspiration that when the chest expands it catches and makes you cough, then this is a problem underwater."

We are booked to travel on a liveaboard to the Red Sea tomorrow, and my wife has been prescribed trimethoprim 200mg for an infection. Can she dive whilst taking it?

It depends what infection she is being given this for. Trimethoprim is used most commonly for cystitis, so if this is the case she will be fine. The only thing she should watch out for here is that it can really make you pee a lot: a bladder infection that is. So to avoid diving dehydrated, and the increased risk of a bend that this entails, she should drink plenty of fluids.

Trimethoprim is occasionally used in treating chest infections. I would not recommend diving with a partially treated chest infection, and would even leave it for a good week or two after the antibiotic course has finished. The infection itself, or the vast amounts of mucus that always seems to occur with a bronchitis, can cause lung problems in a diver: the green gunk could theoretically block off a small airway, so the air trying to get out on exhalation can't. Every dive has to finish with an ascent and the trapped air will expand. Doctors call it pulmonary barotrauma, but you may know it as lung rupture. It's not a lot of fun so make sure you are well clear of the rattley cough phase before you dive after any chest infection.

I would like to know if you can give me some advice after having pneumonia and a pleural effusion. After a follow up appointment a couple of months later I was told that there was still fluid present but that they would like me to try and get rid of it naturally over time rather than drain or syringe it out.

I was told by the non-diving doctor that providing my fitness was OK then there would be no problem diving. Can you confirm this?

A pleural effusion is a potential complication of pneumonia, but one that will often clear up by itself (if the volume of the effusion is not too large). Just to get the anatomy clear (as you know I'm a stickler for these things), the pleurae are membranes that cover the inside of the chest cavity and the surface of the lungs, forming one continuous lining. The space in between the two layers usually contains a small amount of fluid (three to four teaspoons or so), to lubricate the movement of the lungs against the chest wall with breathing. Normally surface tension holds the two layers close together, allowing the lungs to expand maximally. If excess fluid accumulates in this space it effectively squashes down the lung tissue, so reducing the surface area over which gas exchange can take place. Less oxygen makes its way into the blood and if you factor in the increased work of breathing at depth, then it's easy to become dangerously low on oxygen.

Before you dive again it would be important to ensure that all of the fluid has been reabsorbed, and there is no significant scarring of

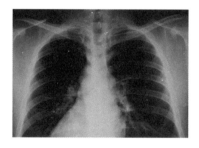

"This is probably going to mean some X-rays to ensure the lung fields are clear, and a set of lung function tests."

the lungs. This is probably going to mean some X-rays to ensure the lung fields are clear, and a set of lung function tests. You might be able to organise these via your GP, but you may require a visit to a local dive doc to get your fit to dive certificate.

I grew up in India and had TB at a young age. Unfortunately I didn't improve despite all the drugs that were given to me (for at least a year I think). In those days the only treatment they could offer me was pulmonary resection: cutting out the infected part of the lung. My parents were very worried I would not survive the procedure. I am now in my 60s and have never had any suggestion of the TB returning. I am fit for my age and two of my sons have qualified as divemasters. Now they want to take me diving, and I would like you to tell me whether this is possible.

Tuberculosis, aka 'consumption' (so-named because of its ability to 'consume' genetically-susceptible sufferers), was the scourge of Europe in the 19th century. Its hardcore statistics make grim reading. 1 in 4 deaths in England was due to TB in 1815. Traces of TB have been found in the spines of Egyptian mummies, so it has been around for thousands of years. Although nearly eradicated in the 1980s, the nasty bacterium is now making a comeback thanks to the emergence of HIV and multi-drug resistant strains.

TB tends to target the lungs but can be found in almost any tissue. It is spread through the air (coughing, sneezing, spitting), producing a new infection at the worldwide rate of one every second. One of its scariest aspects is its ability to lay dormant for many years. It is estimated that a third of the world's current population has been infected, but most cases will luckily remain asymptomatic, with only one in 10 going on to develop active disease.

Treatment consists of a wolf's liver taken in thin wine, the lard of a sow that has been fed upon grass, or the flesh of a she-ass taken in broth. At least it did in Pliny the Elder's time. These days antibiotics are the norm, although they are only barely more palatable. But in the pre-antibiotic days of the 1940s, surgery was the commonest method used to try to cure the disease. You don't say how old you were at the time the scalpel was wielded on your lung, but I would guess 40 to 50 years have elapsed since. Active TB is a complete no-no for diving, but a past history does not necessarily exclude it. The key question is, are there any cavities or scarred areas in the remaining lung tissue that might predispose you to pulmonary

"Treatment consists of a wolf's liver taken in thin wine, the lard of a sow that has been fed upon grass, or the flesh of a she-ass taken in broth."

barotrauma? To find out you would need to see a respiratory physician and have some pretty detailed scanning of the lungs, as well as functional testing (blowing into various machines, usually via a suspicious-looking toilet roll tube). If the tests come back clear, then certainly diving is possible.

My boyfriend has recently been diagnosed with sarcoidosis, which is a bit of a nightmare as we are divemasters and have flights booked to Thailand to do our instructor course.

He has seen a specialist and his lung function tests are better than average, but he has a small amount of scarring on his lungs. He has never experienced any symptoms and we probably never would have known if it wasn't for a chest X-ray needed for an Australian visa.

The specialist has told him that it will probably go away and no treatment is needed, but the big question is: can he dive?

This is a funny old illness of unknown cause which is extremely variable in severity and duration. It gives rise to 'granulomas' (small nodules of inflammation) in any organ, but most commonly the lungs and lymph nodes. Young adults of both sexes are typically affected, peaking in the 20-29 age range. The symptoms are often vague at first; fatigue, dry eyes, a cough, general aches and pains. The sorts of things young adults dismiss, so the diagnosis is sometimes delayed. As in this case, most sufferers are picked up on chest X-rays or breathing tests performed for another reason. You see a classic shadowing on the lungs caused by big lymph nodes in the early stages, but this can evolve into more serious lung disease. And this is why diving might be a problem: our old friend pulmonary barotrauma. Active sarcoid can cause scarring or air trapping, predisposing a diver to burst lung.

Treatment usually involves steroids or other immunosuppressant drugs, but mild cases often remit without therapy. The hope in your boyfriend's case is that, given time, the lung changes will clear up, but it could take many months. My advice is not to dive until you have a clearer idea of the course of his illness.

I have been diagnosed with asbestosis & pleural plaques in its early stages. I am 48 years old and have a reasonable level of fitness and feel I can cope with diving for a few years at least, but will I be able to?

"The symptoms are often vague at first; fatigue, dry eyes, a cough, general aches and pains. The sorts of things young adults dismiss…"

The situation with lung problems and diving can be summed up in a couple of points. Firstly, is your lung function good enough to ventilate you adequately during a dive and also if that dive were to suddenly become more of an exertion than you had originally planned, eg a strong counter current or having to tow your buddy back to a boat a few hundred yards away? This is assessed by lung function studies known as spirometry and should be done by a recognised medical examiner of divers in your area.

Secondly, lung problems that can result in dead air spaces or 'bullae' are a definite contraindication as air gets into these spaces under pressure at depth and as you ascend, because the air cannot be expelled, it expands and causes bad lung damage called pulmonary barotrauma. Your problem is not normally associated with these bullae so you should be fine on that count.

"…could you tow your buddy back to a boat a few hundred yards away?"

However, the bad news is that asbestos can lead to rather a nasty piece of medical grief called a 'mesothelioma'. It can appear several decades after asbestos exposure, so have regular reviews with a respiratory physician. Even every year or two to be safe. If these are OK, if you pass the spirometry, and the asbestosis doesn't affect your fitness, then you should be fine to do the PADI Open Water Course as diving will not make your condition worse.

My father, sister and brother all have marked alpha-1-antitrypsin deficiency (a genetically predisposed deficiency of a protease inhibitor). I have only a mild deficiency, and I have been diving for five years without problems, although I avoid technical diving.

My question regards my younger brother, who is 17 years of age, in good general health, and does not smoke. Is recreational Scuba diving going to be contraindicated for him, or is it reasonably safe to recommend him to take it up?

Alpha-1-antitrypsin deficiency is one of the commoner genetic disorders but is still rarely found. Basically it is a lack of the protein of the same name which has the function of keeping in check another protein called neutrophil elastase. The purpose of this is to digest ageing lung cells or bacteria in the lung. The problem with neutrophil elastase is that once it gets going on these cells it will go on and destroy the healthy lung cells unless the alpha-1-antitrypsin is there to stop it. So people with a deficiency of this will go on and get permanent lung damage, called emphysema.

But the question in your brother's case is how deficient is he, and does this deficiency mean that he will definitely get emphysema? And if so when?

Some research shows that even if he has only 15% of his expected level of alpha-1-antitrypsin then he may well not go on to get emphysema. On top of this there is a replacement treatment called Prolastin that can slow down the lung damage to the same levels as the rest of us.

If he has got any lung damage it would be unwise to dive, as the emphysema results in air pockets in the lungs. This means that air inhaled would not be able to be exhaled and would expand on ascent resulting in pulmonary barotraumas and cerebral arterial gas embolism (CAGE).

As you say it is "marked" then I guess that he is a bad case. Lung function testing and X-rays can tell how bad any damage is. But the only hope would be that if a respiratory physician were to be able to 100% guarantee that there were no lung effects yet then he may be fine at this stage. However, most docs wouldn't risk this sort of call to sign off a diver, so sadly it may be better if he pursued another sport.

"...most docs wouldn't risk this sort of call to sign off a diver, so sadly it may be better if he pursued another sport."

ENDOCRINE

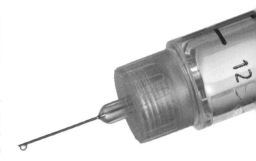

I am a 50 year-old female, insulin-requiring diabetic with hypertension. I take metformin 850mg three times daily, insulin (Novorapid with meals, Levemir at night), simvastatin 20mg daily and quinapril 40mg daily.

Until last year I had no side-effects from the diabetes but now I have developed symmetrical neuropathy (hands and feet) and problems with my eyesight. I have medium proliferative retinopathy with macular oedema in one eye. Apparently the retina is detaching due to extra vessels and I am waiting to see a specialist at hospital to discuss. In the other eye I have spots on the retina.

Is it time for me to give up diving?

Halle Berry, Sharon Stone, Scotty from Star Trek… the list of famous diabetics is long and fruity. For the benefit of the curious, a quick run-through the chequered history of diabetic divers would be a good start here. An incident of DCI involving a diabetic diver in the mid 70s prompted BSAC to ban all divers with the condition (apart from those controlled by diet alone). However, when the case was re-examined in the early 90s, it was found that several factors not related to diabetes (including a PFO) contributed to the accident. Around the same time, a survey of diabetics who continued to dive despite the ban found that none reported hypoglycaemic (low blood sugar) attacks whilst diving. So BSAC began to re-admit diabetics as members in 1992, as long as certain strict medical criteria were met.

The subject of diving with diabetes could fill this whole book but in a nutshell, the greatest potential risk to diabetic divers is having a hypoglycaemic episode (a 'hypo') whilst under water. A severe attack can result in weakness, loss of consciousness or fitting: all potentially catastrophic in the inky blackness. The stresses of diving (hard finning, high work of breathing etc.) can use up a lot of blood

"Halle Berry, Sharon Stone, Scotty from Star Trek… the list of famous diabetics is long and fruity."

sugar and make hypos very unpredictable even in well controlled diabetics. Also, the early symptoms of a hypo (disorientation, euphoria, nervousness) can easily be confused with narcosis and this potential masking of symptoms is why most authorities recommend a depth restriction of 25-30m for a diabetic diver.

So, generally we say that if you have good sugar control (revealed by a blood test called a HBA1C), a good understanding of your disease, are responsible enough to recognise symptoms and can dive with a buddy with at least Rescue Diver skills then there's a good chance a dive doc can clear you as fit to dive...

...Provided there are no manifestations of advanced diabetes, which is where we have a problem here. Secondary complications of diabetes are generally indicative of severe and progressive disease. These can affect any organ of the body, but of most importance diving-wise are the effects on blood vessels. Furring up of the arteries occurs much earlier in diabetics, leading to an increased risk of high blood pressure and heart attack. For the same reason, diabetics can develop early cramping in the legs, with poor exercise tolerance. The eyes, kidneys and nerves are also affected, and function less well. Although this does not directly affect diving ability, it is a sign that the illness is progressing. In your case I think the stage has been reached where it may be best to consider hanging up the fins and looking back at all the enjoyable memories you've accumulated.

"The stresses of diving can use up a lot of blood sugar and make hypos very unpredictable even in well controlled diabetics."

I was recently sent to hospital due to climbing potassium levels and a strong feeling of fatigue, weakness and shortness of breath. This was completely out of character since I usually run five miles every evening after work. After four days I was sent home with a diagnosis of Addison's disease. (I have vitiligo, another auto immune disease which should have helped with the diagnosis, although it seems Addison's is relatively rare).

I have to take fludrocortisone (100mcg) once daily and hydrocortisone three times a day (breakfast 10mg, lunch 10mg and dinner 5mg) to account for the lack of cortisone my body is producing.

Can I continue to dive?

The thing about these endocrine problems, like underactive thyroid as well, is that the medication you take is to replace what's missing. If this is done well and titrated to full effect, then you should be normo-hormonal. The lack of steroid from your underactive adrenal glands, and the consequent electrolyte imbalance, should be corrected by the synthetic steroids you are on. If the balance is right, then you should not suffer any effects of over-steroiding.

So diving should be fine. I would say that it is worth having a blood test to check all your levels before doing a long series of dives. As you know, the fatigue and fluid balance and low blood pressure caused by this disease can affect diving and increase risk, so plan ahead and get in to your GP early so they can do the tests twice. Twice? They always lose the first one.

I am currently in the US Navy and stationed at the Naval Diving and Salvage Training Center in Panama City, Florida. When I reached the school here I was told by the DMO that I was disqualified from diving duty due to Graves disease. I was diagnosed in 1994, treated with radioactive iodine and am now on levothyroxine. I have never experienced a problem with this disease and am a PADI certified diver, so I've had the experience of pressure at depth and have had no problems there either.

I would like your opinion as to whether I am fit to dive.

Graves disease is a relatively rare condition that affects the thyroid gland (a small gland in the front of the neck that is responsible for regulating the metabolism of the body). With this disease, the body's immune system attacks the gland making it overproduce thyroxine, a hormone that acts on every cell in the body. In most cases the condition is picked up quickly and treated with drugs, surgery or radioactive iodine. Usually this results in the gland becoming underactive and not producing enough thyroxine, and it has to be replaced in the form of tablets. Once stabilized there are usually no long-term problems.

During the stage of excess thyroxine production, there can be multiple symptoms: fast heart rates, excessive sweating, intolerance to heat, anxiety and more serious symptoms such as heart disease, and a condition called exophthalmos, where the eyes bulge out.

Provided that you have been checked out, there have been no serious long lasting side effects and you are stable on thyroxine, I see no reason why you should not be able to dive.

I have something called phaeochromocytoma. I went to see my GP because I'd been having lots of headaches, feeling very anxious and even getting hot flushes (I'm not going through the change, I'm a 39 year-old man). My blood pressure was high and after lots of messing about with pills and various tests my GP sent me to see a specialist who diagnosed phaeo. Do I have to stop diving?

Phaeochromocytomas (let's call them phaeos, shall we?) are rare tumours of stuff called chromaffin tissue. In humans this is mainly found in the adrenal glands, just above the kidneys. As you might expect, the adrenal gland secretes adrenaline (and a related compound called noradrenaline), and so a tumour of this sort leads to hugely excessive amounts of these hormones entering the blood. The symptoms that result are those of adrenaline overload: rapid heart rate, high blood pressure, palpitations, anxiety or panic attacks, sweating, headaches, pale skin and weight loss, to name a few. The old test for a phaeo was to see whether a gentle shove of the adrenal gland would trigger off a bout of symptoms; thankfully there are subtler diagnostic tools these days.

The main problem with diving with a phaeo is that the symptoms can come on suddenly in paroxysms or 'episodes', without warning. You can see the problem if this was to occur underwater. But all is not lost. Most phaeo's are actually benign, ie non-cancerous, and although technically challenging, surgical resection of phaeos is undertaken with good success rates these days. Sometimes the tumour itself can be removed, occasionally the whole adrenal gland has to be chopped out, but 95% of people are alive five years after surgery (this is a pretty good statistic). Once you're rid of the pesky thing it should be possible to return to the wet stuff.

> "The symptoms that result are those of adrenaline overload: rapid heart rate, high blood pressure, palpitations, anxiety or panic attacks, sweating, headaches, pale skin and weight loss, to name a few."

CONTAGIOUS

As Training Officer for a BSAC Branch, we teach and practice 'full on 100% contact' mouth to nose artificial ventilation in water, obviously not inflating the casualty's lungs. I am wondering what the medical consequences are with respect to infectious diseases? Are we risking anyone's health and what are the legal implications?

When you use the term "full on" in reference to any physical contact it makes me wanna join your club.

The cases of viral transmission, eg HIV or any of the hepatitis viruses after mouth to mouth or mouth to nose contact are enormously rare. What would be needed is blood to blood contact from each participant, and for long enough to make viral transmission a possibility. To tell you the truth, the only case I saw was on cable TV, on one of those Springer type shows. "I got AIDS from kissing" strap-lined below two of the ugliest people ever to appear on telly. They both had bleeding gums during snogging, and were both stupid enough not to realise how repellent the other one was and to stop. Their best efforts to remove themselves from the gene pool were sadly not rewarded as their mutant progeny sat by their sides.

Mouth to nose should be fine. You really should practise it as you would do it if the situation arose. The paramedics use those mouth guards not so much for viral reasons but rather for blow back of vomit in an unconscious patient.

I am going diving in the Andaman Islands off India, but have heard stories about street beggars having leprosy. Is it possible to catch this disease easily from them if they were to touch me or is it quite safe really?

Your fears, you will be glad to hear, are not well founded. Leprosy, or to give it its other name of Hansen's disease, named after its discoverer, is in fact not transmitted by direct contact with the skin of a sufferer.

> "When you use the term 'full on' in reference to any physical contact it makes me wanna join your club."

Current figures show that leprosy afflicts over 15 million people world-wide. These cases are found around Africa and India mainly, and are seen in the poorer sector of the population.

It's caused by bacteria which live in the lining of the nose and also in the nerves of sufferers, and it is because of the latter that the effects of the disease are seen. Because the nerves that supply the feeling of sensation to various parts of the body get inflamed during the infective process then they cease to function properly. This then results in what we call painless injury. People with this problem can easily cut themselves, pick up objects that are far too hot, and even break bones without realising, and because of this deformities arise all too easily. The skin depigmentation seen in this disease is due to scalding or sometimes the bacteria which can cause inflammation in the skin. The sad thing about leprosy is that it is easy to diagnose and also very easy to treat in the early stages with simple antibiotic treatment, but the problem goes unchecked in the developing world due to lack of resources and also fear of the stigma of the disease.

The way that it is spread is via respiratory droplets full of bacteria being sneezed and then inhaled by the recipient. Early symptoms are non-itching rash or blood stained nasal discharge, and if you are diagnosed at this stage then a course of Dapsone will cure it. But it really is a hard disease to catch and you wouldn't get it from just passing contact but by sharing a room with a sufferer for quite some time, and it is definitely not passed on by touching a person with it. Interestingly, the leprosy bacteria is only able to infect humans and one other animal species, the nine-banded armadillo, which of course is now blamed for the spread of disease in parts of the Americas.

The other myth to dispel here is that parts of limbs do not fall off in this illness, so don't worry, it is a hard disease to get and an easy one to get rid of.

I have glandular fever, which is bizarre as I'm about 35 years too old for it, and haven't been snogging any 17 year-olds since I was 17.

Nevertheless, I do have it; I feel rough in the mornings, and get tired. I am working and manage to get to the City and work (reasonably long days), but don't do much else except come home and collapse in the evenings and weekends. I have stopped running and doing swimming training, although I do

"Because the nerves that supply the feeling of sensation to various parts of the body get inflamed during the infective process then they cease to function properly."

swim a bit in a pool. I have pulled out of a triathlon in two weeks time.

I am due to go diving in the southern Red Sea, on a liveaboard, in a couple of months time. The travel company have requested payment. My doctor said that there is still plenty of time for me to get better, but I couldn't go in my present state. What's your view?

Poor you. Glandular fever (GF), or infectious mononucleosis, to give it its boring name, can be contracted at any age. The virus can get you when you are feeling low, and make you feel lower still. I think the key thing here, as recovery goes, is to have goals to aim for and work up to them slowly. In rare circumstances GF can lead to ME like problems, where constant inability to achieve normal activities sets you back physically and mentally. Depression sets in, physical exertion gets harder, and before you know it you're off work for a year, and Esther Rantzen has to take you to swim with a dolphin 'to get you better'. So, book the dive holiday.

Work your physical activity up to the point where you will be strong enough for the diving by then, and when there take it easy and only take on the easy stuff to start with. GF is no bar to diving, but the inability to do even the lightest of activities would be, so plan your recovery from now with that in mind.

Can you please tell me if HIV prevents you from Scuba diving? I've been positive for about six years, but have been in good overall health (reasonable T-cell count) and have never had to take any medication for my condition. I am considering taking lessons, so I would appreciate your advice.

Having HIV/AIDS shouldn't, in this day and age, prevent you from doing anything, and is certainly not a bar to diving. There are some special considerations though.

Firstly, even in otherwise unaffected individuals, there are often subtle changes in a variety of brain functions, for example behavioural and motor skills, eye movement, coordination and spatial orientation. These may be exacerbated in the underwater environment and could potentially threaten safety.

Secondly, no doubt many divers will relate to the bloodstained snot/ spittle that emerges from masks on surfacing, and this is a potential

"...before you know it you're off work for a year, and Esther Rantzen has to take you to swim with a dolphin 'to get you better'."

(although unproven) route of transmission of the virus.

Thirdly, some of the drugs that are used to treat HIV have side effects that may mimic symptoms of DCI; typically tinglings in the extremities, aches in muscles and joint pains; which may cause diagnostic confusion if a bend is suspected. Indeed, these symptoms can occur as part of AIDS itself.

Finally, there is also the question of an increased susceptibility to infections. Venomous marine critters are no respecters of a compromised immune system and may cause long-lasting and severe illnesses.

All that sounds pretty gloomy, but in reality many of these problems do not seem to have materialised in individuals whose HIV is under control, such as yourself. Suitable assessment prior to diving ought to pick up those with complications likely to endanger themselves or their fellow divers. The virus doesn't survive for more than a few minutes outside the body, so buddy breathing techniques and use of rental regulators (which are regularly disinfected) pose no real risk. So if you are in good overall health, there's no reason you shouldn't start taking lessons.

GENETIC

Our nine year-old son is a keen swimmer and enjoys weekly snorkelling and lifesaving lessons at his local swimming club. My husband is a regular Scuba diver and our boy is starting to take an interest, however he was diagnosed with cystic fibrosis (CF) late last year. He is generally fit and well, pancreatic sufficient, has no persistent cough nor nasal mucus, and apart from when he has a bad cold he is like a normal, happy nine year-old.

Do you have any knowledge of research or views on the potential for children suffering from CF to dive? Would it be totally unsafe for him to participate in this sport when he is older due to lung pressure or would he be safe to Scuba dive to a certain depth?

Apparently in the US, children call this illness '65 Roses' as it's easier to pronounce.

Cystic fibrosis was spotlit recently by 'A Boy Called Alex', a great TV antidote to the currently ubiquitous teenage hoodie tales. The story of Alex's quest to put on a choral performance at Eton (where he is a music scholar) in the face of frequent hospitalisations was one of those inspirational 'life is what you make it' yarns. CF is the most common genetic disease in Europeans. The mutated gene causes production of thickened mucus in the lungs, and similar thickening of digestive juices in the pancreas leads to difficulty absorbing nutrients and vitamins, with consequent malnutrition. Cases can be diagnosed before birth with genetic testing, but unfortunately CF is presently incurable, and many die young: often in their 20s or 30s.

There are several difficulties I can envisage with diving. The thickened mucus tends to clog up sinuses and nasal passages, which increases the chance of infection, polyp formation and equalisation problems. The same thick mucus in the lungs could also cause blockages and plugging in the small airways, with possible air trapping and the risk of pulmonary barotrauma and air embolism. All these thickened

"Our nine year-old son is a keen swimmer and enjoys weekly snorkelling and lifesaving lessons at his local swimming club."

secretions are perfect havens for bugs to breed in, and regulators or snorkels could spread infection to a CF sufferer.

But these days life expectancy is on the increase thanks to new treatments, and in some children there is very little lung involvement. Your son's consultant will be familiar with the condition of his chest in terms of infection, damage and associated asthma. If chest disease is minimal, precautions are taken and any risk is understood, diving might be possible, but you would need to be certain that the problems outlined above were dealt with.

I have a form of muscular dystrophy (FSHD), which means my muscles slowly become weaker over my lifetime. I cannot lift heavy weights and could probably not swim against strong currents. If I am helped to my feet with the weight on my back, then I can manage to stand whilst kitted up. The only time I went Scuba diving was in Fort Lauderdale and we were dropped off and picked up by a boat. I can swim and tread water proficiently, but not strongly. It's not stamina that's the problem, it's the power.

So, would I be accepted to attend the PADI course?

If it is just a question of power, and you cannot totally lift a weighted BCD, or a buddy in trouble, then you are the same as many other divers. The elderly, young and just plain feeble: they can dive so why can't you? Well the problem is you have a whopping great diagnosis, and they do not. So wherever you go there will be problems of admitting your condition on the medical forms in the dive shops.

I think a better solution is for you to enrol into a disabled diving programme. They exist the world over, and in the UK, the Scuba Trust is close to my heart. They would teach you the basics over here. You would be accompanied by professionals who know how to dive with low ability divers, how to watch for problems before they occur and who have a lot of patience. They run trips to the Red Sea, so you can still dive your dream over there and it would be a lot safer than rolling up to a Sharm shop and hoping they have an expert spare.

"The elderly, young and just plain feeble: they can dive so why can't you? Well the problem is you have a whopping great diagnosis, and they do not."

I want to try diving, but when I was pregnant last year I was diagnosed with sickle cell trait. My doctor doesn't know whether it's safe for me to dive. I've heard about sickle cell disease and

I'm not sure what the difference is, if there is one. Can you clear up my confusion, and, better still, tell me I can dive?

OK, let's do a basic biology lesson first. Red blood cells have evolved a particular shape to help them flow easily through blood vessels, the so-called 'bi-concave disc'. Imagine two Frisbees opposite each other and squashed in the middle. Or a doughnut with a thin flat piece filling the hole. Mmm, doughnuts. In sickle-cell disease, an abnormal form of haemoglobin (HbS) means that the red cells become distorted into a sickle shape. These get stuck in blood vessels, cutting off blood supply to tissues further on, which leads to organ damage and painful 'crises', which can be completely incapacitating. It is genetically inherited: if both genes code for HbS, then a person will develop sickle cell disease, but if only one HbS gene is inherited (and the other gene is normal HbA), then you have sickle cell trait. Those with trait only are (relatively) lucky; they don't develop the full-blown disease, but are carriers. It is a lifelong condition, and most often found in those of Afro-Caribbean origin. The reason for this is interesting: having sickle-shaped red cells protects a person from malaria, and so it is relatively common in areas where malaria is endemic. In certain parts of Africa sickle cell disease is known as ogbanjes ('children who come and go'), because the infant mortality rate is so high.

Unfortunately, if you have sickle cell disease, diving is out. The increased risks of DCI and precipitating a sickle cell 'crisis' are too great. For those with the trait the situation is a bit more controversial. Some authorities cite evidence that low oxygen levels can trigger sickling and crises, but others quite reasonably point out that in these conditions (eg out of air/equipment failure situations), drowning would be more of a worry, and the sickling is irrelevant. I tend to agree with this last point. Those with trait are very unlikely to develop any dive-related problems under normal conditions.

Is it safe to dive if you suffer from Marfan syndrome? My 34 year-old husband has this condition and would like advice.

The thought of a 6'5" superwoman hurling a volleyball at you at 110mph is seriously disconcerting, but one of the game's best female players, Flo 'The Clutchman' Hyman, had Marfan syndrome. Some even speculate that the world's favourite terrorist Osama bin Laden was a sufferer, based on his tall stature, use of a cane and rumoured heart disease.

> "Imagine two Frisbees opposite each other and squashed in the middle. Or a doughnut with a thin flat piece filling the hole. Mmm, doughnuts."

Named after the French paediatrician who first described it, it's a genetic disorder affecting men and women equally, which is most often inherited although it can arise from new mutations in 15-30% of cases. The defective gene causes problems with the elastic proteins found in the connective tissues of the ligaments, major blood vessels (the aorta in particular) and many other areas. The resultant symptoms and signs include great height, long, slender limbs and a wide handspan (the composer Rachmaninov was another famous case, as anyone who has tried to play his ludicrously difficult piano music will know). These manifestations would seem to be pretty useful in the aquatic world: carving through the water like the Thorpedo with zero resistance and great big paddles for feet and hands. However, some of the other consequences are of more detrimental import to diving, including chest wall deformities, curvature of the spine, and, more seriously, abnormalities of the aorta and heart valves.

The condition often goes undiagnosed until complications occur: poor Flo was only 31 years-old when she died on the courtside after being substituted during a game in Japan in 1986. Her death was due to aortic dissection (resulting from her previously undiagnosed Marfan), where a tear in the wall of the aorta causes blood to flow between the layers, forcing them apart; a medical emergency which can quickly lead to death. Once diagnosed, treatment of Marfan involves regular heart checks with the aim of slowing the damage to heart valves and the aorta. There are also some procedures that can correct the skeletal problems if they are severe.

The biggest risk in terms of diving with Marfan is its effect on the lungs. The chest wall deformities (including the so-called 'caved in' chest, and spinal curvature) can restrict lung expansion, and Marfan is a risk factor for spontaneous pneumothorax (or collapsed lung). About 10% of patients have some lung abnormality, and there are case reports of lung collapse occurring even with the relatively small pressure changes of mountain climbing and ascent / descent in pressurised planes. So you can imagine that there's quite a significant risk of lung problems given the large pressure changes that occur in the first few metres of a dive. My advice would be to steer clear and adopt a slightly less dangerous activity.

"...symptoms and signs include great height, long, slender limbs and a wide handspan."

NEUROLOGICAL

My girlfriend has passed her PADI Open Water Course but has recently discovered she has multiple sclerosis (relapsing and remitting). She has no symptoms and has had a diving medical. Should she go on to do her Advanced Open Water Course?

Also, can you dive with silicone implants?

MS is a neurological illness involving the central nervous system (brain, spinal cord and optic nerves). The CNS nerve fibres are surrounded by an insulating fatty sheath composed of myelin, which aids in the transmission of electrical impulses. In MS, myelin is lost and replaced by areas of scarring (termed sclerosis) often in multiple disparate areas, hence the disease's name. As a result, conduction in the nerves is disrupted, giving rise to a broad range of symptoms: cognitive impairment (memory difficulties, attention and concentration deficits); sensory manifestations (pins and needles, numbness); bowel or bladder disturbances; and visual problems to name the more common.

Anyone with a passing knowledge of DCI will perhaps recognise all of these as possible symptoms, and historically diagnostic confusion between MS and DCI has been a major issue. Precautions such as keeping an up-to-date record of an MS diver's neurological deficits should allow a clued-up doc to distinguish the two. There's no evidence that diving has any detrimental effect on the disease process, but sometimes MS relapses can be triggered by over-exertion or extremes of temperature. These factors should be borne in mind when considering dive trips and evaluating conditions on the day. As such, I would advise that she limits her depth to 20m: preferably on Nitrox as it is safer when used in conjunction with air tables.

The current regulations are that anyone suffering from MS is allowed back into the water one year after a relapse of the problem, providing they do not experience any symptoms or worsening of

> "Anyone with a passing knowledge of DCI will perhaps recognise all of these as possible symptoms, and historically diagnostic confusion between MS and DCI has been a major issue."

the condition during this time. So if your girlfriend has been free of the problem for 12 months then she is OK to go in again.

As for silicone, I have spoken to a couple of plastic surgeons, and they both say that the modern gel type implants are completely safe, however the old style implants which are silicone bags filled with fluid may have a very small chance of leakage if pressures are extreme.

However, assuming she is not diving to the bottom of the Marianas trench, the only extreme pressure she will get is from a drysuit squeeze... or hands. The former is more likely at the bottom of Stoney Cove, the latter in the bacon sandwich queue.

I am aged 59 and have been receiving treatment as a Parkinson's patient for the last 18 years. The disease is fairly well controlled. Does Parkinson's disease rule out diving for me?

This condition has such a broad range of presentations that the answer to your question is not easy. Parkinson's is one of the 'movement disorders', and results from a loss of cells in the brain, particularly those that secrete a substance called dopamine. The lack of dopamine gives rise to the classic symptoms of impaired motor and speech skills.

To dive or not to dive? As usual, it boils down to individualised assessment. Certainly in its early stages, the disease sometimes has very little noticeable effect, and there is no evidence that diving worsens or accelerates it. The potential problems I can envisage are several though.

Firstly, the physical: Parkinson's is characterised by muscle rigidity, tremor and slowing of movements, often complicated by poor balance. Practical issues such as donning kit, water entry/exit and finning would become tricky.

Secondly, cognitive disturbances: reaction time slows, procedural memory (so-called 'how to' knowledge, used when performing skills) is impaired, and later dementia occurs, with hallucinations, delusions and paranoia developing.

Thirdly, medication: the main drug used to treat Parkinson's is called levodopa, which attempts to replace the lost dopamine in the

"Certainly in its early stages, the disease sometimes has very little noticeable effect, and there is no evidence that diving worsens or accelerates it."

brain. It can cause dizziness, confusion and visual disturbances. Several other medicines used to potentiate or control side effects of levodopa may have their own adverse effects too. All a bit of a worry.

So there are lots of possible hurdles, but I would never give an outright 'no' without seeing a patient first. It would be unfair to deprive an individual with mild and manageable symptoms of the pleasures of diving.

I'm a volunteer instructor for the Scuba Trust (who teach those with disabilities to dive).

A would-be student with Motor Neurone Disease (MND) was turned away last spring from another diving organisation, on the grounds that he had some airway difficulties during initial pool training. In recent years he has dived (untrained) on holiday in Australia and Egypt.

I sent him for (yet another) medical, which confirmed he was fit to dive. Yet, I have spoken to his previous instructor who says I would be mad to take him in the water. This instructor feels the diver is at risk from his bulbar palsy, while the doctor who examined him does not, but says I should trial the diver in the pool on mask and reg removal.

In the past, this man has had some minor difficulty with swallowing when his disease is very active, but at present his gag reflex is intact. His voice is moderately affected. He is very determined to dive, and if it is at all possible for him to do so safely, I will train him on an IAHD level to dive with two trained assistants, but initially I must decide if is safe or not to assess him in the pool.

This is an interesting case where we have to weigh up several issues. MND is a terrible neurological condition where due to degeneration of certain areas of the spinal cord and cells in the nerves that supply the throat, tongue and pharynx, the sufferer can find that they progressively become more disabled but with unaffected mental functioning. Sadly, it is a rapidly progressive disease and if there are symptoms of 'bulbar palsy' ie inability to swallow and problems with speech, then death can often be within two years. So you can see how determined this man may be to dive right now as the future is bleak.

As he has been passed as fit by a diving doctor, then I would agree with their decision, but I would also add that the best person to assess his bulbar palsy and how much airway protection he has at this stage is a speech therapist. Because MND can be rapidly progressive, if the speech therapist confirms the doctor's findings then it's not a situation like other medicals where you are passed as fit for a year or so. The assessments would actually need to be very frequent, even weekly, if he continues to dive.

The real problem with this bulbar palsy is that it affects his ability to protect his airways if he were to swallow or inhale any water. If unaffected people get water in their mouth and throat, then the epiglottis comes down over the upper airways to stop it running down to the lungs. This may not be the case with your diver and it would obviously put him at risk underwater. However, as you know, most competent divers don't need this function as they never lose a reg or let water get in the mouth during a dive.

POST VIRAL FATIGUE (ME)

I am an avid diver and have been diagnosed with ME. As little is known about ME, I need advice as to whether I should continue diving. Most of my dives are 40m plus. The vast majority of time I don't feel well enough, but on the rare occasions I do I would like to.

In 1955 the Royal Free Hospital in north-west London (about two miles from where LDC is based) had to shut for two months due to a mysterious illness which caused fever and persisting fatigue in 292 staff members. Initially called 'Royal Free disease', investigations into the cause led to the coining of the term 'myalgic encephalomyelitis' (ME) for the condition. Interestingly, many veterans with Gulf War syndrome have almost exactly the same symptoms.

Diagnosis is difficult, relying as it does on subjective criteria, but generally it involves unexplained fatigue of six months or more, which is not due to exertion and which is unrelieved by rest. Numerous other symptoms may occur, such as memory problems, sore throats, joint and muscle pains, and unrefreshing sleep. If any other illness could cause the symptoms then ME is excluded. So there's plenty of scope for controversy here, as you can see. Initially the medical community was sceptical even of the existence of the disease, and the stigmatising 'attention-seeking' or 'malingering' labels are still very much a problem in the public arena.

Not surprisingly, as you say, most sufferers do not feel well enough even to contemplate diving. This, in some ways, is the best guide, as due to the fact that the mechanism of the illness is so unclear, it's very difficult to give concrete advice on whether it's safe to dive or not. All sorts of theories as to the cause of ME abound involving hormone imbalances, infections, neurological deficits, lack of childhood exercise, insecticides... the list goes on. The only fact is, no-one knows. As such, the best advice I can give you is if you feel up to diving, then make sure you get a full diving medical first. If you can put in a good showing on the ears, heart, lung and exercise tests, then I'd say you could dip your toe into the water.

"it involves unexplained fatigue of six months or more, which is not due to exertion and which is unrelieved by rest. Numerous other symptoms may occur, such as memory problems, sore throats, joint and muscle pains, and unrefreshing sleep."

VACCINATIONS AND PREVENTIONS

My girlfriend and I are travelling to India to work as diving instructors for up to twelve months.

We have both had jabs for various conditions within the last five years. As far as I can remember we've had, polio, tetanus, hep A and B combined, typhoid, diphtheria and meningitis. I had all three rabies jabs but my partner only had two. Would you mind letting us know what we are missing please?

Secondly, we are having difficulty getting information regarding malaria tablets and which are recommended for divers. Also, we have heard that some malaria tablets have antibiotic properties and are concerned about the effect this may have on the performance of the oral contraceptive my partner takes (Cilest).

You have had all the jabs you'll need for India. The only thing is how out of date some might be after you have had them. Tetanus is 10 yearly, typhoid two to three yearly; the heps should be good for 10 years if you had the boosters before the 12 month run-off period after the shots.

That leaves the rabies really. This is necessary if you are both in the remote wilds of India, however if you are in the dive zone then I guess that you are in Goa where local hospitals will have all the proper rabies shots if you were bitten by a mad salivating dog, so you probably don't need that shot any more. Forget meningitis for India, you will be safe there.

Malaria is the big question. You have three or four options. One is mefloquine (better known by the trade name, Lariam), but that will make you barmy at times. Best to go for Malarone in the short term, but this is expensive as it has to be taken daily and is not off-patent yet. As you are there for a whole year you are better off with the combination of Paludrine and chloroquine. The former daily, the

> "...hospitals will have all the proper rabies shots if you were bitten by a mad salivating dog, so you probably don't need that shot any more."

latter weekly. Go for that, but remember that not getting malaria is more than just taking tablets. Long sleeved shirts, mossie nets and repellent are needed too. You could always just keep wearing your wetsuits all night for total protection.

I'm off to Cancun, Mexico. Could you tell me which injections are mandatory if any and which are recommended? Also, are they checked and could I be refused entry if I cannot prove compliance?

Well perhaps only a reality shot mate. Cancun: probably the farthest we can send the Millwall pie-throwers for a holiday without destroying a fragile ecosystem.

Actually, I have flown there and the key is to go as far south as possible ASAP. The coral is in Cozumel, the culture inshore from Tulum. All you need is a hep A shot as you are out of real rabies/malaria/dengue country. As for the certification of shots don't worry, Mexico has this weird system of arrival etiquette. You will get to push a button on a red/green flashing traffic light thing. Red, and it's off for the rectal with sniffer dog back up, green and its go straight through to the land of Montezuma. But whatever colour you get no-one is going to ask for the vaccinations you have had. How do I know? Well as a good doc I mostly travel in a state of medical disorganisation, and have fought my way past blokes with five litres of Factor 8 and duty-free voddy at the passport queue, to be never asked about what shots I've had before Mexican entry. I shouldn't knock it of course: Cancun is the point of disembarkation for all that cave diving in the crystal clear cenote waters; it's just a shame that most visitors don't get further than their hotel bar.

Recently, at a party, I met a retired consultant physician and our conversation turned to malaria prophylaxis, as it does at parties. This person told me that the 'supposed' neuro-psychiatric side effects of Lariam were unrecorded outside the UK and that the rest of the world used Lariam quite happily. Of course, if this is true and we British divers are all deluded, it would be quite interesting to know. Can you shed any light on the subject?

"Unrecorded outside the UK"? What a load of twaddle. I remember when this medication came out. It was tested in the first Gulf War on bomb wary GIs, who could not tell a drug related side effect from the nuttiness brought on by shell shock.

> "You could always just keep wearing your wetsuits all night for total protection."

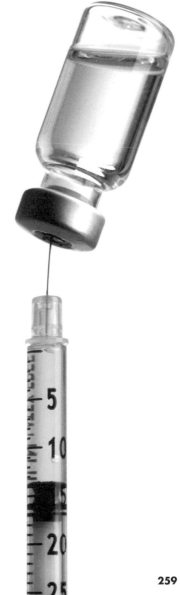

When I spent half a year in Africa in the 90s, about 30% of the travellers on Lariam reported side effects. One Aussie girl woke up in a tree after taking one at night. Another American girl used to dread it when her Lariam dose coincided with her PMT. We witnessed it when it did. Thank God for those big Zulu shields and assegais. Also, some of the associated side effects, such as tremors, dizziness, rashes and joint pains may mimic decompression sickness, and as such are hard to differentiate.

Lariam, though does have its place. A weekly anti-malarial and there's little resistance to it, so I always suggest that if you are going to an area of high resistance, you should take a test dose before you go. If you go nuts on it, then stay clear, but if it has absolutely no side effects with you, then you may be OK to dive on it.

The thing to remember is that when abroad, not getting malaria is more important than diving. I know. I got cerebral malaria in Ouagadougou, which was so bad it stopped me smoking and made me lose two stone. What a bummer of an illness. Thanks to quinine and the Tropical Diseases Hospital, I got better, fatter and back onto the tabs again: healthy at last.

Point of note: Malarone is good for all the areas Lariam is used. It is a daily tablet and expensive, but cheaper than a psych consult afterwards.

I am going cave diving in South America and my doc is not sure what shots I need. Can you help me out?

This is a fairly straightforward question, however there is a little twist which you may find interesting.

The baseline shots to make sure you are always up to date with, even if you are in the UK are tetanus and polio. What you then need to top up with before going out to South America are typhoid, which comes as a single shot in the arm, or there is an oral version for those who don't like the throbbing arm pain that typhoid immunisations always seem to cause. The next is hepatitis A, a single injection giving you a year's immunity followed by another shot after six months which increases your immunity to 10 years.

You are also advised that South America carries a risk of yellow fever, a viral disease spread by forest dwelling mosquitoes, and in many countries it is mandatory that you have a certificate of

"I got cerebral malaria in Ouagdougou, which was so bad it stopped me smoking and made me lose two stone. What a bummer of an illness. Thanks to quinine and the Tropical Diseases Hospital, I got better, fatter and back onto the tabs again: healthy at last."

immunisation against this illness before you enter the country. Yellow fever has recently been spreading into more urban parts of this continent, because human habitation has sadly moved into forested areas, and also the mosquito has been making tracks into areas where it was never found before.

The debate though is whether you need to have a rabies shot. This will not prevent you from getting the disease if you are bitten, but means that if you are you will not need to find the immunoglobulin, which can be very scarce in many parts of South America. You will still need to have a course of rabies injections if you are bitten by a suspect animal but these are easier to get. The chances of getting into contact with a rabies carrying animal are normally fairly rare, but one species that does carry the rabies virus is the bat. The virus can also be present in the excreta of the bat, which is found on the floor of the large caves where they roost during the day. It has been stated that there is a theoretical risk of contracting rabies if this excreta is inhaled. As you are caving, there is a chance that this may happen to you, so in this case I would recommend the rabies shot. The best way to prevent inhaling rabies laden bat excreta is to wear one of those masks that cyclists wear in polluted cities. Likewise, I would always ask any local guides what the current information is on the bat colonies that live in the caves you are about to go deep into, as they will be far better informed than most other sources.

Don't forget your malaria medication and also a good, secure mosquito net. If you are caving in remote areas you are entering vampire bat and also cone-nosed bug territory. We all know about the former, and the latter is the vector that spreads Chagas' disease, so remember a mossie net is not just for keeping off mosquitoes, but all the other biting bugs, bats and animals that would cause many travellers sleepless nights as they lie in fear of what will drop onto their heads at night from the ceiling of their hotel room.

"...so remember a mossie net is not just for keeping off mosquitoes, but all the other biting bugs, bats and animals that would cause many travellers sleepless nights..."

My wife and I are travelling to Roatan, and it has been recommended to us that we take chloroquine as the Bay Islands are in the local malaria zone. Can you please advise whether it is safe to take it whilst diving?

No worries here. Chloroquine is perfectly fine to dive with. It has few side effects, can be bought over the counter, and is taken weekly to prevent malaria.

I spent a long old while in Roatan. Loved it, me. Though my landlord, a local man, demanded no smoking, drinking or any pleasurable activity in his hotel. He and his wife were from some strange religious sect, although when she popped off the island for a few days on urgent family business, I was surprised to find him in a pool of his own vomit, drunk and singing garbled hymns. Faith in action.

Oh, by the way, you must do the night dive in the West End Bay, my top dive ever.

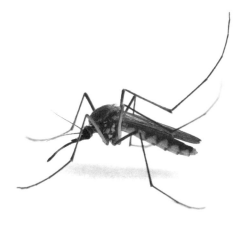

PSYCHIATRIC AND PSYCHOLOGICAL

INTRO

I was guided once, on a dive in Malaysia, by a guy who was teaching an Open Water class at the same time. The current was raging, but he waited until we were 18m down and the same distance from the line before aborting the dive. He did this by giving me (and me alone) the up signal and bolting. I helped his permanently-embarrassed DMT bring the students up. When we reached the surface, the instructor was already 30m away, back on the boat with his wetsuit around his waist, screaming: "Everybody get out of the water, right now!".

It's OK losing your cool if your house goes through a time warp back to the Dark Ages ("Quick! Everyone panic" said Vyvyan in The Young Ones), but the general consensus is that the water is best kept as stress-free as possible. Mind you, I once took some yoof supplied by Camden Council on a try-dive in a pool. They abandoned the karmic approach to diving entirely in favour of the 'mass-brawl' philosophy: ripping each other's masks off and power-inflating their BCDs. I would've stepped in but even though they were only 12, they were bigger than me. At the end of the session, their carer or something shoved them over to me one at a time to mutter "fank-oo" whilst sullenly staring at the floor, so I think they found the experience pleasurable. People generally do.

That said, I did once consider lobbying PADI to put an extra question on their medical form: "Are you learning to dive as the first step in overcoming the paralysing phobia of water you've had since you nearly drowned at the age of six?", but looking back, the real psychological stress in that situation was caused by having employers that insist on three day Open Water Courses.

So I don't think you can deny that diving is therapeutic. Unless, that is, you're wearing a holey hired 5mm in a quarry in February with 4mm vis. In which case, the only sensible thing to do is take Vyvyan's advice. Just make sure you do it before the dive, whilst you're still in the car park and within touching distance of the bacon-sarnie counter.

Tip: It's probably best to ignore any voices you might hear under-water and seek further advice before diving again, unless you're specifically wired up to some sort of surface communications device.

ANXIETY AND DEPRESSION

I am on 30mg of fluoxetine (Prozac) a day. This was prescribed for grief/depression following the loss of my mother and I am also going to counselling. Can I dive on this medication?

I find the whole issue of diving on anti-depressives very interesting. There are some doctors who feel anyone on these sorts of tablets should be barred from diving, whilst others have a far more realistic attitude as we know there have been thousands of divers doing millions of dives over the years without a single hitch whilst taking everything from Prozac to Cipramil.

The key to diving if you are on this medication is that you should have been on it a while so there are no surprises as to the side-effects of the tablets. I would say that a period of three to four months on the Prozac would be enough for you to have got used to being on it.

The other consideration is how well it's controlling your problem. If yours is a grief reaction, then that will probably not manifest itself underwater, but others on anti-depressives have problems that may cause difficulties. Examples are anxious depression that manifests as panic attacks, morbid depression where the sufferer is seriously suicidal, and the worst of all: psychotic depression where the plot has completely been lost resulting in a pseudo-schizoid state that should be treated at The Priory rather than Ras Mohammed. You really need to be assessed by someone who has a good understanding of psychology and diving to see if you are fit enough to dive and unlikely to suffer an episode which could endanger you or your buddy.

The intriguing point here as well is that there are many depressives who only feel well and free of their problem when they are one on one with a nudibranch on a clear blue day at depth. And as someone who has seen plenty of these divers I can only see the benefits of diving for their wellbeing.

> "The intriguing point here as well is that there are many depressives who only feel well and free of their problem when they are one on one with a nudibranch on a clear blue day at depth."

I am currently being treated for clinical depression and want to know if I can dive whilst taking venlafaxine 2 x 75mg in the morning, 1 x 75mg in the evening and carbamazepine 300mg in the evening. I have been on two diving holidays while taking this medication in the past and have had no problems at all.

You are going to wish you never asked me that I'm afraid.

The venlafaxine is debateable depending on how your condition is controlled and any side effects you have. The bigger problem though is the carbamezepine. This is normally used in epileptics as an inhibitor of fits. It potentially causes narcosis at very shallow depths and consequently anyone taking it is barred from diving.

This may annoy you as you may have dived many times on this medication and probably had absolutely no problems. But rules are rules. On top of this if you ever did have a problem and needed your insurance to cover it, they would be loathe to pay up in this sort of situation. So I suggest you go back to whoever put you on this med and see if there's an alternative. Then go and see a diving doctor to discuss the issues of the anti-depressant you are taking.

My doctor has just put me on buspirone for panic attacks. Is it OK to dive on them?

There is no actual problem in taking this particular medication and diving, but the bigger question here is how well the panic attacks are controlled.

I'm sure you understand the implications of having a panic underwater, not just for yourself but for your buddy. If your GP has decided that your condition is bad enough to warrant this sort of treatment, then I think it is better if you don't dive until whatever is causing the attacks has been alleviated.

Most people usually begin to get panics because of job, money, relationship or accommodation difficulties. If any of these are the causative factor, then once you are on top of it and panic free it will be fine to dive again. However if you are one of those people that gets a panic attack for no real reason then I suggest diving is not the thing for you as it most commonly results in a rapid ascent to get out of the water, which will of course bring on a bend. So the medication is fine but the condition isn't until you are more stable.

"I'm sure you understand the implications of having a panic underwater, not just for yourself but for your buddy."

I have been prescribed a course of 28 tablets of the Selective Serotonin Reuptake Inhibitor (SSRI) citalopram to relieve work related stress. I mentioned to my GP that I was a diver and he said that they would not have any side effects and I was to continue diving as it helps me relax. I just wanted to check this advice with a dive doc.

This has been something of a tongue-wagging hot topic recently. SSRIs are drugs often prescribed for depression, but they are used in a number of other conditions. A diver in Egypt who was taking the SSRI citalopram suffered symptoms of 'serotonin storm' – a syndrome of confusion, agitation, sweating, palpitations and hallucinations. This understandably prompted a flurry of visits and calls to LDC. The theory in this case was that the combination of depth and the drug led to the event. There is some evidence in animals that hyperbaric exposure renders the brain more susceptible to the effects of SSRI drugs such as citalopram, so this might be a plausible mechanism, but to my knowledge this is an isolated case. Usually this type of presentation is only seen in SSRI overdose; if the drug is combined with another psychotropic medication; or interestingly, with specific dry wind conditions, such as the Mistral or Sirocco in Europe.

The usual individualised approach is therefore important: why is the diver taking an SSRI, ie is the condition an issue? SSRI drugs are used for two purposes: treatment and maintenance. During treatment diving is unwise, but in the maintenance phase, where a low level of medication keeps a person well, diving is permissible. In general, SSRI's are much safer than the older tricyclic antidepressants, which were sedative and could trigger off funny heart rhythms and seizures. Nevertheless, the diver should have been on a stable dose of an SSRI for at least three months before diving, to allow the body to become used to side effects. Because neurotransmitter levels take time to respond to medication, any change in dose can produce unpredictable effects up to six weeks later, so people are most vulnerable when starting, stopping or changing SSRI dose. Increased effects of narcosis at depth will also produce a bit of a pot-pourri of influences on the brain, so I tend to advise shallow conservative profiles whilst on these meds.

I have been diving for around five years. I took Cipramil for depression for two years and continued to dive regularly during that time without experiencing any problems. I first took 20mg per day then reduced the dose to 10mg and finally stopped taking it altogether around nine months ago.

I think it's probably true to say that the benefit I get from diving feels as though it does me every bit as much good as taking Cipramil did. In fact, the thought of not being able to dive makes me feel really quite down. At the moment, I feel that the depression is returning (although I've never had panic attacks and I've never felt suicidal). I think I'd probably benefit from the support of taking medication again for a while, but I do feel a bit reluctant to start up the drugs again.

I've heard good reports from a friend of how much better he felt after taking St John's Wort, so, after reading about it as well, I have been considering trying it myself. I'm in good health generally and I'm not taking any other medication of any sort. Would it be OK to take St John's Wort and carry on diving?

Sorry to hear you are on a bit of a low, but here's some good news. The newer SSRI type anti-depressives are a whole lot safer than the old ones. So it is accepted that as long as your condition is stable (no one wants a suicidal buddy after all), and there are no odd side effects, that most divers will be OK on Cipramil. You will need a dive doctor to sign you off for this though, not your local GP.

As for St John's Wort, this is a fairly active compound more in line with the old style meds, so I would think it better to go back on to the Cipramil if you want to dive. This drug has been researched far better and we know its full side effect profile.

Or how about nature's own Prozac: dolphins. From what I have heard, a quick dip with Flipper and Mr Gipper (his stunt double; yes really) and your serotonin will be leaking out of your ears.

My brother, a diving instructor, is taking me to do the pool work of an Open Water Course on Saturday. He said that as I had intussusceptions when I was a baby, there might be a chance that I would need a medical before I could do the course. I had the operation when I was six months old and I am now 28. I have not had any intestinal problems since, caused by the operation or otherwise.

I also have suffered from panic attacks after I had glandular fever when I was 18 and again two years ago whilst working in a very stressful job which I left. I have not suffered from anxiety or panic attacks since then. Do you think I need to have a medical?

"From what I have heard, a quick dip with Flipper and Mr Gipper (his stunt double; yes really) and your serotonin will be leaking out of your ears."

The PADI medical has a real catch all statement on the form. "Do you have or have you EVER had..." And one of the questions is about psychological problems. So you will have to answer YES to that. When you present the form to any dive shop after your bro has trained you, it may cause concern, so it's best to collect your 'Get out of jail free' card, otherwise known as the Fit to Dive cert. As all has been OK for a while, I am sure the anxiety will not be an issue, unless you're a total bag of nerves and normal for you is half way between Norman Wisdom and a man about to be electrocuted.

The other issue, intussusceptions, is not a problem now, but an interesting medical problem. That's where your bowel slides into itself, like those odd water filled toys. The bowel then gets its blood supply cut off resulting in agonising pain, gangrene and death. Mainly babies get it and the classic sign is redcurrant jelly-like goo from the anus. A Munchausen's-by-proxy favourite for parents with nothing to do after their lamb roast.

I am currently on 20mg/day of Seroxat (prescribed as a gentle reliever of mild pre-menstrual lows and tensions) and have been for the last two and a half years.

My GP does not foresee a problem combining this medication with Scuba, however the centre I am currently diving with in Egypt insisted I consult with a dive doctor here and he has prevented me from further diving. Can you help?

Interesting this. In your favour is that the Seroxat is for seemingly mild, menstrual related depression rather than the morbid suicidal variety, where you could be a danger to yourself and others diving. Mind you, it's one hell of a drug for that (and one with some bad press recently), but horses for courses and if it works for you, then fine I guess. However, these drugs do have side effects that could cause problems underwater, so you do actually need to see someone for a complete check up as well as an ECG.

Finally, I think as GPs aren't up to speed on all diving issues, it is worth all divers being proactive themselves. Have a look at the PADI form on their website. If you do answer yes to any medical question, then make sure you get a dive doc's fit to dive cert before going all that way to find you can't dive as you haven't got the right paperwork.

I have a mild form of Seasonal Affective Disorder accompanied by rapid mood swings (no mania ever diagnosed). The severity is best described as interfering with social life during the months of November through March. There is no significant impact on work; no suicidal tendencies.

I want to become a dive instructor and as such am faced with the problems of my medication: lithium. It might be a problem with medical checks as there is little to no known data regarding lithium and diving. I have currently four options open to me: continue using lithium with a stringent blood check protocol (I have never ever had any problems using lithium and diving and my levels have always been steady at .70-.78 even after a night of heavy drinking and prolonged usage of NSAID's); quit using lithium (my mood swings have significantly reduced since 1995); switch to carbamazepine; or switch to Depakine.

What do you think?

I think it's going to be tough for you to become an OWSI on this medication. In the UK you need to pass the HSE medical to be allowed to train and actually then instruct. If you are on lithium, you won't get past first base. Firstly, as there is a lack of evidence of how it may affect you at depth, then it is not safe to have students under your care. Secondly, there are strict rules about your underlying condition and diving. Lithium is usually used for bipolar disorder which is not something that is conducive to sharp, quick decision-making in stressful environments.

The other two drugs are a no-no as they are both anti-epileptics and therefore bar you from diving.

However, having rapid mood swings that only affect social functioning in winter sounds like half the population. I wonder if your condition is as bad as you think it is or whether this is a hammer for a walnut case. So, come off the meds, get cleared by a psych as back to normal, and then see a dive doc for assessment.

"…having rapid mood swings that only affect social functioning in winter sounds like half the population."

OTHER

We have a certified diver who dived with us one day prior to starting an Advanced Open Water Course. When filling out the medical questionnaire, he stated he has a prescription for trifluoroperazine and procyclidine prescribed by a consultant psychiatrist. The client says it is to reduce voices that he hears on occasions. Can he dive with us?

Sadly I think that this diver should not really be in the water. The voices that he is hearing are a classic symptom of a psychosis. They are known as auditory hallucinations and are a symptom of schizophrenia. The medication that he is taking is a called a phenothiazine and has a wide side effect profile including seizures and blurred vision. Another side effect is called a 'tardive dyskinesia', where the mouth and lips go into a sort of spasm. So you can see the dangers of diving if these were to occur. The procyclidine part of the treatment s supposed to stop some of the side effects. However, one of the problems with this condition is that the medication is often forgotten and the symptoms come back under stress or anxiety.

Hence my advice is that he would be better off not taking the risk of diving.

This though, does bring up another issue. That of disappointed divers arriving on their holiday only to find that they are unable to dive. I think that it's about time that some of the holiday companies double check the client's medical history before they pay for the holiday. This can so easily be done by simply including the questionnaire from the PADI dive form in the brochure on their websites. If the prospective client answers 'yes' to any of the questions they will know to get medical clearance before going ahead and booking the trip.

This would have saved this person a 4000 mile trip to find out all he could do was lie on the beach.

"This though, does bring up another issue. That of disappointed divers arriving on their holiday only to find that they are unable to dive."

I used to occasionally feel claustrophobic on buses and I had trouble when I went caving once. Whilst I do not, and never have, felt claustrophobic in water, I still had to tick 'yes' to the question on the self-declaration form.

Can I dive?

> This is where a little common sense is needed. Claustrophobia is on the PADI form as a no-no to diving. But there are many shapes and forms of this psychological phenomenon. In most dives the only enclosed space you will find is your mask and the bogs on board a boat. So you would have to have an extreme version of this problem to find this debilitating.
>
> I think that if you are OK with a mask and don't do the swimthroughs, caves or wreck penetration then all will be fine.

"I think that if you are OK with a mask and don't do the swimthroughs, caves or wreck penetration then all will be fine."

I am taking my 16 year-old son on his first try dive within the next few weeks. He takes Ritalin 10mg for Attention Deficit Hyperactivity Disorder (ADHD) and Pimozide for mild Tourette's (symptomised by pacing) and I was wondering if this was safe to dive with.

My son doesn't actually need to take the medication whilst diving but I thought it might be wise as his concentration levels will be affected without it. I can stop the pimozide for the dive day, but thought the Ritalin would be wise whilst going through safety briefs etc. Please advise.

> ADHD has had an extremely bad press over the years. Although mostly thought of as a recent medicalisation of tartrazine-crazed kids, descriptions of ADHD-like symptoms go back to Ancient Greek times: in one individual, Hippocrates noted "quickened responses to sensory experience, but also less tenaciousness because the soul moves on quickly to the next impression". His explanation for this was "overbalance of fire over water". Things have moved on considerably since, and the illness now has a well-defined set of criteria which must be fulfilled for the diagnosis to be made. Some of these involve inattention and, well, hyperactivity and this obviously makes diving with the condition a risk. The last thing you want is your buddy drifting off into a world of their own, or fidgeting hysterically throughout the dive briefing.

Unfortunately, I've gotta be Doctor Gloomy here and break the bad news. I think diving on a medication like Ritalin is unsafe. It's basically an amphetamine: speed if you like. It will increase heart rate, cause dry mouth, whack up the metabolic rate etc. Also there is no research as to the drug's effects at depth, so forget taking him diving for now. Snorkelling should be OK though.

My fiancée takes Stelazine 5mg and procyclidine hydrochloride 5mg once per day. This is to counteract a dopamine deficiency. She is aged 42, otherwise in good health and does not smoke. Would it be safe for her to dive?

I think it's going to be difficult to get her signed off to be fit for diving on this drug combination and also for what it is used to treat.

Stelazine is a powerful tranquillising drug used for treating severe anxious, psychotic and depressive episodes. It also has side effects similar to Parkinson's Disease, which the procyclidine is given to counteract. Stelazine's tranquillising action will inhibit her ability to respond in critical situations, endangering both herself and her buddy, and if this were added to any narcosis then a fatality could happen.

As she is on this treatment for a major psychiatric episode, then this in itself would bar her from diving too.

I suggest she sees her psychiatrist to find out how long they think she needs to take this treatment, and if ever she is off it then a diving doctor would need a clear letter from her psychiatrist that she has fully recovered before passing her as fit to dive.

ARTICLE – THE PSYCHOLOGY OF DIVING

As I sit writing this, only a few yards away through a brick wall and a foot of steel lie two of my patients. They are undergoing a Royal Navy Table 62 recompression. Both have decompression sickness. But what is unique about these two, boyfriend and girlfriend, is that it was all so avoidable.

Nick and Janet had qualified three months previously and apart from the four open water dives deemed necessary to get a certificate of competence, they had done no more. Whilst on holiday last week the opportunity to dive again came up. Both keen to keep their log books ticking over, they went for it. At the dive shop, they told the owner that they were inexperienced and asked to do a simple dive. This was no problem apparently as the shop had two groups going out, one to a 30m maximum depth, and the other to only 15m. They signed up for the latter.

Gearing up, Nick was given a 12 litre tank, whilst everyone else was given 15 litres including Janet. Nick is over 6ft tall, Janet, under 5.5ft. Down they went off the boat and their group levelled out at the prearranged depth. This is when it went wrong. The divemaster proceeded to go after the deeper group and beckoned to his less experienced charges to follow him. They did. They followed him down to 40m. After well over 10 minutes there, Nick noticed he was down to less than 50 bar. In his own words, "I guess I was narked, though I've never experienced that before. So I panicked, over inflated my BCD and went straight up to the surface". He remembered to exhale, luckily, but managed to break the surface water waist high. Janet was dragged up too and hit the top still clutching Nick's leg.

Amazingly neither of them suffered any problems immediately, but later that day, Nick started to get tingling in his arms and also noticed pains in his shoulder joints. He rang the dive shop and told them, but they said it couldn't possibly be a bend as he hadn't

> "He remembered to exhale, luckily, but managed to break the surface water waist high. Janet was dragged up too and hit the top still clutching Nick's leg."

been deep enough for long enough. OK, he thought, they have the experience, they must be right. He still had the problem two days later, and told them again. This time they let him have some oxygen. For five minutes. He flew back home a day after this whereupon everything worsened. And there they both are with about another three hours to go on the table. They have both improved already, but through the chamber intercom they've asked myself and the outside attendant whether we want to buy any dive gear.

There are two lessons to this tale. Firstly, what happened to them both is not isolated: it happens to a diver every day of the year. You are told one profile above water only to have it changed for no reason below. You follow blindly even when you know it's going well beyond your experience. If you go into a bar and ask for a beer and pay for a beer, what would you do if they give you wine instead? Of course you would refuse and demand what you paid for, so why is it OK in diving to pay to do one thing and get something else? Well the answer is it's not. Nick and Janet should have refused to go deeper and indicated to the DM that 15m was where they were staying, because the results of not trusting your own judgement and blindly following the leader are just a few feet away breathing 100% O2. There are situations where profiles have to change, in the event of conditions or emergencies, but that wasn't the case here. Just a misguided shepherd and his flock. So next time you dive, remember it's your dollar or baht and make sure you get what you pay for.

The second lesson is equally important. Dive tables are basically guidelines. Calculated using lean, fit, US Navy volunteers. You can get decompression sickness even if you dive within the limits. Not very often, but you can. The most important thing as a diving doctor is what are the symptoms? If you are recently out of the water, complaining of tingling, numbness, fatigue or whatever, I don't really care exactly how long you were down or what your maximum depth was, all I want to know is could it be a bend from the symptoms you have? It was obvious Nick was bent from his symptoms and he should have been given oxygen as soon as he called the dive shop later that day. However, before we blame the shop for misdiagnosing, we need to make sure our own medical house is in order, and from my experience it's not. I have seen the most obvious cases of DCS sent away from the Emergency Departments of hospitals with a handful of paracetamol. One girl had obvious numbness and loss of power in her right arm, but was told that she was being hysterical. Another told that the joint pain in

"If you go into a bar and ask for a beer and pay for a beer, what would you do if they give you wine instead?"

the ankle was probably a sprain, despite it coming on whilst he was lying on a sofa watching TV.

Why do so many docs get it wrong? Well here's why: when I trained at med school, the sum total of teaching on decompression sickness was one hour and that was in my second year of five. I never saw a case until I actually learned to dive myself, and the symptoms you learn about were always the extreme ones of severe crippling joint pain or total paralysis; never the most common symptoms of fatigue, skin rash, numbness, loss of balance or tingling. So if you have any of these sorts of symptoms after diving and are not sure whether it's a bend or not then take yourself to a diving doctor. You wouldn't ask an eye surgeon to fix a hernia and neither would you try to buy pork from a fishmonger just because he sells 'food'.

I asked Nick what was at 40m anyway. "Nothing" he said "I think the DM was just testing his new computer." Anyone need a cheap BCD?

ANIMAL
HAZARDS

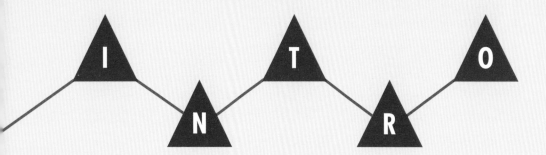

INTRO

I got stung by a scorpion once; a particularly painful variety, apparently. It was quite exciting. First aid (administered on the fly by five people I'd taught EFR to that morning) mostly involved a tourniquet to hold the poison back for five minutes. The scene was made secure and free of further danger by smashing the blighter into crunchy little bits.

Actually, the most crucial part was ensuring you received the correct dosages of medication during that five-minute delay. You fill a glass with three fingers of gin and throw in two soluble codeine tablets of the highest dose available. Neck that and wash it down with as much beer as you can take in one go without burping. After you do belch, drink as much rum as you can without starting a nose bleed and then remove the tourniquet. It's essential you sit down for the removal because a) the subsequent rush of pain through your circulation can be intense, and b) you're absolutely hammered.

I felt nothing when the tourniquet came off. Indeed, someone slapped me in the face several times but I barely noticed. I did suffer from a near-fatal hangover the following day, though, so you see the danger of arthropods can't be underestimated.

Most of the following chapter deals with water-dwelling creatures, as this is the environment in which divers usually reside, but you'll be reassured to discover that there's plenty of life out there on dry land waiting to bite, sting, lay eggs and set up home inside you as well. And most of it's too small to see. We don't want to give you the impression that the whole animal kingdom is on the warpath though (even though it definitely is), always remember there's still plenty of lovely stuff out there like, er... dolphins.

Mind you, they can be vicious.

And we've saved viruses for a different chapter altogether...

Tip: There are many animals that could be dangerous that aren't mentioned here. Just because we don't have anything to say about tigers, it doesn't mean it's safe to climb the fence at London Zoo and flick the testicles of one while he sleeps.

CORAL, JELLYFISH, URCHINS AND STINGERS

I've just got back from Sharm where I was stung by a fire coral. It first went into a swollen bubble and the crew put white vinegar and iodine on it. Since then the swelling has gone down but around the wound there is a red/purple patch. I was given steroid injections, antihistamines and painkillers whilst over there and although it's not painful now, it is very itchy and irritated. Unfortunately it's beneath my bottom and the allergy has gone toward my inner thigh (not nice) as I have to sit on it. Could you please help me?

Not to worry, even professional snorkelers get stung from time to time. Fire corals are so named because of their similarity in appearance to reef-building coral, but in fact they are carnivorous members of the coelenterates (jellyfish). The thing all coelenterates have in common is the development of stinging capsules called nematocysts, which either cling to victims via sticky mucus or a hook, or inject venom into prey by penetrating like a needle. Either way, the purpose of the nematocyst is to immobilise the hapless chump so it can then be eaten.

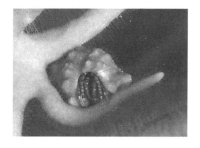

Fire corals have bright calcified skeletal coverings perforated by millions of tiny pores, through which stinging tentacles project. Hence people can be injured by scraping themselves against the skeleton, or by being stung, or often both. The symptoms vary from a mild, burning itch to severe pain, and what you see is a reddish swelling around the site, often surrounded with blisters or weals. Occasionally the blisters become pus-filled but most dry and flake off within 24 hours or so. Sometimes the burn seems to go away completely, but can return weeks later if the area comes into contact with skin irritants.

Plenty of local treatments have fallen in and out of favour over the years. Alcohol was once thought to dehydrate the nematocysts and thus prevent further stings, but studies now suggest it may actively stimulate more discharges. The current fashion is to use vinegar,

"The symptoms vary from a mild, burning itch to severe pain, and what you see is a reddish swelling around the site, often surrounded with blisters or weals."

which seems to reduce the number of stings from a live tentacle, although it does nothing for pain. Local anaesthetic ointment will provide relief, as will antihistamines and steroid creams (such as Fucibet, an antibiotic and steroid cream) for the itch. Local heat, in the form of a hot towel or hot water, can help to denature the stinging toxin too. There is the chance of secondary infection too, so if there is redness and swelling you may need a penicillin-based antibiotic tablet called Magnapen. These are the only remedies for which there is evidence, gleaned from trials involving brave (or foolish) guinea pigs who volunteered to be stung. Lime juice, washing powder and mermaid's milk are unlikely to be of benefit. If left untreated, you could be left with what look like chicken pox marks in the area, which can take years to disappear completely. In all, the best approach is prevention: keep away from the coral and wear, at the very least, a stinger suit, ie a full 1mm Lycra bodysuit.

I am going to Baja California and after a nasty sting in the Red Sea by a jellyfish, would like to know more about how to prevent it happening again, and what to do afterwards.

Fear not, because at least now you are going to a relatively jelly free part of the world. The Sea of Cortez is not as bad as other parts of the Pacific for this problem. What you always need to do when you are swimming or diving in a new area is ask the locals. They should be able to tell you if there are any jellyfish blooms or a sudden influx of these creatures locally. This can commonly happen after a storm or strong onshore wind.

If there are local reports of their presence and you still have to go into the water, the main thing to do is prevent yourself from being stung. This is best achieved by wearing a full wetsuit or a suit called a stinger suit. This is made from Lycra, fits snugly and will stop the jelly from stinging you, but only on the non exposed parts of your body.

The way jellyfish feed is by enveloping their prey in their tentacles and paralysing them with 'nematocysts'. These are tiny bags full of venom that are found on the tentacles, and on contact with a fish or human skin they fire off, releasing the poison into their prey. If this happens to be you or a friend then you need to act quickly.

Get out of the water as soon as you can and have someone help get any tentacles off your skin. They must first of all stop any remaining nematocysts from firing off and the best thing for this is ordinary

"The way jellyfish feed is by enveloping their prey in their tentacles and paralysing them with 'nematocysts'."

household vinegar. Pour this over the area affected and on any remaining tentacles. If there is no vinegar handy then there are other fluids you can use, the best of which is urine, which may seem bizarre but has good medical grounding due to its relative warmth and acidity. Having been doused in whatever liquid, try to take off any remaining tentacles with gloved hands or tweezers so you don't get stings on your fingers. Depending on what sort of jellyfish it was, appropriate action needs to be taken. If you were in eastern Australia, which the deadly box jellyfish frequents, then you need to get some anti-venom as soon as possible. Fortunately most stings are not deadly, just really painful. Take a simple analgesic such as ibuprofen and apply some calamine lotion on the affected area twice a day.

Finally, when you're diving, remember to always look up when surfacing after a dive as this is where most problems happen. Going up headfirst into a Portuguese Man'o'War is not the best way to enjoy Baja.

A few months ago I put my hand and foot on sea urchins. I managed to get most of the spines out but a few remained. One has just exited my finger the opposite side that it went in and two appear to be doing the same in my toe, but there are two at the base of my thumb/palm of my hand that I know are in there but cannot feel anymore. Should I be worried about these remaining bits? The bit that came out of my finger was about 10mm long.

One of the reference texts on marine dangers includes the following helpful advice on sea urchins: "stay away from these creatures". Concise, practical, but not exactly useful when spines are nestling happily in your digits. Bad luck on that front, but you needn't worry too much.

Sea urchins vary considerably in colour, size and venomous potential. They are animals of the phylum Echinodermata, 'urchin' being the Olde English name for hedgehog. The spines are attached by ball-and-socket joints to their globular body, and can waft about menacingly, or converge on a point to deter predators. Unfortunately, the spines are very sharp (often piercing tissues on contact), and very brittle, tending to break off and embed themselves within those tissues. Unsurprisingly, severe pain ensues, out of proportion to that of the piercing alone, and lasting up to four hours. Trying to extract the spines only serves to snap them off deep

"Trying to extract the spines only serves to snap them off deep in the wound."

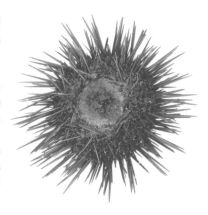

in the wound. The surrounding area then becomes inflamed and swollen over the next few days, with any luck healing up in a week or two.

Sometimes the spines are absorbed by the tissues, but they can also become encrusted and remain for many months before emerging from sites distant from the original puncture site, which has obviously happened with the spines in your finger and toe. Drawing pastes such as magnesium sulphate will often speed this process up. The other possible complication is infection, which is accompanied by the usual signs of increasing pain, redness and swelling. Occasionally the ache spreads to involve the whole limb, making movement difficult.

Traditional Islander remedies include urinating on the wound (nice) or placing it in thick mud. Bathing the area with hot water or methylated spirits has also been advocated. Embedded spine fragments can be crushed up by vigorous pummelling with a fist, which seems to relieve pain, although whether this is by replacing it with a distracting new pain is unknown. Occasionally, if troublesome remnants persist, they can be dealt with surgically: an X-ray of the area should pinpoint where they are, and under local anaesthetic the area can be explored and the pesky fragments removed.

So, in your case I would hold off as those bits in your hand have probably either been broken down, or will work their own way out, and it's a bit late to start peeing on your hand.

"...those bits in your hand have probably either been broken down, or will work their own way out, and it's a bit late to start peeing on your hand."

I have just returned from Sharm and have been attacked by unseen beasts of the deep. I wore a full wetsuit but got stung on my wrists, ankles, face and lips (it was sore when it got me and my fellow divers also felt the stings but didn't have the bad reaction). The next day I had itchy bumps and now they have turned into fluid filled blisters.

This has happened to me before in the Maldives and Thailand but not in the Caribbean. I did not see a jellyfish, nor did I touch any coral. The dive outfit I was with says it is plankton. Any idea of how I can get rid of this horrendous rash and how I can avoid it in the future?

Yup, it's the plankton. Zoophytes or zoon sorts of beasties. Not much use to man or toothed mammal, but I guess they make up some part of a food chain somewhere.

If you are covered in an itchy rash, then the best thing to take is some oral antihistamines, like Clarityn, with calamine lotion. If that doesn't work, use a mild steroid cream over the area; say a 1% hydrocortisone. It may take a while though. I got hit by these critters and it was a good two weeks before I stopped rubbing my back against trees and other tube passengers.

Prevention is always the best way, but you have to be practical. A neoprene gimp suit would raise too many concerns on a Carib boat. Mind you, so would pulling out a pot of Vaseline and handing it over to the divemaster, with the order to "sort me out so the pricks don't hurt." Best to find a middle option: a stinger suit, Lycra gloves (if allowed where you're diving), and Vaseline on any remaining exposed parts of the skin or even one of those full face masks.

I have just returned from Cozumel and have a very strange rash on my leg. While diving on the second to last day I was stung while lying on the bottom taking a picture. The sting was not too bad, and not the first either, so I ignored it. The pain abated after a few hours and I assumed I had rubbed against some fire coral, although I did not see any near where I had settled.

It is now four days later and unlike the other stings it's developed into a long rash about six inches long which is very red and lumpy. It looks a bit like 30 mosquitoes all homed in on the same place. It no longer itches or stings but merely looks unsightly. Is this anything to be concerned about?

I too was in Mexico. Smoothly moving over a bare rock to approach the seal pups when, "Ouch! What the f*** was that?" I had got stung by something invisible. I went back to look and there were a couple of weird looking fronds, like tiny sea bracken. All was OK for a few hours then it kicked in and itched like hell for the next two weeks. And in this way I was introduced to the evil hydroid.

That's what's got you too. God or Darwin put them on this planet to create good copy for diving medical books as they don't seem to do much else. Use a mixed antibiotic/steroid cream and don't scratch. I suggest Fucibet applied twice daily and next time stay mid-water.

Whilst diving off the coast of La Gomera in the Canaries, my daughter suffered a jellyfish sting on her face. We treated it immediately with a sting remedy from the chemist called 'After Bite'. After it calmed down we started applying vitamin E cream

"Ouch! What the f*** was that? I had got stung by something invisible."

to try and repair the skin, which was still quite red and a bit swollen and chafed looking.

Now, nearly five weeks later, it still hasn't disappeared completely and has actually started to hurt again, not only on the site of the sting itself but also around it and across her chin. It seems very dry and there are darkish marks in a patch where she was stung, which become prominent if she gets a bit cold. I think the jellyfish was called a 'medusa' but I don't know the Latin name. Is it possible that there is something remaining in there that needs to be removed?

"Interesting one, this. Pain and deformity five weeks after a jellyfish sting may be the result of scarring."

Interesting one, this. Pain and deformity five weeks after a jellyfish sting may be the result of scarring. It is unlikely that there are any nematocysts still there, but certainly infection is a possibility.

I would try a cream with some antibiotic and steroid, eg Fucibet, twice a day for a week. If this doesn't nail it and there's still a problem then you may be better off seeing a dermatologist for a closer look. From my own experience with a similar beastie called a hydroid, the pain and itchiness can last for a good few weeks.

I was diving in the Gulf of Thailand recently and put my hand on a sea urchin. I removed all the stings but one of my fingers is still swollen and I am still unable to bend it properly. It does not look like I have anything left in there, but it also does not look like it is healing itself. What should I do?

There is a chance something was left in. A tiny fragment from the tip of the spine is most likely, but no surgeon is going to plough in there risking further damage. You have an infection; that much is obvious, so the best way forward is to take antibiotics. Magnapen, four times a day is the best as long as you are not penicillin allergic. The fragment, being made of keratin, like human hair and nails, will disintegrate in time, the infection will be fought, and all will be well.

If it happens again, there is a myriad of potential ways of removing spines. Wax, needles, hot rocks and hammers, that sort of thing. Never urine though.

FRESHWATER AND OUT OF THE WATER

My son and I swam in Lake Malawi this summer. After reading the travel books, we decided to take action, even though we have no bilharzia symptoms. Six weeks after exposure, our GP reluctantly agreed to send off stool samples for testing for 'all egg infestations'. The results have come back normal. Should we take any other action?

Lake Malawi always had the reputation of being bilharzia free, but recently more and more cases of this problem have been reported from there, so, I see your point about getting checked for it now you are back. The area most affected is in the Southern part, around a place called Cape Maclear. This may be as it's the most popular part because it's the most beautiful and hence has most visitors.

Bilharzia, or schistosomiasis as it's also known, is caused by a nasty little worm that has part of its life-cycle in a freshwater snail, and the rest in the human bladder, liver or blood supply to both. It is contracted when you come into contact with the worm after it's come out of the snail. It then burrows through the skin and into the body and... you don't really want to hear the rest.

Many people who are infected do not get any symptoms for a couple of months, but later they may get blood in the urine, a raised fever or blood in the stool. The best test is in fact a blood test for antibodies to the parasite. If this comes back positive then a single dose of a powerful drug called praziquantel is all that is needed.

I don't know what your doc expects to find with a simple stool parasite and egg test. This is normally something you do to look for bowel bugs rather than bilharzia, so I think you need to get your doctor to do the blood test. If you are still asymptomatic after all this time then the chances are that you probably do not have the disease.

If you ever go back to the lake, avoid contact with the snail that is

"It then burrows through the skin and into the body and... you don't really want to hear the rest."

the parasite-human vector by wearing dive boots in the reeds near the shore, and it's best to swim or dive off a boat in the open water.

I am getting married next month and my fiancée is planning a surprise diving honeymoon. My fear is that it's going to be to the Great Barrier Reef as, well, I found the tickets the other day. This is a problem as I have a total phobia about spiders which he doesn't know about yet and I know that Australia is full of them. Am I right in thinking that there are going to be some poisonous spiders out there, even on the coast, which could kill me, or should I not worry at all?

OK, calm down. There are venomous spiders in Australia and they do have the potential to kill you. But as you know, Australia is visited by many millions of people and they have a wonderful time without so much as seeing a spider at all, let alone getting bitten by one of the toxic varieties.

If you are determined to worry about it, then the one to look out for in the part you may be visiting on your not-such-a-surprise honeymoon is the redback spider. This is a close relative of the black widow that is found in the Americas. The redback is not aggressive but contact comes by accident when the unfortunate victim either sits or lays a hand on it. Redbacks are known to live under the seats of lavatories, so it is advisable to always check before you sit down as the consequences can be a trip to the local hospital for a shot of anti-venom.

The really nasty spider out there doesn't live so much in the outback but more in the suburbs of the bigger towns like Sydney and along the east coast. It's called the funnel-web and is an aggressive specimen that can bite you without provocation. It usually lives under raised houses in its funnel shaped web. They have been known to come out from under the house with the sole purpose of biting the foot of any adult or child that may be in the garden. If this happens it is important to lay the victim flat, apply a pressure bandage to the affected area (but not a tourniquet), and make sure they are transported to medical back up with as little fuss as possible. Symptoms that can develop are the local reaction to the bite, with pain and inflammation right through to paralysis of the nervous system with death due to respiratory failure.

So those are the two worst you could encounter, but there are others, such as the white tail, that can inflict a nasty bite, or as one

> "One therapeutic technique is called 'flooding'. Here the phobic is made to face their fear for as long as it takes, so you would have spiders crawl all over you until there was no more screaming."

Australian arachnophobe once said to me "I don't care whether they're poisonous or not doc, just seeing them will give me a heart attack". My suggestion is that you would be in a spider free zone if you went on a liveaboard around the Whitsunday Islands, and the diving would be a lot better than some of the Cairns shore-based round trips to the inner reef that are done.

However, perhaps the best long term option is to get some help with your problem. One therapeutic technique is called 'flooding'. Here the phobic is made to face their fear for as long as it takes, so you would have spiders crawl all over you until there was no more screaming. This technique has been waning in popularity.

I am planning on diving in the Thames and other British fresh water sites; both rivers and lakes. I would like to know of any health risks that might be involved in diving such sites, and any preventative measures, such as vaccinations, I can take to protect myself.

I think you should be fine in our joyous clean waters here in the UK. The only real issue is that of an interesting illness called Weil's disease or Leptospirosis. This is a bug transferred into fresh water from rat's urine. However it's mostly found in still water, such as in wells or small ponds where the only divers are from the supermarkets retrieving their trolleys. If you are diving big lakes or quarries like Stoney then there is little chance of getting this interesting condition. As for rivers, they are pretty clean, even in London as the number of cormorants visible from Chelsea Bridge proves.

For immunisations, always keep up to date with tetanus and polio, which are required every 10 years anyway. That's about all you need look out for but if you are diving near unprocessed sewage, get a hepatitis A shot too. Nowadays, most of the capital's number two's are clean enough to drink after processing by the water authorities. Well that's what they tell us anyway.

I have recently returned from a diving trip to Zanzibar, where due to the fact that all my money was stolen I had to spend a few nights in a dirt cheap hotel until more was wired out to me. Since my return I have had the most awful itching on my hands and feet, but what's odd is that it is mostly at night. Any thoughts on what it could be?

I think I can make a diagnosis here with some assurance. You have

"The only real issue is that of an interesting illness called Weil's disease or leishmanisis. This is a bug transferred into fresh water from rat's urine."

unfortunately contracted one of those skin infestations that seems to be becoming commoner as more people travel over the world: scabies. This is caused by a tiny mite, Sarcoptes scabeii, which is caught by either being in contact with a person or, occasionally, bed sheets where the mite has previously been.

The mite, having got onto your skin, normally finds its way to specific areas of your body, notably the wrists and finger webs, but also the feet and ankles, and finally your genital area. Having got there, it then burrows under your skin leaving a tell tale track to its hiding place. The reason the itching occurs is due to the next part of its life cycle; it comes out of its burrow and lays its eggs on the surface of your skin. This usually occurs at night when those areas where it lives on your body are warm and moist, making a better environment for the eggs and causing an intense itching so that you re-implant them by scratching your skin. This also helps to spread them over other parts of your body.

The usual signs of this disease are the previously mentioned tracks, and also a rash where you have been scratching. I have seen very bad cases of this in the past where the infestation has affected the whole body, and this is what used to happen years ago before any cure was around. In very rare cases it can even lead to death where infection gets into the blood stream from the open scratched sores on the skin.

We are luckier now, though as it is very easy to treat. The basis of the cure is an anti-parasitic cream called permethrin, which you have to apply to your whole body from neck down to the tip of your toes. Leave the cream on for 24 hours then wash it off and reapply again. One day later wash it off and that should finally get rid of it. As the mite can still live on clothing and sheets for a while, you need to wash anything you have worn or slept on since your return on the hottest wash available to kill off any remaining mites or their eggs.

Finally, this rash and itch usually comes on about six weeks after contact. If any diver experiences an itchy rash sooner after diving, then it is wise to make sure it is not a case of skin bends. This though is more often found on the shoulders and trunk and is associated with an odd marbled-looking rash. The only effective treatment for this is recompression in a dive chamber.

"The mite, having got onto your skin, normally finds its way to specific areas of your body, notably the wrists and finger webs, but also the feet and ankles, and finally your genital area."

JUST UNDER THE RIB CAGE ON THE LEFT

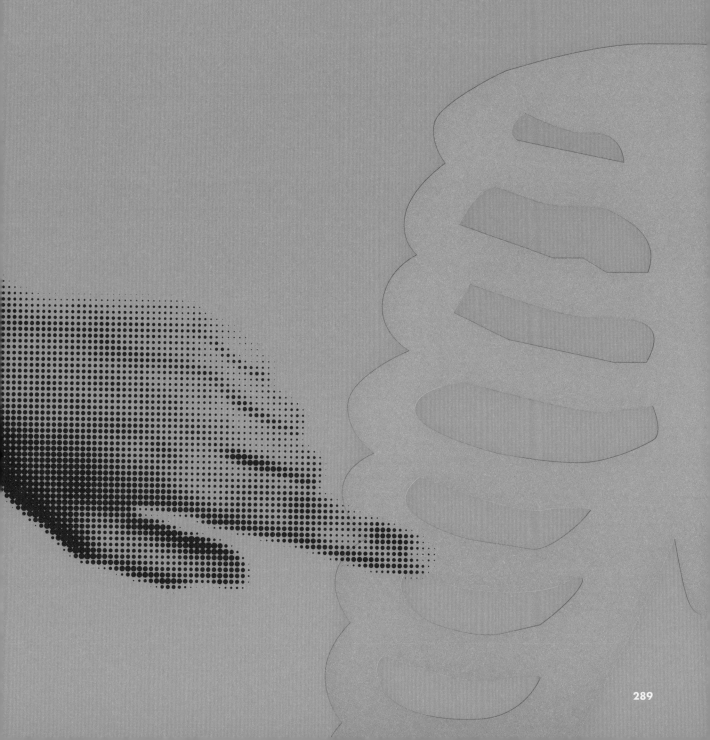

INTRO

"There will be no Miscellaneous section in this book", I trumpeted determinedly to myself at some point in the indiscernible past. Then I came across a question asking when a HSE medical is required. And then one from (presumably) a man who wanted to know if you can dive after taking Viagra. And I realised: this is how it happens. You start off with principles, and then practicalities start getting in the way; just one or two, here and there, so that you hardly notice it at first, you just keep making little adjustments. But it all builds up, slowly and imperceptibly, becoming something solid and real but which you don't really see. Until one day, with seemingly no warning at all, you suddenly find yourself voting Tory. Oh hang on, that's Ben Elton. The miscellaneous git.

The thing is, 'Miscellaneous' covers everything. Every question in this book could rightfully have been put into a 'Miscellaneous' chapter. If there was a 'Miscellaneous' section in the library, they could do away with the Dewey Decimal System altogether and just chuck all the books in a big heap (sometimes they do that anyway). It's not possible to think of an experience or object in the entire history of this or any universe that couldn't rightfully be categorised as 'Miscellaneous'. What's that, you say? Similarities? Patterns in nature? Science? Even if exactly the same thing happens twice, it still happens at different times so it's not exactly the same thing is it? Is it? "Hurts to think about, doesn't it?", my brain said to me on that terrible day when my principles went out of the window, "'Miscellaneous' doesn't seem like such a bad idea for a chapter now, does it?"

Alright, look, it was either this or have a different category for every question, with titles like 'Salty Taste in the Mouth Even After Eating Fruit or Drinking Tea' and 'Being Allergic to Cold'. But I still refuse to call it 'Miscellaneous'. So, what would you do with questions on alcohol, allergies, skin, sleep, age, seasickness and weight? And where does the spleen go exactly?

The answer is: 'just under the rib cage on the left'.

Tip: If a representative of the company you've been diving with claims that your DCS-like symptoms are "just something that's going around", that they will "go away on their own" and that a lot of their divers are "picking up a similar virus" from their dives, headbutt them, push them into a hedge, then call your local chamber.

SEASICKNESS

I have been diving for over 10 years now and suffer from sea sickness. 18 months ago, I went on a liveaboard and was taking Stugeron. I had to seek medical advice in Egypt after a reverse block on ascent ruptured my left tympanic membrane. I was told that it was the medication that contributed to the block and therefore the rupture. I am now diving again with no problems (other than sea sickness) but am going on holiday and need some advice about what medication I can take, as it can be a misery without it.

This is a very interesting question and one which I have been asked a lot. Exactly what is the best treatment for seasickness when you're diving and what other preventative measures you can take?

Stugeron, or cinnarizine as it is known medically, is an antihistamine. It stops seasickness by stabilising the inner ear's balance centres; however as an antihistamine it also decreases any mucus production too. What could have happened to cause your eardrum to blow is an increased mucus production if the drug's effects wore off… This could have blocked your Eustachian tube thus stopping the air from escaping down it as you ascended.

The other thing about cinnarizine is that its antihistamine properties are sedating. The makers don't recommend you drive on them, so I don't think you should dive on them either. Doziness underwater can only lead to errors of judgement so best leave them alone.

So where does this leave the seasick diver?

Well, I would recommend you try one of the homeopathic alternatives, such as ginger or Nelson's Travella which don't sedate, or even those acupressure wristbands to start with, as at least there are none of the side effects of antihistamines. If someone does need something a little stronger then I've found prochlorperazine a good non-sedating medication. It's prescription only though so you need to see a doc to get it.

"Doziness underwater can only lead to errors of judgement so best leave them alone… So where does this leave the seasick diver?"

I've recently returned from a short diving holiday in Spain. Late on in the first dive, I developed bad indigestion and a build-up of saliva. I took out my reg and was sick. I was able to make a slow, controlled ascent and continued to be violently sick at the surface (and for a good 20 minutes afterwards). The same thing happened the following day, even when we got back on to the RIB. The nausea stopped as soon as we were within 20m of the shore. I had no feeling of spinning, dizziness or any other warning signs apart from indigestion and saliva.

I was unable to hold down any food for 24 to 36 hours after but was able to do another dive two days later without any problems. I had recently returned from a week's diving in Scapa Flow without incident and am going on a liveaboard in the Red Sea next month. Although it provides a feast for the wildlife, it's not something I want to do again. Can you help?

I can indeed, but first things first. If you're going to be sick underwater, do not take out your reg. The pressure of vomiting is not enough to prevent water entry into your mouth and upper respiratory tract. Most regs will allow the passage of bits out of them, and even if it did block you can switch quickly to your alternate.

Most reasons to be sick on a dive can be attributed to three areas: middle and inner ear problems for starters, ie if there is unequal air escaping from the middle ears on ascent, you can get vertigo and nausea which can lead to a vomit. But, as you had no spinning feeling, we can rule this out.

Secondly, sea sickness, presenting late, and hitting you underwater. This is more likely but as it was late on in the dive, and with just the vom and no nausea, we can forget that one.

Lastly, and most likely, is some kind of bug, virus or food poisoning. This can cause a vomit alone with few other symptoms, and you feel better once it's all out. And not holding down food is more symptomatic of some food-borne nastie. Why this should get you at depth and at no other time, though, is a mystery.

So, I reckon you should be fine and dandy for the liveaboard.

We've booked to go to Egypt next week, mainly so my daughter, a 14 year-old Rescue Diver, can enjoy the lovely waters there.

"I can indeed, but first things first. If you're going to be sick underwater, do not take out your reg. The pressure of vomiting is not enough to prevent water entry into your mouth and upper respiratory tract."

The dives she'll be doing require her to be on the boat all day. Unfortunately, she gets travel sick. Once she has been ill, she's absolutely fine, but it would be better not to reach that point. She's very fit and does about 10 hours of dancing a week.

Bless, sweet youth. I used to do 10 hours of dancing in my college days, but mainly on car roofs. Still got it on my record.

I think she will be fine. These Egyptian day boats are big mothers, not your rolling RIBs that bob with every ripple. For her it's best to sit at the bow if she can and watch the waves coming. That makes the brain predict the oncoming movement from the swell, and the brain tells the inner ear balance centres what to expect. Result: no nausea, and no embarrassing knocking on the only loo door from the other divers trying to get in.

As for preventatives, if it's a well rough day, I suggest ginger. Nice and natural. Breakfast on ginger nut bikkies. Ginger beer all day for rehydration. A picture of Chris Evans in her pocket and chant a mantra to Chris Fairclough, legendary Liverpool super-sub before each dive. That'll do it.

"Ginger beer all day for rehydration. A picture of Chris Evans in her pocket and chant a mantra to Chris Fairclough, legendary Liverpool super-sub before each dive. That'll do it."

I've never had any problem with sea sickness, until I went out in the sea off the Norfolk coast. All was OK and I was feeling great until I had to gear up and before I knew it my breakfast was over the side.

I had the same thing on the second dive that day and once again when I got to the car. So now I am thinking that I could have contracted sea sickness as an old age problem. Or maybe it was just a tummy bug.

It is impossible to contract sea sickness, so no worries on that count. It is possible, though, to have a bad day: a one off where it all goes wrong. I get that rarely, and like you I come from good stock. Naval parents, and on rare occasions, out of the blue, I will paint the decks with bile. Nice.

So it is probably that, but a dose of food poisoning will cause this too. Give it another go, and if it keeps happening, then go for all the cures.

WEIGHT

I get a lot of students wanting to learn to dive who are overweight, and some hugely so. What are the real risks of diving if you are overweight, and how can I decide which ones are safe to train and which ones aren't?

Obesity is a huge topic (ha ha). Chocolate taxes, fire crews being called out to rescue 30 stone people stuck in the bath, a third of us obese in 2012: the media is full of fat. Briefly, the major issues with diving are:

Increased risk of DCS: nitrogen loves dissolving in fat. Obese divers will produce bigger bubble loads, which can overwhelm the normal lung filter and force bubbles into the systemic circulation. This puts them at higher risk of all forms of DCS.

Increased risk of diseases such as high blood pressure, diabetes, heart attacks and strokes. Every year dive accidents occur as a result of these conditions.

Decreased physical fitness tends to go hand in hand with being overweight, meaning it's going to be harder to rescue yourself or your buddy. It also leads to higher risks of panic and more gas uptake on exertion (increasing DCS risk again).

Decreased lung function: sheer belly bulk can significantly restrict lung capacity, and overweight divers have lower oxygen levels and higher carbon dioxide levels. In extreme situations these gas disturbances can cause breathlessness, confusion, and ultimately drowning.

A little bit of fat is good for you, of course: it helps insulate you against the cold and cushions the internal organs. The much maligned BMI is still the best lay guide to body fat: square your height in metres, and divide that into your weight in kilos. If the result is over 25 then you're overweight, and if it's more than 30

"Obesity is a huge topic (ha ha). Chocolate taxes, fire crews being called out to rescue 30 stone people stuck in the bath, a third of us obese in 2012: the media is full of fat."

then you're officially obese. There are lots of caveats around this method, but if you're worried about training someone because of their weight then just contact your local dive doc to discuss it.

Please can you tell me what my BMI needs to be below for a HSE Medical?

This is a very interesting point as there are several guidelines involved, but also the question of how accurate BMI (Body Mass Index) is as a measure of obesity.

The standard BMI under which you have to be is 30. If you are above this when you learn to dive, then you are passed on to a medical referee who will assess your general health and wellbeing. In BMI terms 30 is the break point above which you are considered obese, below 30 and above 26 you are overweight and below this down to about 20, healthy.

The reason BMI is important if you dive, is like any other sport: if you are obese then there is a greater chance of knock on effects such as cardiac problems. This is why you are referred to a referee: to see whether you are a risk to any diver underwater and also if your fitness is going to pose a risk to yourself.

Having said all of this, I do have personal reservations about the accuracy of the BMI. Basically, it is calculated as a ratio of height to weight but the charts that doctors use are the same for men as for women. Also, and more importantly, they do not take into account body morphism. This is a factor where some people are naturally very big and often their BMI comes out as obese when in fact they are obviously healthy and fit. For example, a prop forward in a rugby team may well be 5'8" and weigh 16 stone, but he would have the same BMI as a woman of the same height and weight who hadn't done any exercise for the last 10 years and whose only pastime was eating pizza and drinking cider. So would they both have to be referred to a medical referee? Of course not, but you can see the problems involved with BMI.

Perhaps in the future, the body fat monitors will increase in accuracy and be used as the standard to pass or fail a diver, but for now if you are below 30 you should be fine, and if you're above it you will be fine so long as you are fit and you have a strong and healthy cardiovascular system.

On a side note, the abundance of miracle weight-loss cures on the net suggests that few if any of them actually work. It's a simple sum really: if calories out exceed those in, you'll lose weight. This translates to diet and exercise (rather than surgical intervention). A couple of tips for anyone that's interested: rather than watered down soup for eternity, make dietary changes that you can stick with and try and build some exercise into your daily routine, so that it doesn't all go to pot once the new gym fad wears off.

Benefits of Exercise:
Feeling less tired after diving; less gas consumption and therefore longer bottom times; decreased chance of injury, back pain and decompression illness; increased ability to tackle more challenging diving; will help avoid cramps.

AGE

Whilst holidaying with my daughter and grandchildren in the Maldives, I was given the opportunity to dive. I had only ever snorkelled previously and Scuba diving was a revelation. But at the ripe old age of 63 how many years of this wonderful sport do I have left?

Potentially plenty. Browsing through a news website recently, I came across an article about 72 year-old Donald Sutherland, the bearded Canadian thespian whose latest flick involved his learning to Scuba dive. Apparently he was taken ill with chest pains during a break and began coughing up blood. After much diagnostic confusion (including being mistakenly labelled with lung cancer) a clued-up physician finally twigged that the blood was due to a fragile lung vessel which had leaked during a dive.

The point of this arduous preamble is that he was then told by the specialist that he shouldn't have been diving past the age of 50. Now in these days of political correctness and disability discrimination the onus is on us docs to justify why someone shouldn't dive. Admittedly anno domini wreaks its mischief on us all in terms of declining strength and agility, but to designate an age past which diving is unsafe is ludicrous. There are some considerations: older divers are more prone to hypothermia as they generally have less fat tissue and a slower metabolism. A higher proportion will have chronic problems, such as lung or heart disease, which need to be managed appropriately, and with medications that are sanctioned safe for diving. Limbs are more fragile and being tossed around in big swells may break bones and DCI gets more common with age, possibly due to slower blood flow through the tissues and arthritic changes. The older diver is also more likely to be on medications and the tablets themselves or their side effects might cause underwater safety issues.

But we all age in time to our individual genetic clocks, and I know several divers in their 60s and 70s who are far fitter than numerous

"Now in these days of political correctness and disability discrimination the onus is on us docs to justify why someone shouldn't dive."

younger lardballs. Plus their wealth of life experience makes them far safer than your average anxious 18 year-old novice. So it's two fingers up at Father Time, all you over 50s divers (including you, Donald). Get some new fins and jump in.

I've just reached my 70th birthday and my wife's promised me a diving holiday in the Maldives to celebrate. I used to be a runner and quite fit up to my retirement, but since then too much fine food and wine has made its way to my waistline. I know I need to lose some weight to dive safely, but how fit should I be? Is there any guidance you can give me?

Physical fitness depends on three main variables: the heart, the lungs and muscle strength. All three decline gradually with age. Increasing blood vessel stiffness causes a gradual increase in blood pressure and a thickening of the heart muscle; the lungs become less elastic and shrink in size; and muscle power lessens by 10-15% per decade. Great. But with regular exercise the rate of decline can thankfully be halved. What this means is that someone who's exercised throughout their life can often be fitter than a sofa-bound slug 20 years their junior, so age alone is not an issue.

> "...someone who's exercised throughout their life can often be fitter than a sofa-bound slug 20 years their junior, so age alone is not an issue."

Rather than sadistic step-test torture, one kinder and oft-used way to assess fitness in the older diver is the timed swim: a 200m swim in less than five minutes, or 1km in less than 30 minutes is acceptable proof of adequate fitness. So take that as your initial target, as it will also strengthen your swimming and general aquatic skills.

Why is it that children can't dive below the age of eight?

To some extent there has to be a cut-off point somewhere, and there will always be exceptions to any rule, but there are various physical reasons why diving below the age of eight is not advised:

Up to about this age, the areas of the lung where gas exchange takes place (the alveoli) are multiplying, and the elasticity of the lung tissue is reduced. Theoretically this puts children at higher risk of barotrauma, particularly when you take into account their emotional immaturity and consequent increased chance of panicking and ascending rapidly.

A small frame, light weight and limited strength make for difficulties handling dive gear, particularly in open water conditions.

Children have a high body surface area to weight ratio. Coupled with a faster metabolic rate, this predisposes them to rapid cooling and dehydration.

Aliquots of weight (on descent) and BCD air (on ascent) will have greater effects on a smaller individual, making buoyancy control more difficult.

Smaller air passages in the ear and sinuses make equalising harder and barotrauma more likely.

The way we 'grow' in childhood is by the ends of our long bones, called the 'epiphyseal growth plates', gradually elongating. This continues until about the age of 18. These plates are mostly cartilage and they don't have much blood supply, relying on diffusion from nearby areas for their nutrients, so if they are damaged, stunting of growth and shortened arms or legs may result. There's no experimental or clinical data on whether diving causes damage to these areas, but looking at saturation divers there is a risk of bone thinning after many years. However, considering the depths and times that children are restricted to, the risk of this occurring is minimal.

The proportion of children with a patent foramen ovale (PFO) is much higher than the 25% of adults who have one. At birth, we all have this passageway between two chambers of the heart, which has been implicated as a risk factor for DCI. Closure after birth can be delayed for many years, so the younger a child is, the more likely they will be to have a PFO.

So, there are several physical issues of concern, but the psychological aspects are arguably more important, yet subtler and more difficult to gauge:

Gas dynamics and the effects of pressure are difficult enough concepts for adults, let alone children, but need to be understood to use equipment properly and dive safely.

The ability to recognise and fully appreciate a dangerous situation is necessary, a skill requiring emotional maturity.

Stressful underwater situations can cause anxiety and panic, and the risk of rapid ascents, dropped regs, and drowning is considerable.

"The ability to recognise and fully appreciate a dangerous situation is necessary, a skill requiring emotional maturity."

Above all, the unpredictable behaviour of children in a potentially lethal environment makes it impossible to guarantee their safety.

Another important factor is sussing out the motivation behind the decision to dive: is it the child's or the parent's? Forcing a child to dive because their parent thinks they will enjoy it is a disaster in the making. All in all a complicated judgement call then, but one that's becoming more and more common. The rate at which children develop varies enormously, and for this reason there are some who would not allow children to dive until twice the minimum age.

Both our children have decided they want to learn to dive. (Lord knows why, having watched their mum and dad unattractively flopping about in Wraysbury). Anyway, one is eight, the other is 10, and we've been trying to find out whether they're more likely to get decompression illness or other problems whilst diving. Can you advise?

I think if any diving doctor decided to dunk kids underwater in the name of research, they'd be struck off quicker than a soggy match trying to light a stove on a weekend's camping holiday in Wales. There's no evidence I'm aware of that suggests children are more susceptible to DCI. That's not to say they aren't, just that it's unethical to do the studies you'd need to find out. Most of the knowledgeable authorities agree that depths and times should be restricted to minimise the risk of bubble formation for this reason, though.

There's also a question about whether children are more sensitive to oxygen toxicity, but if we take the 1.4 bar maximum that applies to adults, and remember that children can't dive on Nitrox, then they would have to dive to 60m plus to be at risk, so we can pretty much discount this too.

> "Forcing a child to dive because their parent thinks they will enjoy it is a disaster in the making."

ALCOHOL

I've noticed recently, in a few dive magazines and forums, that people are saying it's OK to drink beer between dives during a surface interval. Being Australian, I'm partial to a cold stubby or ten, and I know some divers who insist on drinking beer before, during and after their dives. Are there any real dangers in this or is it all scaremongering?

I read somewhere that "alcohol can never make you do a thing better, it can only make you less ashamed of your mistakes." This makes sense when I've had a few beers and then try to play pool. I'd love to tell you it's all a load of rubbish but, sadly, there are good reasons not to overindulge when you're diving.

One of the myths is that small amounts of alcohol aren't a problem. One drink does actually produce a measurable decline in performance, with diminished awareness of cues and reduced inhibitions. Another important point is that the deleterious effects of alcohol are consistently underestimated by people who drink. One study involved videotaping 13 divers performing pool dives at different blood alcohol concentrations and rating their injury risk. They had objective 'sobriety' tests and rated their own performance afterwards: at higher alcohol levels, injury risk was increased but divers weren't aware of their degraded performance. Other research has shown that there is a definite reduction in the ability of the individual to process information, particularly in tasks that require undivided attention, for many hours after the blood alcohol level has reached zero. This means that the risk of injury in a hungover diver is increased significantly, particularly if high blood alcohol levels were reached during the drinking episode. Deaths have been directly attributed to excessive alcohol consumption as it exacerbates the effects of nitrogen narcosis and can lead to drowning.

In addition to these dangers, alcohol can contribute towards:

Dehydration: Alcohol stops production of the body's anti-diuretic hormone, in essence taking the brake off the bladder and causing excessive peeing and fluid loss. The brain is especially sensitive to this dehydrating effect, and this, together with the toxic by-products of alcohol breakdown in the liver, curses us with the throbbing headaches we know and love. Of course, this may be exacerbated by emission of supplementary bodily fluids from either end of the gut (typically in a projectile manner over pavement or porcelain, depending on how quick / posh you are).

Hypothermia: Although a cheeky nip of whisky reputedly warms the cockles, alcohol actually causes the opposite effect. By dilating blood vessels in the skin, blood flow is redistributed from our body's core to its peripheries, where heat is lost more quickly. If you add in the massive cooling effects of immersion in water and the breathing of dry, compressed gas, a diver with alcohol in their system will end up particularly prone to hypothermia. And that post-dive cold one can slow the rewarming process too.

Hypoglycaemia: one cause of the after-binge munchies is a drop in blood sugar (glucose). You might think all the sugar in beer would raise blood levels, and initially it does; but as the body's insulin gets to work removing it from the blood, it overshoots, leading to low glucose levels (commonly rectified by a large portion of chips and chillisausalad with your kebab). Diving puts a considerable amount of strain on the body's muscles, the heart as well as all the skeletal ones, and since their main fuel is glucose, it's not a good idea to start a dive with a low level.

DCS: The explanation goes like this: firstly, alcohol speeds up peripheral circulation, leading to increased uptake of nitrogen. Secondly, it makes the blood thicker, due to the dehydration it causes. And thirdly, it reduces surface tension in bubbles, which might promote their growth and turn 'silent' bubbles into ones that cause symptoms. Although never directly proven, the net effect of all this could be physiologically disastrous, particularly over a period of repetitive diving (your typical week in a hot Sharm, say).

Other toxic effects: unfortunately, alcohol is readily absorbed by all cell membranes, creating widespread side effects in every corner of the body. Muscle aches and pains, stomach irritation (heartburn), palpitations, diarrhoea, vomiting and pins and needles are all pretty

"...as the body's insulin gets to work removing it from the blood, it overshoots, leading to low glucose levels (commonly rectified by a large portion of chips and chillisausalad with your kebab)."

much a direct result of alcohol acting on the linings of various body structures. This also explains brewer's droop or, in Shakespeare's words: "it provokes the desire, but it takes away the performance".

Is there some sort of guide as to how quickly alcohol is eliminated from your system? I'd like to be able to estimate how long it takes for me to be alcohol-free after one beer, two beers, eight beers... If one or two post-dive drinks turns into a big binge night, at least I can then make an educated guess as to when it's safe to dive again.

There are rough guides to the rate of alcohol detoxification but it varies a lot from person to person. Some of the factors involved are:

Age: elimination rates slow as we get older.

Gender: females generally clear alcohol faster than males, although the increased body fat and smaller size of a woman do lead to higher blood alcohol levels.

Race or ethnicity: alcohol is broken down by a liver enzyme called alcohol dehydrogenase. Levels of this enzyme vary between races, being high in Europeans and sometimes almost non-existent in Asians or those from the Americas (hence the violent facial 'flush response' sometimes seen).

Physical condition: the rate of alcohol elimination varies with weight, and increased physical fitness will speed it up to some extent.

Amount of food consumed before drinking: food slows down the absorption of alcohol.

How quickly the alcohol was consumed: multiple shots or drinking games may overwhelm the liver, which can only process about one drink per hour.

Use of drugs or prescription medicines: these can often interact with alcohol and exacerbate its effects.

Having said all that, the average human with an intact liver will burn up about one unit of alcohol (which is 8g) every hour. A pint of 5% beer these days is nearing three units, so reckon on three hours per pint for full clearance. It soon adds up.

"A pint of 5% beer these days is nearing three units, so reckon on three hours per pint for full clearance. It soon adds up."

My diving friends and I are taking our mate to Egypt for his stag night next month. We plan to live it up and party all night and then spend the days taking in the Red Sea highlights. We are bound to still be a bit merry in the morning with what we have planned, any tips on freshening up for the dive?

Being merry in the morning probably means you're still drunk, so I'd lay off diving and do some sight-seeing if this is the case. Vomiting through a regulator is not much fun. But in terms of "what's the best cure for a hangover", the answer is: prevention, or a brace of raw eggs, a hot sauna, kidney dialysis and a lemon wedge rubbed under your drinking arm. Placebo, or just weird for the sake of it, who knows? In the real world, try to pack down some water before you hit the sack, preferably with some painkillers and an antacid or milk. Vitamins and anti-oxidants will help (Berocca or Alka Seltzer get my vote). The next morning, a good dose of O2 (via a run if you're up to it), more fluids and you'll be well on the mend.

ALLERGIES

After the third day of diving on a recent trip to the Red Sea, I started to get an itchiness on my belly and thighs. It became really painful after the eighth day and on my return to the UK, my doctor prescribed some cortisone cream and tablets. I know this is not the kind of treatment you want to take for just anything, so do you have any advice as to what can I do to prevent this rash/itchiness in the future?

This is obviously a suit rash if you are getting it all over the body. There are weird algae blooms and other nasties that lurk in the deep that can cause similar problems, but allergic reactions to neoprene are becoming increasingly common (a lot of neoprene wetsuits contain small amounts of Latex).

Some people I know smother themselves in Vaseline to protect their skin but I'm not sure how effective this is in the long run and it gets pretty messy, so I reckon you have two options. Either you get a Lycra undersuit, as it's less likely to cause problems, or you go the other way and get a drysuit. Under this you can wear whatever you want; even your normal clothes that you know won't cause a rash and itching. It may be a lot of kit to wear in hot countries but you'll get used to it. Just don't dehydrate whilst you stand in 40° heat waiting to get in the water as some muppet takes an hour to put their kit on.

When I go on holiday I take Zirtek antihistamine to prevent a heat rash. Am I OK to dive and take them?

Some antihistamines sedate. Others don't according to the packet. But in my experience it's a personal thing. If you find Zirtek makes you tired, then do not use it when you dive. If you are OK; fine and alert enough to respond to emergencies on it, then great, you're in the blue. Alternatives are heat rash powders or just wearing loose cotton clothing.

"Some people I know smother themselves in Vaseline to protect their skin but I'm not sure how effective this is in the long run and it gets pretty messy."

After every dive I get pimples/acne on the nose and forehead. The longer/deeper/more frequently I dive, the worse the problem gets. I have been treated for acne over the last year (to avoid this situation when I dive as I do not usually have pimples) but I went diving last week and the same thing happened again. Do you have any idea what it can be?

I think the only thing this could be is a reaction to the silicone in your mask. When it happens again, see if the distribution of the rash is in the same place as the mask lining and the nose piece. If it is then either find a barrier cream you can rub on the inside of the mask, like Vaseline or try a non silicone mask lining. Sadly, hypoallergenic masks have yet to be invented.

If the above doesn't work then maybe other factors are at play. Stress is a great inducer of acne like rashes. If you find diving stressful, and we all have at times, then think long and hard about what brings it on: bad buddies, diving beyond your limits, or the fact that you are being cajoled into it against your better judgement; then treat the cause.

I dived in a lot of wetsuit in New Zealand this summer (15mm of neoprene so I could hardly bend my knees or elbows). Despite all the rubber I still felt really cold on the dives, and the dive guide poured flasks of hot water down our backs during the surface interval. When I got back to the campsite I found a strange rash on my arms and legs, lots of little raised bumps of different sizes, which were really itchy. I went straight back to the dive shop and they sent me to a doctor. Thankfully, she didn't think it was DCI but an allergic reaction to the cold instead. However, this is not something I've ever had before and whilst I didn't get any other symptoms, the bumps are still there, four months later. Should I come to the chamber?

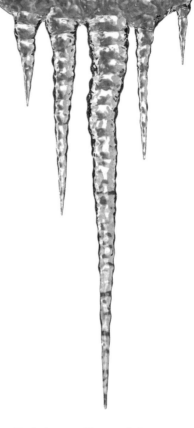

"I felt really cold on the dives, and the dive guide poured flasks of hot water down our backs during the surface interval."

I have a feeling she was right, actually. The rash you're describing sounds very unlike the classic mottled appearance of a skin bend, and I've never heard of one lasting four months. This sounds to me like something called cold urticaria. It is indeed a form of allergy, triggered by exposure to cold, where hives, weals or bumps form on the skin. They can be incredibly itchy, and last for anywhere from minutes to months. Strangely, it can be inherited or it can develop later in life, most commonly in the early 20s. The diagnosis is usually made by the aptly named 'cold test': an ice cube held against the arm will produce characteristic hives after a few minutes. The

treatment is pure rocket science: stay warm. The quicker the skin is warmed, the sooner the reaction will disappear. Antihistamines will sometimes help the itch and possibly reduce the number of hives.

Although it sounds trivial, cold urticaria can sometimes result in serious anaphylactic shock, which can be fatal, so more severe sufferers should carry an adrenaline injection around with them. In your case, if the bumps are still present, I would strongly advise you see an allergy specialist to get a concrete diagnosis. Probably best to avoid cold water diving until then, too.

SKIN

I am currently taking minocycline on prescription for acne. I have been taking this for about a year now and have had two blood tests to check for liver problems due to it. Both have been fine. Am I OK to dive?

You should be fine to dive if you are on this medication. It's very good stuff for acne and will not cause you any side effects underwater. The only thing it may affect that could be construed as diving related is that it can make the skin hypersensitive to sunlight. As most diving is done in sunny climates then I assume you may well be going to get some exposure to higher levels of UV than we get here in the UK. So make sure you wear plenty of sun block or even a light stinger suit to cover you above water.

Early last year I had a case of acute dermatitis. My whole body was covered with the exception of hands, feet and face. After much application of various creams, lotions etc. I healed, although it took two weeks. I have recently taken up Scuba diving and all my dives to date have been in a semi-dry suit with hood. During my last two weekends of diving I noticed a rash forming on my neck, underarms and groin area. These were itchy and I consulted my doctor. He said the dermatitis had returned, probably due to the chaffing of the hood combined with salt water. The rash on my neck has subsided, although the other places are still there but not quite as bad as before. I am now in the process of changing from a semi-dry suit to a dry suit. Is there anything on the market today that I can buy to minimise the effect of the chafing/salt water? My doctor said I could possibly use petroleum jelly as a barrier. Would this work?

Ah back to my old friend the tub of Vaseline again. If you are about to switch to a dry suit then your problem is going to solve itself. As you can wear normal clothes underneath, that will spare your groin and armpits. That just leaves your neck and wrists. And if it's chafing

"My whole body was covered with the exception of hands, feet and face. After much application of various creams, lotions etc. I healed, although it took two weeks."

you hate, may I recommend a crushed neoprene suit with neoprene on the cuffs and collars. This is a lot softer on those body parts, and with my joyous O3 brand you use copious amounts of aqueous jelly to slip them over, thus creating a nice barrier to prevent the chafing.

Problem sorted. Sort of, there's still the hood to think of and that can cause problems on your head area. A good barrier here is maybe some light cotton. So get down your local Puff Daddy franchise and purchase a do- rag, direct from the Crips in Compton, LA. Put it on, hood over, and baddabing, the God of Bling, no dermatitis.

"…purchase a do-rag, direct from the Crips in Compton, LA. Put it on, hood over, and baddabing, the God of Bling, no dermatitis."

My wife is 49 years old and is in general good health although she takes ACE-inhibitors for high blood pressure. She now has about 130 dives but in the last eighteen months she has suffered terrible dry skin on her feet that cracks and splits, becoming quite painful, whenever we go on our diving jaunts and she dives for more than a couple of days. This has now started to spread to her fingertips.

We have tried all sorts of barrier creams, plastic bags on her feet before putting on dive boots and in case it is a combination of salt water immersion reacting with the dive boot materials/glue she has tried full foot fins. The pharmacist in El Gouna believed the problem to be immersion in salt water. Can you suggest any possible remedy to prevent or even delay the problem?

A tough one this as you seem to have tried everything sensible. So we are in the realms of exclusion. To see if it is the salt water, why not spend your next holidays in Leicestershire. Go for several dives at Stoney Cove. If, with the same kit, she has absolutely no problems, then you know it is the salt water. If she gets the same, then if could be the water/boot/fin angle. And so on, you could replace each item with an alternate to find a cause. However, if none of the above work, then I suggest moisturizer. Not a little bit, but shed loads, worked into the skin at the beginning and end of each day. That's all that can prevent skin drying and cracking. A couple of the better ones are Unguentum or Diprobase. You can get them at certain pharmacies.

Just wanted some information, could you help please? I am currently half way through a Trimix course and I've got a tattoo planned on my back. Is it still OK to dive with a tattoo and if not how long would I need to leave it? Thanks so much.

Beckham-style wings? 'APNOEA' in bold Cyrillic up your spine? A pod of dolphins leaping playfully across your trapezii? I've seen plenty of tats in the course of doing daily dive medicals, some pretty cool, others just unfathomable.

Freshly tattooed skin is quite raw and susceptible to infection, so you need to wait until it's fully healed up. How long that is depends on your individual metabolism and immune system: it probably takes at least a week or two though. Submerging the new tattoo too early in water might also cause the colours to fade or leech out completely. Then you'd have to go through all the pain again. Rather you than me.

I'm in my 60's and over the years have developed deep laughter lines and creases around my brow and eyes. They say laughter keeps you young, but annoyingly it also causes my mask to leak. I've tried a couple of different brands but there's always a trickle that gradually fills up my mask. It probably doesn't help that I've got a fearsome set of whiskers too. Any tips on how to stop this?

The single page website of the BLF (Beard Liberation Front) seems to suggest the organization is now sadly defunct. Which is a shame since previous 'Beard of the Year' winners have largely been cricketers who've gone on to do great things; Flintoff and Panesar, to name but two. What you need, however, is a prominent and fulsome silicon skirt on your mask. This, coupled with judicious gobs of Vaseline or silicone grease in the areas that typically leak, should halt the ingress of water. If not, then it's probably worth trying a few other models (change sizes as well as brands) as there's no one-size-fits-all in the mask world. Over-tightening is a common culprit. Get your local dive shop to take you through correct sizing and fitting. While you're there, you could investigate purge masks, which allow water out through a one-way valve, thus easing the arduous task of constant mask clearing. If all else fails, one solution remains: targeted depilation of the immediate under-nose area, which permits a tight seal and shouldn't disrupt your hirsute visage to any noticeable degree.

Is it safe for me to dive whilst taking Roaccutane (isotretinoin) tablets for my acne?

For those not in the know, this is serious anti-acne treatment. So strong it can only be prescribed by named dermatologists. It basically dries up any oil production by the sebaceous glands on the face. It also

> "...previous 'Beard of the Year' winners have largely been cricketers who've gone on to do great things; Flintoff and Panesar, to name but two."

dries all the mucous membranes of the body. That's eyes and mouth. So the only downside with diving, where your mouth can get pretty dry with the regulator, is super-dryness there. You may have to peel your tongue and lips off the rubber of the mouthpiece. But hey, at least that means it'll stay in place when you are underwater. You can dive on this medication, just don't have babies on it: it's a powerful teratogen.

I have a suspect mole on my upper central chest which I have arranged to have removed. They will also be performing a biopsy (spudgun stylee) on my arm on another suspect area of skin. Due to a delay on the surgery, the stitches will be removed just before I head off to Egypt. Can I still go? Is there any way to speed up the healing process?

By a staggering (and quite unbelievable) coincidence, I actually found my old spud gun at home recently, complete with a shrivelled nubbin of potato hanging forlornly from its muzzle. Cue flashbacks to the playground and making a girl cry with it after she pulled my hair… these days the joys of firing starchy projectiles at people would no doubt be roundly condemned for encouraging a life of crime. I suppose the potatoes are happier though.

Er, anyway, normally mole removal is safe, uncomplicated surgery so you won't have many stitches. Healing rates depend on the site and the individual, but central or upper chest wounds are reasonably quick (ballpark figure 7 to 10 days). So with any luck, once the stitches are out the wound edges should be bound together tight enough to hold.

If there's another delay and the stitches are still in, then there are potential risks with infection in tropical water, which can cause the wound to dehisce (burst open). Some divers put Tegaderm or other adhesive dressings over the wound but they can't be guaranteed waterproof. If diving is 'unavoidable' then all you can do is rinse the wound with fresh water and clean it with iodine or a similar antiseptic after the dive.

Speeding up healing: the holy grail of many forms of medicine. Unfortunately, this particular prize is still being sought. A healthy diet is about all the scientific community has come up with so far. Any strain on the wound is more likely to cause it to burst though, so keep the dives shallow and non-strenuous if possible; no chest expanding exercises or pulling on the stuck anchor.

"…these days the joys of firing starchy projectiles at people would no doubt be roundly condemned for encouraging a life of crime. I suppose the potatoes are happier though."

The day before I flew to Egypt, I came down with painful lumps under both arms and quite a bad head cold. The doctor diagnosed the lumps as abscesses and told me that they would probably come to a head, which luckily they didn't. I began a course of antibiotics and they went down but didn't fully disappear.

I had a week of fantastic diving then on the last day the lumps reappeared. I rang my doctor as soon as I could when I got home. One arm has cleared up completely, but under the other I have what looks like a tendon or gland that is visible beneath the skin. It is painful if I lift anything too heavy or stretch my arm up too much. I have been referred to the local hospital but am still waiting for an appointment. Can I dive with this as I was told that I can't with any swelling?

Good news. You can dive if you want.

There is no problem with what you have as regards to all the usual diving medical factors. It's just a question of how you take the pain. It can be bloody painful, having a throbbing red pus-filled swelling under your arm. The neoprene will rub and the BCD will too, but diving won't worsen it and the salt water may even improve it. Armpits are a notoriously good breeding ground for abscesses. Lots of hair follicles, sweat and friction; a bit of shaving (if you're not German) and there are your causes. It would be pertinent to check for diabetes as this can make them frequent after adolescence. If your sugars are fine then dive away and in time they will get better, making the whole experience less painful.

I had a face lift and eyes done and am looking to go to the USA to do my divemaster and instructor courses. When will it be safe for me to dive please?

GO.

Right now. Go girl. Unless you are a bloke, in which case, shame on you, nothing wrong with that gritty Eastwood look of a gnarled face.

I am not super au fait with all forms of cosmetic surgery, but I assume they cut some skin off your forehead, and yanked it all up. Then replaced your eyes. Like in Terminator. All I would say is that if it's all healed you are OK to dive, but for others out there, the only thing to

"Armpits are a notoriously good breeding ground for abscesses. Lots of hair follicles, sweat and friction; a bit of shaving (if you're not German) and there are your causes."

watch is a mask squeeze, especially after collagen injections. If you get enough negative pressure in your mask on descent, I reckon it could pull bits out of shape, making your beautiful youthful features resemble most of my previous girlfriends.

So, a loose mask, and let's say four to six weeks post op for all you Ipanema Beach bunnies out there.

SLEEP AND SPLEEN

I have some Stilnoct (which I believe is zolpidem tartrate), which I would like to use in order to sleep on the plane to Sharm. How long should I wait before diving afterwards?

Tough life, but here's some hope: sleepers are fine. Zolpidem is one of the stronger ones that purport not to cause a hangover the next morning, unless you have been on the lash as well. It gives six hours nice sleep and you feel fine on waking, so a lot of people use it to counter jetlag when flying, or if they're still building the other half of the hotel you're in at night. The only diving implication is that if you were getting up way early, like on a Thistlegorm run, you would be too woozy to think straight.

So you have the OK to use them before midnight, say, the night before a dive, and on the plane there and back.

My boyfriend recently had his spleen removed. He is taking antibiotics for life, but still wants a career in diving. Is this still a possibility?

I always like a little historical background to place things in context. In the 17th century the spleen was thought to be the repository of "ill humour and melancholy", and was particularly applied to women in bad moods who were said to be "afflicted by the vapours of spleen". Venting it was the term given to an angry (so-called 'splenic') person letting rip.

The spleen is in fact a vastly underrated pear-sized organ which lies just under the rib cage on the left hand side of the body. It acts as a reservoir of blood and is the site of destruction of worn out red blood cells. Interestingly horse spleens contain litres of blood which are squeezed out when the horse pelts off. The spleens of diving mammals are even more well adapted; the spleen of the Arctic Weddell Seal contains so much extra oxygenated blood that it often is referred to as a Scuba tank. When it dives the blood ejected leaves the spleen up to 85% smaller.

"In the 17th century the spleen was thought to be the repository of 'ill humour and melancholy', and was particularly applied to women in bad moods..."

The spleen is also full of special cells called macrophages that filter out bacteria and other blood-borne nasties. Hence its absence does lead to a predisposition to infection (generally estimated at around 12 times the rate of individuals with a spleen), and the need for lifelong antibiotics. And this is the issue with a commercial diving career: your boyfriend may be working in remote locations with poor (if any) access to medical facilities. Any minor ailment (a sniffle or a cut for example) may turn into a major infection requiring heavy duty antibiotics, so access to appropriate treatment is a must. Apart from this risk and its practical implications, there's no reason your boyfriend can't pursue his diving ambitions.

I have been diagnosed with obstructive sleep apnoea and have been using a CPAP machine for two years. I've never had a problem underwater, but have recently been asked by my insurance company to obtain a physician's opinion as to the effects of the condition with regards to diving.

So when they talk about the 'tired diver tow', that'll be you mate. Sleep apnoea, or to give it its other name Pickwickian syndrome, after the fat geezer in the Dickens novel, is all about sleep. And being apnoeic. Put them together and you basically cannot breathe so well when you sleep. This decreases the oxygen to your body at night, so you wake up tired, as well as waking up through the night grunting as you snore. It's a problem that only occurs at night though.

So how does it affect diving? Well I suppose, as long as you are not so knackered in the morning that you can't think straight, or as long as you are not expecting to sleep on a dive, then you will be OK.

The CPAP (Continuous Positive Airways Pressure) should help: a tube up your nose blowing in air, to make you breathe, should reverse tiredness.

Dive on, sleepyhead.

"I suppose, as long as you are not so knackered in the morning that you can't think straight, or as long as you are not expecting to sleep on a dive, then you will be OK."

UNUSUAL

Extremely sorry to be here at your busy hour. One of my friends got the following problem, need a consultation with a confidential approach to proceed. He was on holiday on an island. Local mafia people counted him as a big time agent and put an electronic tag on his body to trace him every single day. Still now this group following him and breaking his privacy. What is the procedure to find the tag from his body and take it off, please? Thanking you.

This is for real, seriously. This guy has cc'd every medical website in the UK. Here's a reply:

Electronic tagging is commonplace now on most islands. Since the release of Casino Royale, foreign visitors and holiday makers must be assumed to be big time agents. In the past it was usual to drip poison off a thread of cotton, or put a tarantula in the same bed as the agent, however islanders are more sophisticated now, and the insertion of a tag is deemed both cheaper and easier for one who would use a local volcano to launch a nuclear missile strike on a nearby superpower.

My suggestion for removal is to get off with a stunning girl, avoid sharks and lasers, and somehow, unbelievably, all will be OK in the end. Especially as you snog her in a dinghy as the President of the World is watching you from satellite and trying to thank you.

"Since the release of Casino Royale, foreign visitors and holiday makers must be assumed to be big time agents."

I suffered a bend during my first dive whilst on holiday in Mexico. The sea conditions were rough and I appear to have struck my side when entering the dive boat causing injury to my rib and bruising to my lung.

According to the dive specialist in Mexico, I developed pneumonia and septicaemia whilst diving and this caused the bend to occur. I do not fully understand why. My dive profile appears good. About an hour after the dive I started shaking, which I put down

to shock. I told the dive centre that I felt unwell and that my neck hurt, but they didn't do anything. About four hours after this I passed out with high blood pressure, red skin on the side of my face and loss of co-ordination. The doctor was called and took an hour and a half to stabilise me before I could go into the ambulance for transportation to Cancun private hospital.

When I arrived my wife pressured the doctors for a dive specialist. He arrived 10 minutes later and took me to the chamber, where I was recompressed for 6 hours. After this I was declared clear of DCI. Four hours later, I returned to the hospital when I started to shake and had difficulty breathing. This occurred again 12 hours later and the next day as well. I thought I was going to die.

The day after I returned home I had myself checked by my GP and Colchester hospital. Both said my lungs and baseline functions were normal. I need to book a HSE medical for my IDC but would like to do a dry dive where I can be monitored for any conditions as I am fearful this will happen again.

> Hmmmm. Lots more questions from me here. Did you whack yourself before or after the dive? Were you given antibiotics: ie was it really a pneumonia? Did the recompression heal any of your symptoms? Fainting with high blood pressure? Normally fainting occurs when it's low.
>
> So you see, a few things don't really add up here. Certainly neck pain, a rash and poor co-ordination are symptoms of DCI, and if they got better after treatment then that is diagnostic. But it seems you were all over the place afterwards as well, and as for developing pneumonia and blood poisoning during a dive. Well unlucky that, or perhaps the doc was full of s***.
>
> Either way, what you need to do is come in for a chat before the HSE medical, bring all your notes from Mexico, and we will try to unravel the truth. If all is OK, then you can roll into the HSE examination afterwards.

I began Scuba diving recently and soon afterwards I started having a salty taste in my mouth almost all the time, particularly after eating or drinking. Even after fruit or tea. Do you think that the salty taste might be related to diving?

"Four hours later, I returned to the hospital when I started to shake and had difficulty breathing… I thought I was going to die."

Why should you get a salty taste in your mouth after diving, even after you've eaten a fruit?

The only way to tell is to go for a freshwater dive. If you still get a salty taste in your mouth then, as a doctor, I would be really confused.

If you want to stop it, try breathing through your regulator rather than sipping round the edges.

I was shot six months ago whilst trying to avert an armed robbery. The bullet went into my back near the shoulder blade and came out above my left nipple. It hit my ribs but did not break them. The lung was not punctured but there was some bruising (a pleural rub).

What tests would I need to be allowed to dive again?

You might go down in history as one of the most fortunate men alive. From the look of the entry and exit wounds, it's unbelievable that the bullet only bruised your lung: an inch in any direction and it could have penetrated your heart, punctured the lung, and generally left you in a far more mashed up state. A set of chest X-rays to exclude a pneumothorax (collapsed lung) and any retained foreign material would have been done at the time. The functional integrity of the lung tissue could be assessed by normal spirometry and if in doubt, a CT scan to look for any areas of scarring that might predispose pulmonary barotrauma. But provided the emergency staff are sure that there is no damage to heart and lungs, then off you go, unrestricted, back to the pleasures of the deep. Whatever your lucky charm is, start bottling it and selling it now.

Is it OK to use Viagra half a day before Scuba diving?

Hmmm. Depends whether you can still get that wet suit on. But then again, it's a good way to stop your weight belt from slipping off.

Viagra will result in the widening of the vessels responsible for the blood flow to your old man. Users can still get facial flushing, headaches and gastritis, but some people do not, so if you are free of all these side effects and not a priapic monster any more, 12 hours is safe enough.

"But provided the emergency staff are sure that there is no damage to heart and lungs, then off you go unrestricted back to the pleasures of the deep. Whatever your lucky charm is, start bottling it and selling it now."

WHICH DIVE MEDICAL

I have a number of dive trips planned over the next 12 months, at least two of which will be abroad, and I thought that having a certificate would be useful (and it's years since I had any sort of medical, so it would be a useful 'MOT' too). I was wondering what sort of format would be needed for the certificate to be valid pretty much anywhere. Will an 'I certify... fit to dive' be enough? Should I take the PADI info sheet along?

They will work out whether you are fit or not, and sign you off on the PADI form (which you can download from their website).

The British Sub Aqua Club (BSAC) have a different form, which you can get from their website. It's always a good idea to check the questionnaire on their site before a trip just to make sure there's nothing you might have a problem with. If there is, then you need to see an Approved Medical Examiner of Divers (an AMED). A list of these is on the UK Sport Diving Medical Committee's website (they provide medical advice to BSAC and a few other diving organisations too).

Diving in France, regardless of health or experience, requires a mandatory CMAS medical, which is a similar thing to the above but requires a different form. In Spain, Malta and Gozo, all divers have to have a cert to say they are fit to dive too, but usually a PADI form will do. All these forms need to have been completed within the last twelve months.

And remember, the rules and regs change all the time, so the best advice is to confirm what the current state is with the dive operator you're planning to use at your destination.

"…remember, the rules and regs change all the time, so the best advice is to confirm what the current state is with the dive operator you're planning to use at your destination."

I have just about finished my Divemaster Course in Gran Canaria but am unsure of the medical facilities around me and what medical to ask for at these Spanish facilities. Can you enlighten me?

This is easy mate. When you do the DM internship, or DMT as it's known, there is the basic PADI medical proforma in the pack. That needs to be done by a doc at some point along your DMT. Most divers seem to arrive at my door for this at the end of their course, the logic being that if they're gonna flunk it for non-medical reasons, then at least they realise this before coughing up for the doc's fees for the medical. However, most divers have no problems, either diving or medical and can get this part of the form done by a normal GP, or a dive doc. So if you are in Spain, simply take this form to a local GP, get the basic medical and all should be fine. However, if you tick a yes to any part of the medical questions, eg you are on regular meds, have had a bend, are asthmatic etc, then it's best to see a dive doc on the island, or have seen one before going there in the first place.

That's the Euro and rest of the world rules. It's different over here in the UK though. Here a DMT (or a DM, or an instructor) needs to have the full-on commercial diving medical. It's known as the HSE (Health and Safety Executive) medical, is more thorough and more expensive to have. That is because Blighty rules are that a DMT has responsibility over live divers and so is seen as diving commercially. This rule also applies to DMs/instructors arriving in the UK who have qualified abroad and who are looking to do diving work over here.

Simple really. If you answer all NOs on the form, see any doc there. Any YES's and it's a dive doc you need. And if you come back here, get the HSE to supplement it.

I'm a paraplegic who qualified as an Advanced Open Water diver last year. I had a medical done by my GP prior to diving but can you tell me how long the medical is valid? It was a PADI medical.

On the PADI medical, unlike the BSAC one, there's no box for an expiry date. So unless your doctor actually wrote "valid to..." then it will usually last one year. However, with your paraplegia it would be an idea to get yourself reviewed by a dive doc regularly.

"...the logic being that if they're gonna flunk it for non-medical reasons, then at least they realise this before coughing up for the doc's fees for the medical."

I'm a GP and I'm getting more and more people coming in with dive medical forms asking me whether this or that drug is okay to dive with. A lot of them are older and are on more than one medication. Is there a list somewhere of what is safe to dive with and what isn't?

No, but I wish there was, it would make our lives a lot easier. These sorts of questions are very common, but very few medications have been tested for problems under pressure, so there's often no simple answer. For a start, every drug affects every individual differently: the Lariam one diver takes with no problems may give the next one vivid hallucinations and psychotic nightmares.

What is the condition the medication is needed for? Sometimes the dangers of that are far worse than any medication side effects. On that note, are any of the side effects likely to be of concern? Sedation, nausea, dizziness or a tendency to bleed are just a few of the possibilities. Multiple drug combinations get more common with increasing age, and the unpredictable reactions these produce could be fairly catastrophic mixed with nitrogen at depth. So best advice is to consider all the above, and if you can't come to a conclusion, send your conundrum to someone like me, so I can get a good headache mulling it over.

My partner and I are going to book a trip in May to El Quesir. We are both PADI Open Water divers and last had a dive medical in 1999. We thought that since we are both 50 plus we needed a medical every two years.

We were told by the doctor's surgery that the process is now self-certifying. However, we have since heard that self certification is not always accepted. The dive centre in El Quesir is CMAS affiliated.

Please can you clarify?

Errr... no. I think the deal with any of these resorts is to make sure you know before you go.

Email them and ask whether a self-certification will do as the last thing you want is to be running around an Egyptian town on arrival looking for a doctor to get a cert. It may be cheaper there but the hassle isn't worth it in my book. I don't know what the El Quesir rules are, but from my experience Egypt isn't a problem area, although I suppose there is

"...very few medications have been tested for problems under pressure, so there's often no simple answer."

a chance they'll want to see a CMAS medical, even though they're not actually in France, if that's the agency they're affiliated with. Malta, Gozo and some of the Maldive Islands are well known for needing a doctor's note. Just check first.

ARTICLE – HEALTH AND AEROBIC FITNESS

WHAT IS HEALTH?

A wise wag once declared that health was "the slowest possible rate at which to die". The World Health Organisation prefers this: "a state of complete physical, mental, and social well-being, not merely the absence of disease or infirmity." So how can we apply this to diving?

PHYSICAL FITNESS

Any of you who've had your medical with LDC might fondly recall our cherished step test box, which can reduce your fiercest sat diver to a wibbling heap in under five minutes. Our intent is not to humiliate (although it does somewhat sate ones sadistic tendencies), but to illustrate the importance of some semblance of cardiovascular fitness to diving.

One of the sports' strange paradoxes is that we spend a lot of time trying to relax, breathe slowly, hang gracefully and neutrally buoyant and generally expend as little energy as possible underwater. So how physically fit do you need to be to do this? During an uneventful dive, not particularly; but it's the before and after, and sometimes during (if equipment fails or buddies get into trouble), that can put sudden and intense demands on us. Think gearing up, de-kitting, finning furiously in unexpected currents. Your fat, 50-a-day diver may be fine drifting in calm water, but short, hard bursts of exertion might easily sink them with an arrhythmia from a heart unable to cope. Contrary to popular belief, diving itself doesn't make you fit. In general there's more calories going in than out, and all that sitting about on RIBs outweighs the odd bout of gentle finning, so a bit of extra work is required. Distant memories of finishing a half-arsed cross country run at school won't cut it as, sadly, fitness can't be stored: the old adage of 'use it or lose it' applies.

But the benefits are huge. Anyone looking to become a better diver, extend their bottom times or take on more challenging diving should put fitness near the top of their 'to do' list. Just under 'stop smoking' (which shoots straight in at number one) and 'lose weight' (which will usually be part and parcel of exercising).

Fast walking, running, swimming or cycling are all fine variants on a cardiovascular workout. As well as getting the ticker pumping, they will help develop flexibility, tone and strength in the core muscles of the back, abdomen and legs. A few minutes warming up (with some star jumps, jogging on the spot etc) followed by stretches of the limbs and torso are always advisable before the hard stuff of press-ups, lunges and crunches. Alternatively, jump on your Wii Fit Snowboard and carve for an hour: a good way to build up the quads. And remember a short cool down at the end.

After a mothballed winter layoff it's probably not the best idea to tackle that 100m wreck in the inky blackness for your first venture (even if it is full of lost bullion). It sounds obvious, but I've seen bends occur as a direct result of simply biting off a bit more than is chewable early on in the season. A few easy, shallow dives in known waters will help smooth the passage back to fitness and allow you time to get used to the quirks of the shiny new reg and computer you unwrapped at Christmas.

Finally, pre-dive exercise and its potential to reduce DCI risk has been a vogue topic in recent years. Large decreases in bubble counts were seen in fit military divers who ran for 45 minutes, 24 hours before, and in another study, two hours before, diving. How applicable this is to your average, ah, 'well-built' UK specimen is up for discussion (perhaps a few warm up stretches are more realistic than a 45 minute run), but the principle has been shown in several different studies. More controversial is exercise after diving: some claim it speeds bubble clearance; others that it might increase bubble formation. I'd steer clear of the gym straight after a dive for now.

MENTAL FITNESS

The roof's blown off, the MOT's overdue, teenage daughter is going out with a pierced freak from hell and the drysuit's sprung a leak. Psychological health is often overlooked but is equally as important as our corporeal condition. Although diving can be a big stress reliever, anxiety or longer term conditions such as depression can cause instinctive and dangerous behaviours underwater: breath holding, removing dive gear, uncontrolled ascents etc It's always a good idea to give yourself a quick mental check-up: "Am I in the right frame of mind for this dive?". One of the big benefits of breathing exercises and

"It's always a good idea to give yourself a quick mental check-up: 'Am I in the right frame of mind for this dive?'."

yoga is their ability to focus the mind; you can take plenty of lessons from freedivers on this.

SOCIAL WELL-BEING

More often than not, this involves that well-known lubricant alcohol, in varying and often substantial quantities. The post-dive debrief wouldn't be the same without a few cold ones although the perils of over-indulgence are many: dehydration, clouding of judgment, slowed reaction times, poor co-ordination, impairment of self-control, and diminished inhibitions. Not to mention the shocker between the eyes afterwards. Keeping a lid on the booze in the run-up to, and during, a series of dives is safer all round.

NUTRITION

Bacon butties, beers and between-dive chocolates do not make a fit diver. You didn't expect me to say anything different, did you? If you want to put your body into the high pressure, alien environment of the deep, probably best to feed it some fuel it can work with effectively. Ideally this needs to be done a few days before diving. Carbohydrate loading should be of the healthy variety: rice, pasta, veggies; and get some protein in there too: lean meat, fish, beans. Steering clear of fatty foods will help avoid that heavy-stomached lethargy on dive day.

Hydration is key: the golden rule is to keep your wee copious and clear. Much like equalising, the best way to hydrate is 'little and often'. Sipping on bottles will spread the intake of the two to three litres of liquid you need over the course of a day. Diluted juice is better absorbed than plain water, and if the squits are in full effect then rehydration salts are better still.

"Bacon butties, beers and between-dive chocolates do not make a fit diver. You didn't expect me to say anything different, did you?"

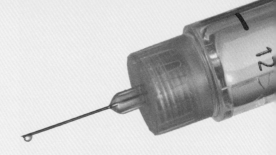

ARTICLE – WHAT DRUGS TO TAKE WHEN DIVING

See one, do one, teach one. That's how you learn to be a surgeon. Easy really, but from my experience a far better route to being a good doctor is: read about it, contract it yourself, diagnose it in others. My old pharmacology tutor used to take it to extremes and try every drug before lecturing on it to us. This was in the pre-Viagra days and if he hasn't retired by now then I guess he's done away with his old laser pointer.

The point of this though, is that one of the most frequently asked questions I get is along the lines of, "I'm going on a liveaboard and want to take some medicines for any illness I may get". Well you've got the expert here, but mainly because on my travels over the world I haven't had anything on me and consequently have gotten most of the diseases available in the countries visited. I speak from experience dear reader. Malaria in Mali, amoebic dysentery in Egypt and ear infections every time I seem to dive. So from these experiences I came up with a list of the must-have medications for every diver to take with them.

There is a greater issue here too, and that is if you go off on a dive holiday and get sick enough to have to stay topside, I don't see the insurance companies paying up. They'll argue that you still have the suntan and were able to snorkel so how come you need reimbursement? So it's up to us to make sure we stay as healthy as possible when we dive. Here are my thoughts on what every diver ought to be packing along with their BC and reg on the long flight to the longer liveaboard.

The medication I can least do without are antibiotic ear drops. Something I always seem to get around the fifth day of diving is the beginning of pain in my outer ear canal. This is called 'otitis externa' or OE. It is due to all the bugs and plankton floating around the sea that get lodged in your outer ear canal. After a few repetitive dives they eventually cause the skin in the canal to swell up and exude this gunk onto the pillow at night. It won't stop you equalising

> "…on my travels over the world I haven't had anything on me and consequently have gotten most of the diseases available in the countries visited."

and so won't stop you diving but it's painful and annoying. The way to stop it is to really clean out your ear canals after each dive with Swim Ear or one of the other ear astringents. If you forget to do this and OE sets in, my favourite ear-drop is a combination of gentamicin and hydrocortisone. The first part is a good antibiotic and the second a steroid that helps get rid of the inflammation that causes the pain. Using two drops, three times a day will stop the OE in a couple of days. Often, if the water where I'm diving looks a bit polluted, then I'll use the drops as a precaution to ward off the ear problem. It's cheap and can be bought at the pharmacy in most Asian countries.

Well, from that end of the body to the other. It's not just the embarrassment of having diarrhoea in close confines on a boat, but the fact that the volume depletion of fluids in the body can really contribute to a bend. You need blood to carry all that nitrogen back to the lungs from the tissues as that's where it's exhaled. But if your usual volume is lessened as your fluid intake seems to reappear seconds later from your bottom, then forget those tables or computer algorithms. They were designed using fit Naval 'volunteers' and not tired, dehydrated, occasional divers. So how do we stop the dreaded D? Well, research now shows us that the main causative organisms of traveller's diarrhoea can be effectively combated by a single 1g dose of Ciproxin. This is the antibiotic that was so in demand during the anthrax scares in the US and it's just as effective against the runs. We all know the reality of diving and that is very few people will stop doing it if they aren't well, so rather than risk a bend, simply take the Ciproxin, load up on fluids, and dive really conservatively. A good rehydration fluid is flat Coke with some salt in it as it has all the salts and sugars your body has lost. The only element you need to add is potassium, which is found in bananas, so eat those too.

The next addition to a basic medical kit is a decent painkiller. I know you can buy ibuprofen or paracetamol at the pharmacy and these are good for a simple headache or sprain, but what happens when you've dropped 10 kilos of lead on your foot? Or, as happened to me, a tooth abscess blows up out of nowhere? A couple of tablets of tramadol are worth more than their weight in gold. The whole thing about pain relief is that it's supposed to relieve pain. Ask anyone who is munching through a pack of over the counter tablets if they are working and more often than not they'll say "no". So there's no point in taking them really, but make sure what you do have will work for long enough to get you to a

"A good rehydration fluid is flat Coke with some salt in it as it has all the salts and sugars your body has lost."

doctor for some treatment. As I mentioned, tramadol is effective and strong, but another good one is 30mg of codeine. I know there is addictive potential, but what we are talking about here is short term emergency use in remote areas and you will rue the day you left them at home when your fellow divers try to stifle your screams. However, if you are worried about crossing borders with these in your pocket then a good workhorse painkiller is co-codamol. The only issue with this is that the effective equivalent to tramadol is eight of these tablets in a day. Quite a mouthful.

So, where next in this cornucopia of medication? It's got to be seasickness. This is the bane of many a diver and can hit you out of the blue, even on some of the calmest of days. Some tablets like cinnarizine can be sedating and I can't recommend you dive on them as they can make you woozy underwater, but a good one is Stemetil or prochlorperazine. This is used for nausea and vomiting, and can settle you down quickly before you paint the decks with your breakfast. An issue here though is that if you take an oral tablet with a little water when you are chucking up, the likelihood is that you will throw the cure up as well. So come on, be brave and take the suppository version. If you can't bring yourself to do it: that's what a good buddy is for. Having said that, a good prevention of seasickness is ginger, available in tablets or biscuits. Your call.

You may not want to take my next suggestion, but I think a dive boat ought to have it for someone who knows to use it. Local anaesthetic and a small needle. I used it twice on one dive once. One poor diver got his finger jammed between the hull and a pole on the boat and was screaming in agony until I blocked the nerve in his finger. And after the dive, a poor old American lady surfaced with a handful of urchin spines. Only one cure for that and the local helped. Of course, not every boat will have a doctor, but if there is one then they will need their tools. It's also great for stonefish stings, lionfish as well, and the occasional bad jelly sting.

This next one is going to sound really weird, but it works. There's a spray you can get for good old fashioned piles. It was designed so you wouldn't get your fingers dirty when trying to treat the little nasties, but its contents are pretty good for a far wider range of conditions. There are two things that make up the contents of grape spray: one, a steroid which is a potent anti-inflammatory; the other, a local anaesthetic for quick pain relief. You can see why it's so good for Sigmunds. I use it for any wetsuit rash, sunburn, irritant

"[Stemetil] is used for nausea and vomiting, and can settle you down quickly before you paint the decks with your breakfast."

skin reaction to underwater beasties like jellies or hydroids and it's really good after fire coral contact. Spray it on three to four times a day. Bliss.

There's been some research recently that shows that over 70% of people going abroad will get ill. 'Ill' can be anything from getting hit by a bus, all the way to sunburn, so you can see why it's so important to take some medication to remote locations. But there's one thing more that is so often forgotten at the last moment. It's not a tablet, it's travel health insurance. We had a US diver in our chamber recently with a bend. Poor guy, he'd forgotten to arrange his insurance whilst on his holiday in Thailand and the bill after the treatment almost caused him to visit the Coronary Care Unit. Treatment in a chamber is expensive. You've doctors on standby, technicians in and out of the chamber with you, and a bed in the hospital too. The dollars mount up, so never ever forget the travel insurance. It's not just for the bends, but for making sure you have the best treatment available to you wherever you are.

"Unless there's a whale shark of course, in which case only death will stop me from getting kitted up."

There are a few more additions to the dive medical kit I could suggest, but these would be the icing on the cake. A single course of penicillin for the middle ear infection for one, but this is a lot rarer in divers than seems to be 'diagnosed'. In the UK, if any diver goes into casualty with ear pain they always seem to end up being told it's a case of otitis media or OM. Wrong call, Emergency Doc. The redness you are seeing is more likely to be a barotrauma from poor equalisation on descent rather than bacteria in the middle ear. However, if it does happen and you have pain in the ear with a complete inability to equalise, then it probably is OM so take the penicillin ASAP.

Waterproof dressings. In my experience they all seem to fall off after the rigours of suiting up, so just make sure any wound doesn't start to go puss-ey, in which case you need to take the penicillin and stop diving. Unless there's a whale shark of course, in which case only death will stop me from getting kitted up.

I'm going to finish on a contentious issue. We all know about the dangers of deep vein thrombosis and flying. Well there is a theoretical risk of diving and thrombosis too. This is based on the assumption that there are microbubbles left in the body after any dive. All bubbles can cause increased clotting of the blood by activating the enzyme cascade that causes blood clots in the body. Add a long flight to this and you can see the potential of the problem. The only thing is that it has not been proven yet, so I would say to anyone who is coming home from a lot of dives and the flight is over six hours: take the aspirin. A dose of 150mg at least should keep you clot free. And if you are high risk, ie you've had them before or have a family history of embolic stroke, then you MUST take the tablet.

So there you go. My list of goodies in a bag to keep you fit and healthy so your trip of a lifetime doesn't end up with zero dive time.

SYMPTOMS OF DECOMPRESSION ILLNESS

Decompression Illness (DCI) is a term encompassing all bubble-related illness. It combines Decompression Sickness (DCS), where bubbles precipitate in the blood and tissues, and Arterial Gas Embolism (AGE), where bubbles may come from lung rupture eg breath holding on ascent. In summary, DCI = DCS + AGE. DCS is commonly called 'the bends'. DCI mimics many other medical problems.

Classical symptoms include:
- Joint or muscle pains
- Tingling and/or numbness anywhere in the body
- Fatigue, headaches

However there are many other presenting symptoms eg:
- Vertigo, dizziness and deafness
- Shortness of breath and chest pain when breathing
- Skin discolouration and itching
- Breast swelling
- Poor memory and irritability
- Confusion and disorientation

As there are so many ways it can present there is a simple mantra:
"Any new symptom present after a dive should be presumed to be due to DCI until proven otherwise"

Always contact a dive doctor if you feel unwell after a dive.

TREATMENT AT THE SCENE

- Lie the diver FLAT
- Administer 100% oxygen
- Give oral fluids at 1 litre per hour
- If unconscious give i.v. fluids if possible
- Pain relief may be given eg ibuprofen or stronger
  – but remember NOT to let this make you 'feel you are better'
- Contact the emergency medical services at your location

In all but the mildest cases, recompression in a hyperbaric chamber will be needed. Do not delay in contacting the nearest facility as soon as possible, as bubbles can shift easily and worsen the problem. The sooner recompression is administered, the better the ultimate result.

"The unpredictability of outcome at the onset of any DCI means that each case must be managed as a medical emergency"

IF YOU ARE IN THE UK OR ABROAD PLEASE CALL:
+44 (0)7940 353 816 FOR ANY DIVE MEDICAL ADVICE